Exploring in Chinese

中文探索

Exploring in Chinese
中文探索

A DVD-based Course in Intermediate Chinese
Volume 1

Cynthia Ning

University of Hawaii

Yale University Press
New Haven and London

Publisher: Mary Jane Peluso
Development Editor: Brie Kluytenaar
Manuscript Editor (English): Karen Hohner
Manuscript Editor (Chinese): Dong LIU
Production Editor: Ann-Marie Imbornoni
Production Controller: Maureen Noonan
Marketing Manager: Timothy Shea

Cover designed by Mary Valencia

Printed in the United States of America.

ISBN: 978-0-300-11569-7
Library of Congress Control Number: 2007925854

A catalogue record for this book is available from the British Library.

The paper in this book meets the guidelines for permanence and durability of the Committee on Production Guidelines for Book Longevity of the Council on Library Resources.

10 9 8 7 6 5 4 3 2 1

Contents 目錄／目录

Unit C Handling Meals
第三單元　飲食 / 第三單元　饮食

Unit D Shopping
第四單元　購物 / 第四單元　购物

Acknowledgments

Production of the DVD and accompanying texts was made possible by a generous two-year grant from the U.S. Department of Education's Office of International Education. For this I am extremely grateful, and for the numerous no-cost extensions of the grant as well.

I also express abiding gratitude to the following: Wang Qinghong, Ruby Yang Jochum, Tian Chenshan, Cui Yue, K.T. Yao, and Chen Shan of the University of Hawaii for many of the notes and letters that constitute the reading tasks in the text; David Blythe and Matthew Olson, then students of Chinese at the University of Hawaii, for many suggestions on content and presentation; Peng Qiong and her father Peng Shuyu, and Shi Lei and his mother Shi Junying, all of Beijing, for assisting with production and appearing on-camera; old friends Hao Ping (then vice president of Peking University, now president of Beijing Foreign Studies University) and Zhang Shenlan (professor emeritus of Lanzhou University) for serving as advisers to the project and also appearing on-camera; to my daughter Robyn Xiuming Ning Yee, my former student Todd Pavel, and James Yao (son of my colleagues and good friends Tao-chung and K.T. Yao) for their courage in using their Chinese on-camera, even when they felt they "looked stupid"; to Robyn for the beautiful line drawings that appear throughout the text; to Kathy Campbell of the Hawaii Department of Education, independent videographer Gene Kois and Yang Zhigong of Peking University—our producer and camera-people; and to Daniel Bernadoni, Stephen and Daniel Tschudi, and Lu-Chen Jung-ying for post-production assistance. The students of two classes of experimental second year Chinese at the University of Hawaii allowed me to test successive drafts on them and provided feedback—some of their written work is featured in the text; and graduate students Cui Yue and Wang Qinghong served as teaching assistants in these sections. Wang Qinghong and Liu Dong (of Tsinghua University) read the finished manuscripts cover-to-cover, checking for consistency in the *pinyin* transcription and overall authenticity in content.

My heartfelt thanks are due to the University of Hawaii's Center for Chinese Studies and our partner institution—Peking University, for their unstinting support. I am also grateful to the University's Department of East Asian Languages and Literatures for its encouragement over the years. John and Pat Montanaro of Yale University's erstwhile Far Eastern Publications were supportive throughout this project; since FEP has been absorbed by Yale University Press, I have been pleased to work with publisher Mary Jane Peluso, development editor Brie Kluytenaar, manuscript editor Karen Hohner, production editor Ann-Marie Imbornoni, and marketing manager Timothy Shea. I am also grateful to independent reviewers John Chang of the University of Southern California, Stephen Tschudi of the University of Hawaii, and Yea-fen Chen of the University of Wisconsin-Milwaukee for their positive reviews and suggested adjustments to an early draft of the manuscript.

Finally, I am grateful to my now-adult daughter Robyn, for pointing out that the video segments in this curriculum are reminiscent of "reality TV," and therefore likely to be attractive to people of her generation, and for never letting up in urging me to complete the manuscript!

Introduction

Exploring in Chinese is a DVD-based course in intermediate Chinese divided into two volumes of one semester each for the college level, or one year each for the high school level. This curriculum aims at moving the Intermediate Low student towards Intermediate High, particularly in listening, speaking, and reading. It is expected that the student's ability in writing in Chinese characters will remain somewhere between the Intermediate Low and Intermediate Mid levels.

Creating the DVD

The curriculum is based on edited video footage filmed in Beijing, China, in the summer of 1999. Its content includes interviews, filmed interactions among two or more people, and records of common transactions, all of which were purposely unrehearsed and unscripted, in order to maximize the "naturalness" and spontaneity of the interactions. The on-camera interviewers included three U.S. students: Robyn Yee, a high school junior and an Intermediate Low speaker of Chinese; Todd Pavel, graduate student in Asian Studies and an Intermediate Mid speaker of Chinese; and James Yao, graduate student in Asian Studies and an Advanced speaker of Chinese. Each of the interviewers was given a variety of assignments ("Go in this store and buy some snacks," "Ask that security guard about his background"). We also interviewed a variety of Chinese people about their lives. The cues were general: "Tell us about how you spend an average day," or "How should an American student go about making friends?" The Chinese respondents very naturally adjusted their level of speech downwards since they were faced with "foreigners," so that what we recorded was more nearly at the optimal "i+1" level for the intermediate-level learner, rather than the normally "too high" level recorded as native-speaker speech. Also, since all segments were unrehearsed and unscripted, what we preserved is a record of people interacting in authentic and lively fashion—trying to decipher what each other is saying, asking for confirmation, working around miscues—all the elements of a real-life conversation.

The curriculum is based on a DVD of 37 video segments arranged by topic and function. The first 20 lessons (Volume 1) are more characteristic of the Intermediate Low/Mid level, focusing on daily life interactions and transactions. The remaining 17 lessons (Volume 2) gradually become more descriptive and narrative, as is appropriate to moving toward the Intermediate High level. Each lesson offers two sound-tracks—the original sound recorded live (which is authentic and more interesting but sometimes harder to understand), and a dubbed soundtrack recorded in a studio (which is clearer but contains none of the color of the original, and does not quite match the cadence of the visuals). My suggestion is that users listen to the authentic soundtrack as much as possible, and certainly for all the first times they contact the material; the dubbed soundtrack can serve as a backup, perhaps as a final listening tool.

Contents of the Student Text

The DVD is correlated with the two volumes of the student text, with learning activities divided into 37 lessons—20 lessons in Volume 1 (third semester college or third year high school) and 17 in Volume 2 (fourth semester college or fourth year high school). The lessons follow the format described below:

•Previewing Activity: generally, predicting the content of the video, to "activate schemata" (bringing to mind sets of previously learned information about any given topic, to aid in comprehension).

•First Viewing, in which the focus is on understanding the *main ideas* in the segment. (Each "viewing" may actually include multiple viewings, of course.)

•Second Viewing, to tease out *supporting details* included in the segment.

•Third Viewing, to support linguistic work: focusing on specific useful new vocabulary and selected structural items. Cultural discussions may also be included here, although information on culture may be derived throughout the lesson.

•Postviewing Activities, including Speaking activities (in which students spiral the content of the lesson into speaking about their own lives); Reading activities including notes/letters written by native speakers pertaining to the objectives of the lesson, and a series of exercises beginning with top-down strategies (in which students try to decipher the main ideas of the reading) and progressing to bottom-up strategies (in which students work on vocabulary and detailed comprehension); and a brief Writing activity, in which students take the content of the Reading unit and write something about themselves.

•Transcript of the video segment, given in traditional characters, simplified characters, *pinyin*, and English. This is provided for the convenience of both the teacher and the students, who might want to read quickly through *after* all the other exercises have been completed, to pick up more information about the content of the segment, and perhaps to answer any remaining questions about what was said.

Within each section, students are encouraged to view the segment as many times as necessary to complete the assigned tasks. Our suggestion is *not* to read the transcript *before* doing all the exercises provided, or else students will not have the opportunity to develop comprehension strategies for authentic (or simulated authentic) situations. Students need to develop their tolerance for native-speaker speech, as well as their skills in *guessing the meaning* of what is said. The exercises throughout the curriculum are aimed at developing both tolerance and skills. Skipping ahead to the transcripts nullifies these benefits.

Overall, all texts provided within double borders (see pages 20–23, for example) are for reference; we suggest that students look at them only *after* doing the exercises provided.

Issues of Coverage

It has been commented that the contents of some of the DVD segments seem elementary, particularly in the early lessons and especially when compared with the contents of other Chinese language textbooks for the second year that are currently on the market. This is the result of a conscious choice regarding this curriculum: it is an implementation of the adage *"Less is more!"* of the proficiency approach, which advises in part that *less* be focused on (introduced for the receptive skills of listening and reading, for example) so that *more* can be done with it (using the productive skills of speaking and writing, for instance).

Conversely, it has also been noted that the long lists of vocabulary that appear in the text in order to encourage students to express their own meaning in speech and writing far exceed similar lists in other second-year textbooks. Here, we are simply enabling the students to express themselves: the lists are for them to choose from, selectively, to enable them to spiral through **conceptual, partial,** and *full control* of the material. That is to say, students may scan through the lists and gain *conceptual* control of perhaps 60% of the material. Then they may hear classmates use some key terms, and through repeated exposure via interactions with the teacher and other students they will gain *partial* control of perhaps 40% of the material. Finally, because they themselves find a certain subset of the material particularly meaningful in their own lives, they will choose to use perhaps 20% of the material repeatedly, thereby gaining *full* control of it.

(A caveat to the teacher: when the time comes to test the students, then, it is important to allow for individual expression by the students. Rather than asking, "Write the Chinese terms for baseball, basketball, bicycling and billiards," for example, you might ask, "Write the Chinese terms for four of your favorite sporting activites." A perfectly acceptable answer might then be "qiánshuǐ 潜水 / 潛水, huá xuěbǎn 滑雪板, rēng fēipán 扔飛盤 / 扔飞盘, zuò yújiā 做瑜珈."]

You might also notice that these vocabulary lists include a certain amount of redundancy in them, that certain terms that have appeared in a previous lesson reappear in later ones. This is to support the principle of moving from conceptual to partial to full control. We don't expect students to master new terms the first time they encounter them, and so repeat them as necessary.

Concerns with Errors

Where the American student interviewers or Chinese native respondents make errors in their speech, or state something in a non-standard way, the student exercises will note this, and suggest alternative forms of expression. Errors and miscues have been preserved in the text, because negotiating errors and extracting meaning is an essential skill in real life, and deserves classroon attention.

Pinyin Orthography

As for the *pinyin* orthography used, we have tried to adhere to the principles listed and the corpus provided in John DeFrancis's groundbreaking *ABC Chinese-English Comprehensive Dictionary*. Whereas in my previous text for the first year—the *Communicating in Chinese* series—I indicated tone sandhis (e.g., when one third tone follows another, the first one moves to second), in this volume I've moved to orthographical conventions, following which original tonal values are indicated on syllables. Thus, the number "one" always appears as "yī" rather than "yí" in front of a fourth tone and "yì" elsewhere, and the negative particle "bù" is always "bù," even before a fourth tone. Two third tones together are each marked by the third tone. We trust that by now, students who are going to be able to master tone sandhi principles have already done so, and have decided to privilege *pinyin* orthographical conventions instead.

Traditional and Simplified Characters

This volume continues the tradition of *Communicating in Chinese*, in that students are encouraged to become familiar with both simplified and traditional characters, and to write in either one or the other format. To this end, glosses are provided in both formats. Many students I have taught have chosen first to read through one transcription (say the traditional) with the help of many handwritten notes, and then fold the page in half and "test" themselves by reading the other transcription in the other character format, without any notes.

PRC and Taiwan Usage

Since the DVD was recorded in Beijing, PRC usage is privileged in this text; however, to the extent practical, Taiwan usage is included as well. Glosses indicate alternate forms of expression, and some of the simulated authentic notes included in reading sections were produced by Taiwan speakers.

Student Work as Teaching Material

The inclusion of the work of the learner (edited by native speakers) in the reading sections is intended to 1) valorize the voice of the learner in the learning process; 2) provide an example of ideal i+1 texts [the original composition by the student being representative of the "i", and the minimal corrections made by the teacher constituting "+1"]; and 3) motivate learners to write for an intended audience (their classmates, in the immediate context).

Finally, supplementary materials to this text (such as indices) will be included at the end of Volume 2 and at yalebooks.com/eic.

If you have any comments, questions, or suggestions, please feel free to contact the author, Cynthia Ning, at <cyndy@hawaii.edu>.

Unit A-1: Making Friends

Lesson 1: *Three Students Introduce Themselves*

Three male students at the Peking University Middle School make impromptu remarks to introduce themselves. They were instructed to mention their names, hobbies, favorite subjects, and career goals.

Previewing Activity

1. List (in English) five items you think the students might mention in each of the categories below.

	Hobbies	**Favorite Subjects**	**Career Goals**
a.			
b.			
c.			
d.			
e.			

2. Work with your classmates and instructor(s) to put what you have listed into Chinese (*pinyin* and/or characters).

	Àihào 愛好 / 爱好	Zuì xǐhuān de kēmù 最喜歡的科目 / 最喜欢的科目	Zhíyè mùbiāo 職業目標 / 职业目标
a.			
b.			
c.			
d.			
e.			

3. Work with your classmates and instructor(s) to come up with five items in each category listed, which you as a class think are most likely to be mentioned by the Chinese students.

爱好 / 爱好

a. _____

b. _____

c. _____

d. _____

e. _____

最喜歡的科目 / 最喜欢的科目

f. _____

g. _____

h. _____

i. _____

j. _____

職業目標 / 职业目标

k. _____

l. _____

m. _____

n. _____

o. _____

First Viewing: Global/Specific Information

View the segment one or more times to complete the following tasks.

4. Count the number of times each item in your list for Exercise 3 was mentioned by the students on the DVD. Use the boxes provided above.

5. Collectively, the students name six hobbies, two favorite subjects, and three career goals. What are they? Write in Chinese, using *pinyin* and/or characters.

爱好 / 爱好	最喜歡的科目 / 最喜欢的科目	職業目標 / 职业目标
a. _____	_____	_____
b. _____	_____	_____
c. _____		_____
d. _____		
e. _____		
f. _____		

Unit A-1

6. Match the students with their career aspirations.

Sòng Xiáng
宋祥

Yán Jīng
嚴京／严京

Zhèng Chéng
鄭成／郑成

guǎnlǐ réncái
管理人才

diànnǎo gōngsī de lǎobǎn
電腦公司的老板／电脑公司的老板

qǐyè guǎnlǐ rényuán
企業管理人員／企业管理人员

diànnǎo shèjì shī
電腦設計師／电脑设计师

Second Viewing: Linguistic Information

7. This segment names a number of activities, mainly sports. If you wanted to incorporate these activities into verbal expressions ("*to play* soccer"), which of the following action terms would you add to each noun? Fill in the blanks in the sample sentence below with "a," "b," or "c."

a. tī 踢 (*to kick*) b. dǎ 打 (*to hit*) c. nothing more; the term can serve as a verb by itself

Wǒ huì 我會／会 ____*a*____ zúqiú 足球

_____ yóuyǒng 游泳

_____ pīngpāng qiú 乒乓球

_____ yǔmáo qiú 羽毛球

_____ chànggē 唱歌

_____ lánqiú 籃球／篮球

8. Sòng Xiáng says he likes to "play with computers." What is the *pinyin* for "play" (玩)?

_____ jìsuànjī 玩計算機／玩计算机

9. Sòng Xiáng and Yán Jīng each say, "I am very happy to see you"— "Hěn gāoxìng jiàn dào nǐmen." Zhèng Chéng intensifies this; he says, "I am extremely happy to see you." What is the *pinyin* for this expression in Chinese?

"_____ gāoxìng jiàn dào nǐmen."

"非常高興見到你們／非常高兴见到你们"

Lesson 1

10. Match the students' career aspirations with the English equivalents of these careers.

guǎnlǐ réncái
管理人才

diànnǎo gōngsī de lǎobǎn
電腦公司的老板／
电脑公司的老板

qǐyè guǎnlǐ rényuán
企業管理人員／
企业管理人员

diànnǎo shèjìshī
電腦設計師／
电脑设计师

business manager

computer programmer

management specialist

head of a computer company

Post-Viewing Activities

Speaking

11. Prepare a brief introduction of yourself. Mention
   •your name,
   •favorite pastimes,
   •favorite subjects, and
   •career aspirations.

Reference vocabulary (*select terms relevant to yourself*):
Favorite pastimes

dancing	tiàowǔ	跳舞
going to the mall	qù gòuwù zhōngxīn,	去購物中心／去购物中心
	guàng shāngchǎng	逛商場／逛商场
going to the movies	qù kàn diànyǐng	去看電影／去看电影
hanging out with friends	gēn péngyǒu dāi zài yìqǐ	跟朋友待在一起
playing computer games	wán diànzi yóuxì	玩電子遊戲／玩电子游戏
reading	kàn shū	看書／看书
singing karaoke	chàng kǎlā ōkēi	唱卡拉ＯＫ
sleeping	shuìjiào	睡覺／睡觉
working out	duànliàn	鍛煉／锻炼

Unit A-1

Favorite subjects

biology	shēngwù	生物
business administration	shāngwù guǎnlǐ	商務管理／商务管理
chemistry	huàxué	化學／化学
economics	jīngjì	經濟／经济
education	jiàoyù	教育
engineering	gōngchéng	工程
geography	dìlǐ	地理
history	lìshǐ	歷史／历史
law	fǎlǜ	法律
language & literature	yǔyán wénxué	語言文學／语言文学
mathematics	shùxué	數學／数学
philosophy	zhéxué	哲學／哲学
physics	wùlǐ	物理
psychology	xīnlǐ	心理
political science	zhèngzhì	政治
religion	zōngjiào	宗教
sociology	shèhuìxué	社會學／社会学

Career goals

accountant	kuàiji	會計／会计
actor / actress	yǎnyuán	演員／演员
athlete	yùndòngyuán	運動員／运动员
chief executive officer	zhíxíng zǒngjiān	執行總監／执行总监
computer programmer	jìsuànjī shèjìshī	計算機設計師／计算机设计师
dentist	yáyī	牙醫／牙医
doctor	yīshēng	醫生／医生
engineer	gōngchéngshī	工程師／工程师
fashion designer	shízhuāng shèjìshī	時裝設計師／时装设计师
filmmaker	zhìpiānrén	制片人
journalist	xīnwén jìzhě	新聞記者／新闻记者
lawyer	lǜshī	律師／律师
professor	jiàoshòu	教授
psychiatrist	xīnlǐ yīshēng	心理醫生／心理医生
scientist	kēxuéjiā	科學家／科学家

Lesson 1

Reading / Writing

12. Glance through the following self-introductions and fill in the chart below.

我非常喜歡跳舞，
希望將來能當演員。
我最喜歡的科目是
文學。

馬順德

我平时爱看有关哲学与历史
的书。
今后想当一名大学教授。
最喜欢的科目是人文科学。

陈莉

我对经济特别感兴趣。
我希望自己能成为一名会计。
我没事的时候喜欢逛商场。

林敏

name	fav. subject	pastimes	goals

13. Write a brief paragraph (3–5 sentences) to serve as a self-introduction, using Chinese characters.

Sample answer

(written by a student from Taiwan)

你們好！我的名字叫張林，今年十八歲。我現在是台灣大學中文系一年級的學生。很高興認識你們！

我的愛好有看電影、看書、打籃球、打網球、逛商場和玩電子遊戲。

我最喜歡的科目是語言、文學和歷史。

我希望畢業以後能成為一名新聞記者或者教授。

Unit A-1

宋祥： 你好，我的名字叫宋祥。我今年十八歲。
嗯，我的愛好有乒乓球、羽毛球和足球。
很高興見到你們。
嗯，我最喜歡的科目是計算機。呃，下課以後，我經常到機房去，呃，玩計算機。
呃，我以後想當一個，嗯，電腦設計師或者是，嗯，電腦公司的老板。

嚴京： 你好，我叫嚴京，今年十八歲。很高興見到你們。
我的愛好是足球、游泳和唱歌。
我最喜歡的科目是數學。
我今後的志向是做一名企業管理人員。

鄭成： 你好，我叫鄭成，今年十八歲。
呃，我喜歡籃球、足球和乒乓球。
非常高興見到你們。
我最喜歡的科目是計算機與數學。我希望以後能作爲一名管理人才。

宋祥： 你好，我的名字叫宋祥。我今年十八岁。
嗯，我的爱好有乒乓球、羽毛球和足球。
很高兴见到你们。
嗯，我最喜欢的科目是计算机。呃，下课以后，我经常到机房去，呃，玩计算机。
呃，我以后想当一个，嗯，电脑设计师或者是，嗯，电脑公司的老板。

严京： 你好，我叫严京，今年十八岁。很高兴见到你们。
我的爱好是足球、游泳和唱歌。
我最喜欢的科目是数学。
我今后的志向是做一名企业管理人员。

郑成： 你好，我叫郑成，今年十八岁。
呃，我喜欢篮球、足球和乒乓球。
非常高兴见到你们。
我最喜欢的科目是计算机与数学。我希望以后能作为一名管理人才。

Lesson 1

Sòng Xiáng: Nǐ hǎo, wǒ de míngzi jiào Sòng Xiáng. Wǒ jīnnián shíbā suì. En, wǒ de àihào yǒu pīngpāngqiú, yǔmáoqiú hé zúqiú. Hěn gāoxìng jiàn dao nǐmen.
En, wǒ zuì xǐhuan de kēmù shì jìsuànjī. E, xiàkè yǐhòu, wǒ jīngcháng dào jīfáng qù, e, wánr jìsuànjī.
E, wǒ yǐhòu xiǎng dāng yī ge, en, diànnǎo shèjìshī huòzhě shì, en, diànnǎo gōngsī de lǎobǎn.

Yán Jīng: Nǐ hǎo, wǒ jiào Yán Jīng, jīnnián shíbā suì. Hěn gāoxìng jiàn dao nǐmen.
Wǒ de àihào shì zúqiú, yóuyǒng hé chànggē.
Wǒ zuì xǐhuan de kēmù shì shùxué.
Wǒ jīnhòu de zhìxiàng shì zuò yī míng qǐyè guǎnlǐ rényuán.

Zhèng Chéng: Nǐ hǎo, wǒ jiào Zhèng Chéng, jīnnián shíbā suì.
E, wǒ xǐhuan lánqiú, zúqiú hé pīngpāngqiú. Fēicháng gāoxìng jiàn dao nǐmen.
Wǒ zuì xǐhuan de kēmù shì jìsuànjī yǔ shùxué. Wǒ xīwàng yǐhòu néng zuòwéi yī míng guǎnlǐ réncái.

Song Xiang: Hello, my name is Song Xiang. I'm 18 years old. Ah, my hobbies are playing Ping-Pong, badminton and soccer. I'm very happy to meet you.
Ah, my favorite class is computers. After school, I always go to the computer lab, ah, and play computer games. Uhm, in the future, I want to become a, uh, computer designer or a, uhm, the owner of a computer firm.

Yan Jing: Hello, my name is Yan Jing and this year I'm 18. I'm very pleased to meet you.
My hobbies are soccer, swimming, and singing.
My favorite class is math. In the future, I want to become a business manager.

Zheng Cheng: Hello, my name is Zheng Cheng and I'm 18 years old.
Ah, I like playing basketball, soccer, and Ping-Pong. I'm extremely happy to meet you.
My favorite classes are computers and math. In the future I hope to become a member of a management team.

Unit A-1

Unit A-1: Making Friends

Lesson 2: *Interviews with Two Security Guards*

In the first portion of this segment, Robyn Yee, a U.S. high school senior, interviews the guard at an entrance gate to Peking University. In the second portion, Todd Pavel, a U.S. graduate student, interviews the supervisor of the security guards.

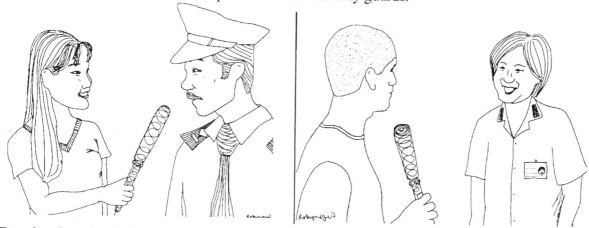

Previewing Activity

1. If you were assigned to find out some basic personal information about a Chinese person you had never spoken to before, which questions might you ask? **List five questions below in Chinese** (write *pinyin*, characters, or a combination of both).

a. _____

b. _____

c. _____

d. _____

e. _____

First Viewing: Global Information

After you have viewed the segments one or more times, complete the following tasks.

Segment A:

2. Indicate how many of the questions you listed were asked by Robyn. _____

3. List below the topics of Robyn's questions. Write in English:

   a. **Name**   b. _____   c. _____

                d. _____   e. _____

4. How many of the questions you listed in Exercise 1 were asked by Todd? _____

5. List the topics of Todd's questions:

   a. *Name*   b. _____   c. _____

                 d. _____   e. _____

                 f. _____   g. _____

Second Viewing: Specific Information

View the segments again as necessary to complete the tasks below.

Segment A:

6. Write five facts about the security guard Robyn interviewed.

a. _His name is Hóu Jiànqiáng._ _____

b. _____

c. _____

d. _____

e. _____

Segment B:

7. Write seven facts about the supervisor Todd interviewed.

a. _____

b. _____

c. _____

d. _____

e. _____

f. _____

g. _____

Unit A-1

8. Write three facts about the supervisor's daughter.

a. _____

b. _____

c. _____

Third Viewing: Linguistic Information

View the segments again as necessary to complete the tasks below.

9. Error correction

The same particle is missing in a question posed by Robyn and one posed by Todd. Please insert it in the blanks provided.

Robyn: Ng, nǐ shì zuò shénme _____?

Todd: Nà nǐ shénme shíhòu kāishǐ zhèige gōngzuò _____?

10. Todd often confirms what he understands of what he hears by restating it.

Example: Todd: Nǐ jiào shénme míngzi?

            Supervisor: Wǒ jiào Zhā Ānfēn.

            Todd: Zhā Fēn?

            Supervisor: Zhā Ānfēn.

            Todd: Zhā Ānfēn.

List three more examples of what Todd confirms by restating:

a. _____

b. _____

c. _____

11. Please transcribe the Chinese equivalents of the sentences indicated below, using *pinyin*, characters, or a mixture of both.

Segment A

Robyn: How old are you this year? _____

Guard: My (type of) occupation is called "security guard."

_____

Robyn: Do you like your job?_____

Guard: I like it very much indeed. _____

Robyn: Are you married? _____

Guard: Not yet. _____

Robyn: Okay, thanks. _____

Guard: You're welcome._____

Lesson 2

Todd: Then, where are you from?   _____

Supervisor: I'm from Shanghai.   _____

Todd: You come from Shanghai?   _____

Supervisor: Right.   _____

....

Supervisor: My daughter's a junior, seventeen years old.

....

Todd: Then, how old are you this year?   _____

......

Todd: Oh, is that so! Okay, thanks!

_____

12. Fill in the missing pieces of the following chart.

English	*pinyin*	characters
occupation		行業／行业
	bǎo'ān	保安
be married		結婚／结婚
	gōngzuò	工作
begin		開始／开始
	dìfang	地方
	àirén	愛人／爱人
be transferred to		調／调
child, children		孩子
high school		高中
	niánjì	年紀／年纪

Unit A-1

Post-Viewing Activities

Speaking

13. Work with your classmates to interview/be interviewed on the following topics:
   •name
   •age
   •occupation / where you go to school
   •do you like your school / job
   •how long you have been at your school / job
   •parents' occupations
(See following for hints....)

13a. Name

Question (informal; generally said by young people to someone their own age or younger):

   Nǐ jiào shénme míngzi?   *What is your name?*

   Nǐ de míngzi jiào shénme?

Answer: Wǒ jiào ⸺⸺⸺⸺⸺⸺⸺⸺

   My name is ⸺⸺⸺⸺⸺⸺⸺⸺

Question (polite; used by adults with strangers likely to be of equal or superior social status):

   Nín guì xìng?   *What is your (honored) surname?*

   Qǐngwèn, guì xìng?   *May I ask your (honored) surname?*

Answer: Miǎn guì xìng⸺⸺⸺ . Wǒ jiào ⸺⸺⸺⸺ .

      (last name)   (last name, then first name)

   Dispense with the "honored," my last name is ⸺⸺. *My (full) name is* ⸺⸺⸺.

Sample conversations:

   1.   A: Nǐmen jiào shénme míngzi?   *What are your names?*

      B: Wǒ jiào Wáng Dàtóng.   *I am Wang Datong.*

      C: Wǒ jiào Sabrina Brown.   *I am Sabrina Brown.*

   2.   A: Nín guì xìng?   *What is your honored last name?*

      B: Miǎn guì xìng Brown. Wǒ jiào Sabrina Brown.

      Dispense with the "honored," my last name is Brown. I am Sabrina Brown.

Lesson 2

13b. <u>Age</u>

Question (generally asked of a child):

Nǐ [jīnnián] jǐ suì le?   *How old are you [this year]?*

Question (generally asked of an adult):

Nín [jīnnián] duó dà le?   *How old are you [this year]?*

Nín [jīnnián] duó dà niánji le?   *What's your age [this year]?*

Nín [jīnnián] duó dà suìshu le?   *What's your age [this year]?*

Answer: Wǒ [jīnnián] _____ suì le.

Sample conversation:

      A: Nín jīnnián duō dà suìshu le?   *How old are you this year? (asked by an adult of an elderly person)*

      B: Wǒ yǐjīng jiǔshíjiǔ suì le.   *I'm already 99.*

      A: Nǐ ne? Nǐ jǐ suì le?   *How about you? How old are you? (asked by an adult of a child)*

      C: Wǒ cái sān suì!   *I am only three!*

13c. <u>Occupation</u>

Question:

      Nǐ / nín shì zuò shénme de?   *What do you do?*

      Nǐ / nín de gōngzuo shì shénme?   *What is your work / occupation?*

      Nǐ / nín shì zuò shénme gōngzuò de?   *What work do you do?*

      Nǐ jiānglái xiǎng zuò shénme?   *What (occupation) do you want, in the future?*

Answer: Wǒ shì _____.   *I am a _____.*

      Wǒ jiānglái xiǎng zuò _____.

      In the future, I intend to be a _____.

(The following vocabulary is for your reference only. You might choose several to remember for your own purposes; the remainder can be handy if your classmates choose to use them.)

      accountant kuàiji 會計／会计

      actor / actress yǎnyuán 演員／演员

      administrative assistant xíngzhèng zhùlǐ 行政助理

      architect jiànzhúshī, shèjìshī 建筑師，設計師／建筑师，设计师

      artist yìshùjiā 藝術家／艺术家

      astronaut yǔhángyuán (PRC) 宇航員／宇航员

         tàikōngrén (T) 太空人

Unit A-1

athlete yùndòngyuán 運動員／运动员

author zuòzhě, zuòjiā 作者，作家

baker miànbāoshī 麵包師／面包师

banker yínhángjiā 銀行家／银行家

bartender jiǔbǎo (old term); tiáojiǔshī (new term) 酒保，調酒師／调酒师

beautician měiróngshī 美容師／美容师

bus driver qìchē sījī 汽車司機／汽车司机

businessperson shāngren 商人

buyer cǎigòuyuán 採購員／采购员

cab driver chūzūchē sījī (PRC) 出租車司機／出租车司机

　　　　jìchéngchē sījī (T) 計程車司機／计程车司机

carpenter mùjiang 木匠

cashier chū'nàyuán 出納員／出纳员

chef dàchú; chúshīzhǎng 大廚／大厨，廚師長／厨师长

chief executive officer zǒngzhíxíngguān 總執行官／总执行官

coach jiàoliàn 教練／教练

company president gōngsī zǒngcái 公司總裁／公司总裁

computer programmer jìsuànjī chéngxùyuán 計算機程序員／计算机程序员

counselor fúdǎoyuán 輔導員／辅导员

dancer wǔdǎojiā 舞蹈家

delivery person sònghuòyuán 送貨員／送货员

dentist yáyī 牙醫／牙医

doctor yīshēng 醫生／医生

electrician diàngōng 電工／电工

engineer gōngchéngshī 工程師／工程师

fashion designer shízhuāng shèjìshī 時裝設計師／时装设计师

firefighter xiāofángyuán (PRC) 消防員／消防员

　　　　jiùhuǒyuán (T) 救火員／救火员

filmmaker diànyǐng zhìzuòrén 電影制作人／电影制作人

flight attendant kōngzhōng fúwùyuán 空中服務員／空中服务员

florist huāshāng 花商

Lesson 2

gardener yuánlín gōngrén, huājiàng (PRC) 園林工人／园林工人，花匠

yuándīng (T) 園丁／园丁

graduate student yánjiùshēng 研究生

hairdresser fàxíngshī 髮型師／发型师

high school student gāozhōngshēng 高中生

housewife jiātíng zhǔfù 家庭主婦／家庭主妇

interior decorator shìnèi shèjìshī 室內設計師／室内设计师

janitor qīngjiégōng 清潔工／清洁工

journalist jìzhě 記者／记者

judge fǎguān 法官

lawyer lùshī 律師／律师

librarian túshū guǎnlǐyuán 圖書館理員／图书馆理员

manager jīnglǐ 經理／经理

masseur /masseuse ànmóshī 按摩師／按摩师

mechanic jìgōng 技工

military officer jūnguān 軍官／军官

military personnel jūnrén 軍人／军人

nurse hùshì 護士／护士

pilot fēixíngyuán 飛行員／飞行员

police officer jǐngchá 警察

postal carrier yóudìyuán (PRC) 郵遞員／邮递员

yóuchāi (T) 郵差／邮差

professor jiàoshòu 教授

principal / college president xiàozhǎng 校長／校长

psychiatrist xīnlǐ yīshēng 心理醫生／心理医生

sailor hǎiyuán; shuǐshǒu 海員／海员，水手

salesperson tuīxiāoyuán; shòuhuòyuán 推銷員／推销员，售貨員／售货员

scientist kēxuéjiā 科學家／科学家

secretary mìshu 秘書／秘书

security guard jǐngwèi 警衛／警卫

Unit A-1

singer   gēchàngjiā   歌唱家

stockbroker   gǔpiào jīngjìrén   股票經紀人／股票经纪人

surgeon   wàikē yīshēng   外科醫生／外科医生

teacher   jiàoshī   教師／教师

technician   jìshùyuán   技術員／技术员

telephone operator   diànhuà jiēxiànyuán   電話接線員／电话接线员

truck driver   kǎchē sījī   卡車司機／卡车司机

tour guide   dǎoyóu   導遊／导遊

undergraduate student   běnkēshēng (PRC)   本科生

　　　　dàxuéshēng (T & PRC)   大學生／大学生

waiter / waitress   fúwùyuán   服務員／服务员

Answer: Wǒ shì zuò _____ de.　　*I am in* _____.

　　shēngyi   生意　　　　　　　　　*business*

　　fángdìchǎn   房地產　　　　　　*real estate*

　　bǎoxiǎn   保險／保险　　　　　*insurance*

13d. <u>Do you like your job?</u>

Question:

Nǐ xǐhuan nǐ de gōngzuò ma?　　　*Do you like your job?*

Nǐ xǐhuan dāng _____ ma?　　　*Do you like being a _____?*

Nǐ juéde dāng _____ hǎo ma?　　*Do you think being a _____ is good?*

Answer:

Wǒ hěn xǐhuan wǒ de gōngzuò.　　*I like my job very much.*

Wǒ juéde wǒ de gōngzuò bùcuò. Qián　*I think my job isn't bad. The money's not*
　bù duō, kěshì hěn yǒu yìsi.　　　　*great, but it's interesting.*

Wǒ bù xǐhuan wǒ de gōngzuò. Wǒ　　*I don't like my job. I'm thinking of changing.*
　xiǎng huàn yí ge.

Wǒ bù xǐhuan wǒ de gōngzuò, kěshì　*I don't like my job, but I don't have a choice,*
　méi bànfǎ, děi chīfàn!　　　　　　*I have to eat!*

Lesson 2

13e. <u>How long have you had this job?</u>

Question:

Nǐ shénme shíhòu kāishǐ zhèi fèn
    gōngzuò de?

When did you start this job?

Nǐ (zuò) zhèi fèn gōngzuò zuò le duō
    cháng shíjiān le?

How long have you been doing this job?

Answer:

Wǒ shì _____ kāishǐ (zhèi fèn gōngzuò) de. *I started (this job) _____.*

    qùnián   *last year*

    jiǔ'èr nián   *in 1992*

Wǒ (zuò zhèi fèn gōngzuò) zuò le _____ le. *I've had (this job) for _____ already.*

                 yī nián   *a year*

Wǒ gāng kāishǐ (zhèi fèn gōngzuò). *I just started (this job).*

13f. <u>School</u>

Question: Nǐ zài nǎr shàngxué?   *Where do you go to school?*

Answer: Wǒ shàng _____.   *I'm at _____.*

The following are some of the largest university / high school Chinese language programs in the U.S., for your reference.

<u>Universities</u>

Columbia University Gēlúnbǐyà Dàxué 哥倫比亞大學／哥伦比亚大学

Cornell University Kāngnàiěr Dàxué 康奈爾大學／康奈尔大学

Duke University Dùkè Dàxué 杜克大學／杜克大学

Harvard University Hāfó Dàxué 哈佛大學／哈佛大学

Indiana University Yìndì'ānnà Dàxué 印第安納大學／印第安纳大学

North Carolina State University Běikǎluóláinà Zhōulì Dàxué 北卡羅萊納州立大學／
    北卡罗莱纳州立大学

Ohio State University Éhài'é Zhōulì Dàxué 俄亥俄州立大學／俄亥俄州立大学

Princeton University Pǔlínsīdùn Dàxué 普林斯頓大學／普林斯顿大学

Stanford University Sītǎnfú Dàxué 斯坦福大學／斯坦福大学

University of California, Berkeley Jiāzhōu Dàxué Bókèlái Fēnxiào 加州大學柏克萊分校
    ／加州大学柏克莱分校

Unit A-1

University of California, Los Angeles Jiāzhōu Dàxué Luòshānjī Fēnxiào 加州大學洛杉磯分校／加州大学洛杉矶分校

University of California, Santa Barbara Jiāzhōu Dàxué Shèngbābālā Fēnxiào 加州大學聖芭芭拉分校／加州大学圣芭芭拉分校

University of Chicago Zhījiāgē Dàxué 芝加哥大學／芝加哥大学

University of Hawaii Xiàwēiyí Dàxué 夏威夷大學／夏威夷大学

University of Illinois Yīlìnuòsī Dàxué 伊利諾斯大學／伊利诺斯大学

University of Kansas Kānsàsī Dàxué 堪薩斯大學／堪萨斯大学

University of Michigan Mìxiēgēn Dàxué 密歇根大學／密歇根大学

University of North Carolina Běikǎluóláinà Dàxué 北卡羅萊納大學／北卡罗莱纳大学

University of Pennsylvannia Bīnxīfǎníyà Dàxué 賓夕法尼亞大學／宾夕法尼亚大学

University of Pittsburgh Pīzībǎo Dàxué 匹茲堡大學／匹兹堡大学

University of Southern California Nánjiāzhōu Dàxué 南加州大學／南加州大学

University of Washington (Seattle) Xīyǎtú Huáshèngdùn Dàxué 西雅圖華盛頓大學／西雅图华盛顿大学

University of Wisconsin Wēisīkāngxīng Dàxué 威斯康星大學／威斯康星大学

Washington University (St. Louis) Shènglùyì Huáshèngdùn Dàxué 聖路易華盛頓大學／圣路易华盛顿大学

Yale University Yēlǔ Dàxué 耶魯大學／耶鲁大学

High schools

Breck School, Minneapolis, MN Bóruì Zhōngxué 博瑞中學／博瑞中学

Bronx High School of Science, Bronx, NY Bùlǎngshì Kēxué Gāozhōng 布朗市科學高中／布朗市科学高中

Choate Rosemary Hall, Wallingford, CT Chóngdé Zhōngxué 崇德中學／崇德中学

Enloe High School, Raleigh, NC Yīngluò Gāozhōng 英洛高中

Highland Park Senior High School, St. Paul, MN Gāoshān Zhōngxué 高山中學／高山中学

Indiana Academy, Muncie, IN Yìndì'ānnà Zhòngdiǎnzhōngxué 印第安納重點高中／印第安纳重点高中

Lesson 2

Iolani School, Honolulu, HI Yìàolánní Xuéxiào 意奧蘭尼學校／意奧兰尼学校

Landon School, Bethesda, MD Lándùn Xuéxiào 蘭頓學校／兰顿学校

Lakeside School, Seattle, WA Húpàn Xuéxiào 湖畔學校／湖畔学校

Livingston High School, Livingston, NJ Lǐwénsīdùn Gāozhōng 李文斯頓高中／
李文斯顿高中

Lowell High School, San Francisco, CA Luòwēiěr Gāozhōng 洛威爾高中／洛威尔高中

Minneapolis South Senior High School, Minneapolis, MN Míngchéng Nán Gāozhōng
明城南高中

Phillips Academy, Andover, MA Fěilìpǔsī Xuéyuàn, Ānduōfú

菲利浦斯學院，安多福／菲利浦斯学院，安多福

Phillips Exeter Academy, Exeter, NH Fěilìpǔēnzé Gāozhōng

菲利浦恩澤高中／菲利浦恩泽高中

Punahou School, Honolulu, HI 96822 Púnàhé Xuéxiào 菩納菏學校／菩纳菏学校

St. Paul's School, Concord, NH Shèngbǎoluó Gāozhōng 聖保羅高中／圣保罗高中

Reading / Writing

14. Following is a letter written to you by a student in Hong Kong. Highlight what you can understand of it.

你好！

我是香港中文大學的一名本科生，專業是商務管理。我今年２１歲。我不太喜歡我的專業，但我的父母和朋友都說這個專業很好，所以我就學了這個專業。我最喜歡的科目是外語。現在我會說英語和德語，以後我還想學法語和日語。我將來想當一名記者，可以走遍世界各地。我的家並不在北京，而是在廣州。我很想家，想爸爸、媽媽和哥哥。

到現在，我從未出過國。因此，我很想知道在美國的同齡人是怎樣生活的。如果你有空，能給我回信嗎？我想知道你的專業是甚麼？你和你的家人住在一起嗎？你平時最喜歡做甚麼？你來過中國嗎？

對了，我想畢業後去美國讀碩士，你能給我推薦幾所有名的大學嗎？我只聽說過哈佛大學和耶魯大學。除此之外，還有哪些呢？

期待你的回信！

李明

15. The letter from Lǐ Míng can be divided into six sections. Match the number of the section with the description of its content.

section 1

section 2

section 3

section 4

section 5

section 6

_____ solicitation of information about U.S. universities

_____ signature

_____ greeting/salutation

_____ solicitation of information about you

_____ closing salutation

_____ basic information about self

Lesson 2

16. Scan Section 2; then fill in the blanks below, providing information about the author of the letter.

Name: _____*Lǐ Míng*_____   University: _____

Level (circle one): *undergraduate / graduate*   Major: _____

Age: _____   Favorite subject: _____

Foreign languages spoken currently: _____ & _____

Foreign languages to be learned in the future: _____ & _____

Career goals (circle one): *teacher / journalist*

Hometown (circle one): *Hong Kong / Shanghai / Guangzhou / Beijing*

Family members (circle all mentioned):

 mother / father / older brother / older sister / younger brother / younger sister / other

17. Now scan Section 3, and complete the following tasks.

    a. Circle one: Lǐ Míng *has / has not* traveled abroad.

    b. Which questions does Lǐ Míng ask of you? Check all that apply.

    _____ What is the name of your university?

    _____ What is your major?

    _____ Do you live with your family?

    _____ Who is there in your family?

    _____ What do you like to do, usually?

    _____ Have you ever been to China?

    _____ Which foreign languages do you speak?

18. Scan Section 4, and complete the following tasks.

    a. Circle one: Lǐ Míng would like to come to the U.S. and study for a

    Bachelor's / Master's / Doctoral degree

Unit A-1

b. Circle all that apply: Lǐ Míng has heard of the following U.S. universities—

Princeton University / Ohio State University /
University of California at Berkeley / Notre Dame University /
Harvard University / Cornell University / Yale University

19. Scan Section 5, and respond to the following.

What is the closing salutation? Check one:

_____ Looking forward to your response.

_____ Please write soon.

_____ I hope you will write me back.

20. Fill in the blanks by guessing the missing information (characters, *pinyin*, or English) in the vocabulary list below, which is keyed to Lǐ Míng's letter. The first two items have been completed for you.

名 _____*míng*_____ *(slightly formal measure word for persons)*

本科生   běnkēshēng **undergraduate student**_____

專業 / 专业   zhuānyè _____

商務管理 / 商务管理   shāngwù guǎnlǐ *business management*

但 _____ *however, but*

科目   kēmù _____

_____ jiānglái *in the future*

記者 / 记者 _____ *journalist, reporter*

_____ zǒubiàn *travel throughout*

世界各地   shìjiè gèdì _____

並不在 X, 而是在 Y / 并不在 X, 而是在 Y _____

   to not really be at X, (but instead) to be at Y

想家 _____ *to be homesick*

_____ cóngwèi *to have never (same as* 從來沒 / 从来没*)*

_____ yīncǐ *because of this*

同齡人 / 同龄人   tónglíngrén _____

生活   shēnghuó _____

如果　　rúguǒ _____

回信　　_____ *write back*

一起　　_____ *together*

平時 / 平时　píngshí _____

碩士 / 硕士　shuòshì _____

推薦 / 推荐　tuījiàn _____

_____ suǒ *(measure word for universities and other institutions)*

有名　　_____ *to be well-known, famous*

哈佛大學 / 哈佛大学　Hāfó Dàxué _____

耶魯大學 / 耶鲁大学　Yēlǔ Dàxué _____

除此之外　_____ *except for this, in addition to this*

期待　　_____ *to look forward to*

21. Following is the completed vocabulary list. Re-read the letter, and see how much of it you can understand now.

名　míng *(slightly formal measure word for persons)*

本科生　běnkēshēng *undergraduate student*

專業 / 专业　zhuānyè *major*

商務管理 / 商务管理　shāngwù guǎnlǐ *business management*

但　dàn *however, but*

科目　kēmù *subject*

將來 / 将来　jiānglái *in the future*

記者 / 记者　jìzhě *journalist, reporter*

走遍　zǒubiàn *travel throughout*

世界各地　shìjiè gèdì *everyplace on earth*

並不在 X，而是在 Y / 并不在 X，而是在 Y　bìng bù zài X, ér shi zài Y

　　to not really be at X, (but instead) to be at Y

想家　xiǎngjiā *to be homesick*

從未　cóngwèi *to have never (same as* 從來沒 / 从来没*)*

因此　yīncǐ *because of this*

同齡人 / 同龄人　tónglíngrén *people of the same age*

Unit A-1

生活　shēnghuó *to live*

如果　rúguǒ *if*

回信　huíxìn *write back*

一起　yīqǐ *together*

平時 / 平时　píngshí *normally, usually, most times*

碩士 / 硕士　shuòshì *Master's degree*

推薦 / 推荐　tuījiàn *to recommend*

所　suǒ *(measure word for universities and other institutions)*

有名　yǒumíng *to be well-known, famous*

哈佛大學 / 哈佛大学　Hāfó Dàxué *Harvard University*

耶魯大學 / 耶鲁大学　Yēlǔ Dàxué *Yale University*

除此之外　chúcǐzhīwài *except for this, in addition to this*

期待　qīdài *to look forward to*

22. Write a letter back to Lǐ Míng, responding to his questions.

Lesson 2

Sample Answer

(edited from American student compositions)

你好！

我很高興收到你給我們寫的信。你的英語一定很好，比我的中文好。以後我們可以用英語寫信，怎麼樣？

我的專業還沒決定。我父母讓我讀管理，可是我跟你一樣，對管理不感興趣。我想學拍電影。可是我爸爸不同意。所以我還不知道我應該怎麼辦。你說呢？你說我應該學管理嗎？

美國有很多很好的大學。比如說，很多州立學校又便宜又好。俄亥俄州立大學、印第安納大學、密歇根大學還有夏威夷大學都是好學校，學費也不貴。值得考慮。

期待你的回信！

你的美國筆友

安娜

Unit A-1

余修明：你好，你的名字叫甚麼？

侯建強：我叫侯建強。

余修明：你今年多大了？

侯建強：我今年二十歲。

余修明：呃，你是做甚麼（的）？

侯建強：我們這種行業叫做保安。我們屬於是北京市保安服務總公司，門安分公司管理。

余修明：呃，你喜歡你的工作嗎？

侯建強：對，非常喜歡。

余修明：哦，你結婚了嗎？

侯建強：沒有哪。

余修明：哦，你 ... 好，謝謝 你。

侯建強：不客氣。

彭德：您好！你叫甚麼名字？

查安芬：我叫查安芬。

彭德：查芬？

查安芬：查安芬。

彭德：查安芬。那你甚麼時候開始這個工作（的）？

查安芬：呃 ...九零年。

彭德：九零年。你喜歡你的工作嗎？

余修明：你好，你的名字叫什么？

侯建强：我叫侯建强。

余修明：你今年多大了？

侯建强：我今年二十岁。

余修明：呃，你是做什么（的）？

侯建强：我们这种行业叫做保安。我们属于是北京市保安服务总公司，门安分公司管理。

余修明：呃，你喜欢你的工作吗？

侯建强：对，非常喜欢。

余修明：哦，你结婚了吗？

侯建强：没有哪。

余修明：哦，你 ... 好，谢谢 你。

侯建强：不客气。

彭德：您好！你叫什么名字？

查安芬：我叫查安芬。

彭德：查芬？

查安芬：查安芬。

彭德：查安芬。那你什么时候开始这个工作（的）？

查安芬：呃 ...九零年。

彭德：九零年。你喜欢你的工作吗？

Lesson 2

Yú Xiūmíng: Nǐ hǎo, nǐ de míngzi jiào
                   shénme?

Hóu Jiànqiáng: Wǒ jiào Hóu Jiànqiáng.

Yú Xiūmíng: Nǐ jīnnián duōdà le?

Hóu Jiànqiáng: Wǒ jīnnián èrshí suì.

Yú Xiūmíng: E, nǐ shì zuò shénme (de)?

Hóu Jiànqiáng: Wǒmen zhèzhǒng hángyè
                   jiàozuò bǎoān. Wǒmen shǔyú shì
                   Běijīngshì bǎoān fúwù gōngsī ménān
                   fēngōngsī guǎnlǐ.

Yú Xiūmíng: E, nǐ xǐhuan nǐ de
                   gōngzuò ma?

Hóu Jiànqiáng: Duì, fēicháng xǐhuan.

Yú Xiūmíng: O, nǐ jiéhūn le ma?

Hóu Jiànqiáng: Méiyǒu na.

Yú Xiūmíng: O, nǐ ... hǎo, xièxiè nǐ.

Hóu Jiànqiáng: Bù kèqì.

Robyn: Hello, what's your name?

Hou Jianqiang: My name is Hou Jianqiang.

Robyn: How old are you this year?

Hou Jianqiang: I'm twenty.

Robyn: Er, what do you do?

Hou Jianqiang: This occupation of ours is
                called "security guard." We work for
                the "Door Security" Branch of the
                Beijing Security Service.

Robyn: Er, do you like your job?

Hou Jianqiang: Yes, I like it very much.

Robyn: Oh. Are you married?

Hou Jianqiang: Not yet.

Robyn: Oh. You ... Okay, thank you.

Hou Jianqiang: You're welcome.

Péng Dé: Nín hǎo! Nǐ jiào shénme
            míngzi?

Zhā Ānfēn: Wǒ jiào Zhā Ānfēn.

Péng Dé: Zhā Fēn?

Zhā Ānfēn: Zhā Ānfēn.

Péng Dé: Zhā Ānfēn. Nà nǐ shénme
            shíhòu kāishǐ zhège gōngzuò (de)?

Zhā Ānfēn: E ... jiǔlíng nián.

Péng Dé: Jiǔlíng nián. Nǐ xǐhuan nǐ
            de gōngzuò ma?

Todd Pavel: Hello, what's your name?

Zha Anfen: My name is Zha Anfen.

Todd Pavel: Zha Fen?

Zha Anfen: Zha Anfen.

Todd Pavel: Zha Anfen. When did you start
           this job, then?

Zha Anfen: Er ... 1990.

Todd Pavel: 1990. Do you like your
              job?

Unit A-1

查安芬：我喜歡。

彭德：那您是甚麼地方人？

查安芬：我是上海的。

彭德：從上海來的？

查安芬：對。

彭德：啊，你的家裏都在這兒嗎？

查安芬：我的家裏我愛人在這兒，我就調北京工作了。

彭德：那你有沒有孩子？

查安芬：有。

彭德：幾個？

查安芬：一個小女孩。

彭德：啊，是嗎？她多大？

查安芬：今年高二，十七歲。

彭德：十七歲。所以她在高中上學。

查安芬：高中，啊，在師大二附中。

彭德：啊，那你今年有多大年紀了？

查安芬：我今年四十八歲。

彭德：啊，是麼！好，謝謝你呀！

查安芬：我喜欢。

彭德：那您是什么地方人？

查安芬：我是上海的。

彭德：从上海来的？

查安芬：对。

彭德：啊，你的家里都在这儿吗？

查安芬：我的家里我爱人在这儿，我就调北京工作了。

彭德：那你有没有孩子？

查安芬：有。

彭德：几个？

查安芬：一个小女孩。

彭德：啊，是吗？她多大？

查安芬：今年高二，十七岁。

彭德：十七岁。所以她在高中上学。

查安芬：高中，啊，在师大二附中。

彭德：啊，那你今年有多大年纪了？

查安芬：我今年四十八岁。

彭德：啊，是么！好，谢谢你呀！

Lesson 2

Zhā Ānfēn: Wǒ xǐhuan.

Péng Dé: Nà nín shì shénme dìfang rén?

Zhā Ānfēn: Wǒ shì Shànghǎi de.

Péng Dé: Cóng Shànghǎi láide?

Zhā Ānfēn: Duì.

Péng Dé: A, nǐ de jiālǐ dōu zài zhè(r) ma?

Zhā Ānfēn: Wǒ de jiālǐ wǒ àirén zài zhè(r), wǒ jiù diào Běijīng le.

Péng Dé: Nà nǐ yǒu mei yǒu háizi?

Zhā Ānfēn: Yǒu.

Péng Dé: Jǐ ge?

Zhā Ānfēn: Yī ge xiǎo nǚhái(r).

Péng Dé: A, shì ma? Tā duō dà?

Zhā Ānfēn: Jīn nián gāoèr, shíqī suì.

Péng Dé: Shíqī suì. Suǒyǐ tā zài gāozhōng shàngxué.

Zhā Ānfēn: Gāozhōng, à, zài Shīdà Èrfùzhōng.

Péng Dé: A, nà nǐ jīnnián yǒu duō dà niánji le?

Zhā Ānfēn: Wǒ jīnnián sìshíbā suì.

Péng Dé: A, shì me! Hǎo, xièxie nǐ ya!

Zha Anfen: I like it.

Todd Pavel: Where are you from, then?

Zha Anfen: I am from Shanghai.

Todd Pavel: You come from Shanghai?

Zha Anfen: Yes.

Todd Pavel: Is your family here?

Zha Anfen: My family ... my husband is here, so I transferred to Beijing.

Todd Pavel: Do you have kids, then?

Zhang Anfen: Yes.

Todd Pavel: How many?

Zhang Anfen: One young girl.

Todd Pavel: Oh, really? How old?

Zhang Anfen: A sophomore in high school, 17.

Todd Pavel: Seventeen, so she is in high school.

Zhang Anfen: High school, yes, the Second Attached High School to Beijing Normal University.

Todd Pavel: Er, then how old are you this year?

Zhang Anfen: I'm 48 this year.

Todd Pavel: Ah, really! Okay, thank you!

Unit A-1

Unit A-1: Making Friends

Lesson 3: *Three Students Name Favorite Pastimes*

Three students of the Attached Middle School to Peking University introduce themselves.

Previewing Activity

1. List (in English) five topics you think the students might touch upon in their self-introductions.

    a. _____*Name*_____   b. _____

    c. _____   d. _____

                          e. _____

2. Work with your classmates and instructor(s) to put what you have listed into Chinese (*pinyin* and/or characters).

    a. _____*Xìngmíng*_____   b. _____

    c. _____   d. _____

                          e. _____

3. Work with your classmates and instructor(s) to come up with five topics that you as a class think are most likely to be mentioned by the Chinese students.

    a. _____*Xìngmíng*_____   *(The boxes are for the next task.)*

    b. _____

    c. _____

    d. _____

    e. _____

First Viewing: Global Information

4. Count the total number of times each topic in your list for Exercise 3 was mentioned by the students on the DVD. Use the boxes provided.

5. What topics did the students on the DVD touch upon (in addition to their names)? List them for each person below.

Lǐ Yàowěi	Shī Huá	Ān Shūmǐn
_____	_____	_____
_____	*the benefits of travel*	_____
		_____
		making friends with Americans

Second Viewing: Specific Information

6. Match the students with their names, ages, and what they said.

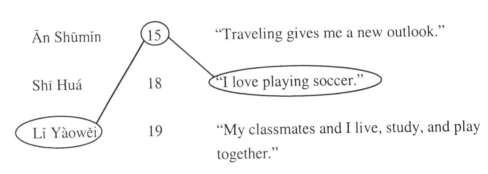

Ān Shūmǐn	15	"Traveling gives me a new outlook."
Shī Huá	18	"I love playing soccer."
Lǐ Yàowěi	19	"My classmates and I live, study, and play together."

Third Viewing: Linguistic Information

7. Fill in the blank below, using *pinyin*, based on what Shī Huá says.

"Wǒ xǐhuān lǚ, _____." ("I like to tra-, travel.")

8. Shī Huá says that traveling has many benefits, including the three below. Match the English with the Chinese expressions.

"Wǒ juéde lǚxíng néng...
"我覺得旅行能／我觉得旅行能。。。

•gěi wǒ xīn de shìyě."
給我新的視野／给我新的视野。"

•ràng wǒ qù jiēchù shèhuì."
讓我去接觸社會／让我去接触社会。"

•ràng wǒ qù jiēchù rénshēng."
讓我去接觸人生／让我去接触人生。"

"I feel that traveling can ...

•let me come in contact with society."

•give me a new field of vision."

•let me come in contact with life."

Unit A-1

9. Ān Shūmǐn says she was born in Hebei Province. Fill in the blank below.

"Wǒ _____ zài Héběi." "我出生在河北。"

10. Ān Shūmǐn is enthusiastic about her relationship with her classmates. She says she does everything with them, including the following (match the English to the Chinese):

•yīkuàir zhù zài sùshè lǐ
一塊兒住在宿舍裡／一块儿住在宿舍里

•yīqǐ shēnghuó
一起生活

•yīkuàir xuéxí
一塊兒學習／一块儿学习

•yīkuàir wánshuǎ
一塊兒玩耍／一块儿玩耍

•yīkuàir huòqǔ zhīshi
一塊兒獲取知識／一块儿获取知识

•play together

•study together

•obtain knowledge together

•live together in the dorm

•live (our) lives together

11. In other words, Ān Shūmǐn "gets along very well" with her classmates:

"Wǒmen _____ de hěn hǎo." "我們相處得很好／我们相处得很好。"

12. She also "hopes to make friends with our friends from America":

"Wǒ xīwàng _____ Měiguó de péngyoumen _____ péngyou."
"我希望跟美國的朋友們交朋友／我希望跟美国的朋友们交朋友。"

Post-Viewing Activities

Speaking

13. Prepare another brief introduction of yourself. Say where you were born, whether or not you like to travel (and why), and something about your relationships with your friends. Note: reasons why perhaps you might NOT like to travel—

"Wǒ méi shíjiān." *(No time)*

"Lǚxíng tài guì le." *(Too expensive)*

"Lǚxíng tài máfán le." *(Too much trouble)*

"Wǒ duì lǚxíng bù gǎn xìngqu." *(Not interested)*

Lesson 3

Reading / Writing

14. Following is an installment in your correspondence with Zhào Míng, a penfriend in Taipei. Highlight what you can understand of it.

親愛的美國筆友，

你最近好嗎？

你的上一封信我收到了，謝謝。你的信寫得很有意思，讀你的信就像在面對面與你交談。

我最近加入了學校的足球隊。自從參加了球隊以後，我交了很多的朋友，我們一塊學習，一塊玩耍，相處得非常好。

你呢？你喜歡踢球嗎？我聽說在美國，一個人可以有很多朋友，但真正的知心朋友卻很難找到，是嗎？

你的中國筆友 趙明

Unit A-1

15. The letter from Zhào Míng can be divided into six sections. Match the number of the section with the description of its content.

section 1	_____ Thank you and comments on your last letter
section 2	_____ Salutation
section 3	_____ Questions about you and your environment
section 4	_____ Closing salutation
section 5	_____ Greeting
section 6	_____ News about self (the writer)

16. Respond to the following questions, which pertain to specific information about Zhào Míng.

Sec. 1. How does Zhào Míng address you? Write in English: _____

Sec. 2 Zhào Míng writes (check one): [ ] How have you been recently?
[ ] Did you receive my last letter?

Sec. 3 Which of the following does Zhào Míng say about your last letter? Check all that apply.

[ ] What you write is very interesting.

[ ] What you write is funny and amusing.

[ ] It makes me feel like I'm talking to you face-to-face.

[ ] Your letter is long, and provides many details.

Sec. 4 Zhào Míng recently joined the (circle one) basketball / soccer / table-tennis team. Since then, he has (check one)

[ ] been very busy

[ ] made lots of friends

[ ] had a lot of fun

Sec. 5 Zhào Míng asks whether you enjoy (circle one) basketball / soccer.

He also asks whether, in the U.S., it is difficult to (check one)

[ ] make a really close friend

[ ] socialize generally

Sec. 6. How does Zhào Míng sign off? Write in English: _____

Lesson 3

17. Fill in the blanks by guessing the missing information (characters, *pinyin*, or English) in the vocabulary list below, which is keyed to Zhào Míng's letter.

筆友 / 笔友　bǐyǒu _____

最近　_____ *recently*

_____ fēng *(measure word for letters)*

收到　shōudào _____

有意思　yǒuyìsi _____

_____ xiàng *be like, resemble*

面對面 / 面对面　_____ *face-to-face*

與 / 与　yǔ _____

交談 / 交谈　_____ *converse, chat*

加入　_____ *enter into, join*

足球　zúqiú _____

隊 / 队　duì _____

自從...以後 / 自从...以后 _____ *ever since ..., after ...*

參加 / 参加　cānjiā _____

交朋友　jiāo péngyou _____

學習 / 学习　_____ *study*

玩耍　wánshuǎ _____

_____ xiāngchǔ *get along*

非常　_____ *unusually, extraordinarily*

_____ tī *kick*

聽說 / 听说　_____ *hear it said, hear it told*

但　_____ *however, but*

真正　zhēnzhèng _____

知心朋友　_____ *bosom friend, "friend who knows your heart"*

_____ què *(expressing that something is contrary to expectation)*

很難找到 / 很难找到

_____ *difficult to find*

18. Following is the completed vocabulary list. Re-read Zhào Míng's letter, and see how much more you can understand.

筆友 / 笔友　bǐyǒu *penfriend*

最近　zuìjìn *recently*

封　fēng *(measure word for letters)*

收到　shōudào *receive*

有意思　yǒuyìsi *be interesting*

像　xiàng *be like, resemble*

面對面 / 面对面　miànduìmiàn *face-to-face*

與 / 与　yǔ *with*

交談 / 交谈　jiāotán *converse, chat*

加入　jiārù *enter into, join*

足球　zúqiú *soccer, (European) football*

隊 / 队　duì *team*

自從...以後 / 自从...以后　zìcóng...yǐhòu *ever since ..., after ...*

參加 / 参加　cānjiā *participate in*

Unit A-1

交朋友　jiāo péngyou *make friends*

學習 / 学习　xuéxí *study*

玩耍　wánshuǎ *play*

相處 / 相处　xiāngchǔ *get along*

非常　fēicháng *unusually, extraordinarily*

踢　tī *kick*

聽說 / 听说　tīngshuō *hear it said,*
　　hear it told

但　dàn *however, but*

真正　zhēnzhèng *true, real*

知心朋友　zhīxīn péngyou *bosom friend,*
　　"friend who knows your heart"

卻 / 却　què (*expressing that something is*
　　contrary to expectation)

很難找到 / 很难找到　hěn nán zhǎodào
　　difficult to find

19. Write a response to Zhào Míng's letter, saying something about what you like to do in your spare time, and answering the questions posed.

Lesson 3

Sample answer

(based on real student responses)

親愛的中國筆友：

　　我很高興收到你的信。我覺得你寫得很有意思。

　　我不喜歡踢球。對不起，我們不能在一起踢球。我跑得不快。你喜歡玩電子遊戲嗎？要是你喜歡的話，我們將來可以一起玩。

　　你喜歡上網嗎？你能給我寫電子信嗎？能的話，請寫給abcd@efg.com.

　　你信裏寫的是對的。我的朋友很多，可是真正的知心朋友沒有一個。希望你會成為我的好朋友。

　　　　你的美國筆友　　　林森

李躍偉：嗯，我叫 ... 呃，我叫李躍偉，今年十五歲。我非常喜歡踢足球。

施華：呃，我的名字是施華。呃，我今年十八歲了。呃，我喜歡旅，旅行。我覺得旅行能夠帶給我，呃，新的視野，讓我去接觸社會和人生。

安淑敏：我叫安淑敏。我今年十九歲。我出生在河北，這是中國北方的一個省份。我不是北京人。我在北京市的北大附中學習。我非常喜歡我們的學校。我跟我的同學，呃，一塊兒住在宿舍里。我們相處得很好。在，我們在一起生活，一塊兒學習，一塊兒玩耍，一塊兒，呃，獲取知識。我，我們，我喜歡交朋友。我希望跟美國的朋友們，美國朋友交朋友。

李跃伟：嗯，我叫 ... 呃，我叫李跃伟，今年十五岁。我非常喜欢踢足球。

施华：呃，我的名字是施华。呃，我今年十八岁了。呃，我喜欢旅，旅行。我觉得旅行能够带给我，呃，新的视野，让我去接触社会和人生。

安淑敏：我叫安淑敏。我今年十九岁。我出生在河北，这是中国北方的一个省份。我不是北京人。我在北京市的北大附中学习。我非常喜欢我们的学校。我跟我的同学，呃，一块儿住在宿舍里。我们相处得很好。在，我们在一起生活，一块儿学习，一块儿玩耍，一块儿，呃，获取知识。我，我们，我喜欢交朋友。我希望跟美国的朋友们，美国朋友交朋友。

Lesson 3

Lǐ Yuèwěi: En, wǒ jiào ... e, wǒ jiào
Lǐ Yuèwěi, jīnnián shíwǔ suì.
Wǒ fēicháng xǐhuan tī zúqiú.

Shī Huá: E, wǒ de míngzi shì Shī Huá.
E, wǒ jīnnián shíbā suì le.
E, wǒ xǐhuan lǚ, lǚxíng. Wǒ
juéde lǚxíng nénggòu dài gěi
wǒ, e, xīn de shìyě, ràng wǒ
qù jiēchù shèhuì hé rénshēng.

Ān Shūmǐn: Wǒ jiào Ān Shūmǐn. Wǒ
jīnnián shíjiǔ suì. Wǒ
chūshēng zài Héběi, zhè shì
Zhōngguó běifāng de yī ge
shěngfèn. Wǒ bù shì Běijīng-
rén. Wǒ zài Běijīng Shì de
Běi Dà Fù-Zhōng xuéxí. Wǒ
fēicháng xǐhuan wǒmen de
xuéxiào. Wǒ gēn wǒ de
tóngxué, e, yīkuàir zhù
zai sùshè lǐ. Wǒmen xiāngchǔ
de hěn hǎo. Zài, wǒmen yīqǐ
shēnghuó, yīkuàir wánshuǎ,
yīkuàir, e, huòqǔ zhīshi.
Wǒ, wǒmen, wǒ xǐhuan jiāo
péngyou. Wǒ xīwàng gēn
Měiguó de péngyoumen,
Měiguó péngyou jiāo
péngyou.

Li Yuewei: Ah, my name is ... er, my
name is Li Yuewei, and I'm 15
years old. I really like playing
soccer.

Shi Hua: Ah, my name is Shi Hua.
Um, I'm 18.
Uh, I like traveling. I feel that
traveling can bring me, um, new
points of view that will bring me
into contact with society and
human life.

An Shumin: My name is An
Shumin. I'm 19 years old this
year. I was born in Hebei, which
is a province in northern China.
I'm not a Beijinger. I study at
the Middle School Attached to
Peking University in Beijing City.
I really like our school.
My classmates and I, er, we live
together in the dormitory.
We get along very well.
In, we live together,
play together,
and er, gain knowledge together.
I, we, I like making friends.
I hope ... with
our American friends ...
I hope to make friends with our
American friends.

Unit A-1   54

Unit A-1. Making Friends

Lesson 4: *American Students Interview a Chinese Woman*

Todd Pavel and Robyn Yee interview Ms. Mǎ Yùpíng on the campus of Peking University.

Previewing Activity

1. In the previous segment, Robyn and Todd asked the interviewees their name, age, and occupation. They would like to interview Ms. Mǎ in slightly greater depth. If you were doing the interviewing, what else would you ask? Write five additional questions using *pinyin*, characters, or a combination of both.

a. _____

b. _____

c. _____

d. _____

e. _____

First Viewing: Global Information

Segment A:

2. Indicate how many of the questions you listed in the previewing activity above were in fact asked by Todd or Robyn. _____

3. Check the topics discussed in this segment:

◯ Name?   ◯ Age?   ◯ Marital status?   ◯ Occupation?

◯ Place of Origin?   ◯ When did you come to Beijing?   ◯ Daily routine?

◯ Any children?   ◯ Any siblings?   ◯ Parents alive?

◯ Favorite book?   ◯ Favorite movie?   ◯ Favorite color?

◯ Favorite sport?   ◯ Favorite food?

Second Viewing: Specific Information

4. Write five facts about Ms. Mǎ Yùpíng.

a. _____

b. _____

c. _____

d. _____

e. _____

5. What does Mǎ Yùpíng say about American food?

_____

6. What does Mǎ Yùpíng say about the U.S. in general?

_____

Third Viewings: Linguistic Information

Clearing up a miscomprehension.

7. Robyn's first question was about Ms. Mǎ's age, and the second about where she came from. What do you think she was trying to ask in in her third question? (Answer in English, please.)

_____

Ms. Mǎ's response was, "I'm getting on-the-job training. Studying." What did she understand the question to be? (Answer in English, please.)

_____

Following are some ways of asking what Robyn wanted to ask, so that there would have been no misunderstanding. Check the one you prefer.

⭕ Nǐ měitiān dōu shì zěnme ānpái de?
你每天都是怎麼安排的 / 你每天都是怎么安排的？

⭕ Nǐ měitiān de rìchéng ānpái shì shénme?
你每天的日程安排是甚麼 / 你每天的日程安排是什么？

8. Mǎ Yùpíng uses two terms that fall along the continuum described below. Identify them, by writing them in pinyin in the spaces provided.

yǒu yīdiǎr xǐhuan ==> _____ ==> hěn xǐhuan ==> _____

有一點兒喜歡 /   比較喜歡/   很喜歡 /   最喜歡 /
有一点儿喜欢   比较喜欢   很喜欢   最喜欢
(like a little)   *(rather like)*   *(like very much)*   *(like most of all)*

Unit A-1

9. Write the *pinyin* equivalents of the following terms, one of which was used by Mǎ Yùpíng. Then match the English and *pinyin* with the character equivalents.

_____ high in fat content   脂肪含量還/还可以

_____ low in fat content   脂肪含量高

_____ the fat content is okay   脂肪含量低

10. Circle Mǎ Yùpíng's favorite kind of Chinese food. (Then draw a square around yours.)

湘菜 / 湘菜   Xiāngcài   *Hunan cuisine*

粵菜 / 粤菜   Yuècài   *Guangdong cuisine*

川菜 / 川菜   Chuāncài *Sichuan cuisine*

魯菜 / 鲁菜   Lǔcài   *Shandong cuisine*

11. Mǎ Yùpíng mentions a city and a province. Match the following cities to the provinces in which they are located. [Note: two of the cities are autonomous municipalities. Circle them.]

西安 Xī'ān

北京 Běijīng

廣州/广州 Guǎngzhōu

南京 Nánjīng

青島/青岛 Qīngdǎo

上海 Shànghǎi

貴林/贵林 Guìlín

杭州 Hángzhōu

廣西/广西 Guǎngxī

江蘇/江苏 Jiāngsū

浙江 Zhèjiāng

陝西/陕西 Shǎnxī (Shaanxi)

山東/山东 Shāndōng

廣東/广东 Guǎngdōng

12. Write out questions (using *pinyin* and/or characters) to obtain the following information.

•place of origin _____

•favorite foods _____

•favorite sports _____

•favorite movies _____

•daily routine _____

Lesson 4

Post-Viewing Activities

Speaking   Do the next set of exercises so that you will be able to interview your classmates on the following topics:

•place of origin   •favorite foods   •favorite sports   •favorite movies

Place of origin   *Reference vocabulary*

13. Circle the U.S. state in the list below to which you feel the closest affiliation—perhaps where you were born, where you are now, or where you spent time in the past. Then try to write the English equivalent next to NINE other states. Finally, pool your results with those of one or more classmates, and see how many of the fifty entries you can "decode."

Ālābāmǎ 阿拉巴馬/阿拉巴马

Ālāsījiā 阿拉斯加

Ākěnsè 阿肯色

Yàlìsāngnà 亞利桑那/亚利桑那

Jiālìfúníyà 加利福尼亞/加利福尼亚

Kēluóláduō 科羅拉多/科罗拉多

Kāngnièdígé (PRC) 康涅狄格

Kāngnǎidígé (T) 康乃狄格

Tèlāhuá 特拉華/特拉华

Fóluólǐdá 佛羅里達/佛罗里达

Qiáozhìyà 喬治亞/乔治亚

Xiàwēiyí 夏威夷

Àidáhé 愛達荷/爱达荷

Yīlìnuò 伊利諾/伊利诺

Yìndì'ānnà 印第安納/印第安纳

Yī'āhuá (PRC) 依阿華/依阿华

Ài'āhuá (T) 愛阿華/爱阿华

Kānsàsī 堪薩斯/堪萨斯

Kěntǎjī 肯塔基

Lùyìsī'ānnà 路易斯安那

Miǎnyīn 緬因/缅因

Mǎlǐlán 馬里蘭/马里兰

Másàzhūsài 麻薩諸塞/麻萨诸塞

Mìxiēgēn (PRC) 密歇根/密歇根

Mìxīgēn (T) 密西根

Míngnísūdá 明尼蘇達/明尼苏达

Mīxīxībǐ 密西西比

Mìsūlǐ 密蘇里/密苏里

Měngdàná 蒙大拿/蒙大拿

Nèibùlāsījiā 内布拉斯加

Nèihuádá 内華達/内华达

Xīn Hǎnbùshí'ěr (PRC)
新罕布什爾/新罕布什尔

Xīn Hǎnbùxià (T) 新罕布夏

Xīn Zéxī 新澤西/新泽西

Xīn Mòxīgē 新墨西哥

Niǔyuē 紐約/纽约

Běi Kǎluóláinà 北卡羅來納/北卡罗来纳

Běi Dákētā (PRC)北達科他/北达科他

Běi Dákēdá (T)北達科達/北达科达

Éhài'é 俄亥俄

Ékèlāhémǎ 俄克拉荷馬/俄克拉荷马

Élègāng 俄勒岡/俄勒冈

Àolègāng 奥勒岡/奥勒冈

Bīnxīfǎ'níyà 賓夕法尼亞/宾夕法尼亚

Luódé Dǎo 羅德島/罗德岛

Nán Kǎluóláinà 南卡羅來納/南卡罗来纳

Nán Dákētā 南達科他/南达科他

Tiánnàxī 田納西/田纳西

Dékèsàsī 德克薩斯/德克萨斯

Yóutā 猶他/犹他

Fóměngtè 佛蒙特/佛蒙特

Fújíníyà (PRC)弗吉尼亞/弗吉尼亚

Wéijíníyà (T)維吉尼亞/维吉尼亚

Huáshèngdùn 華盛頓/华盛顿

Xī Fújíníyà (PRC)西弗吉尼亞/西弗吉尼亚

Xī Wéijíníyà (T)西維吉尼亞/西维吉尼亚

Wēisīkāngxīng (PRC) 威斯康星

Wēisīkāngxīn (T)威斯康辛

Huái'émíng 懷俄明/怀俄明

Favorite foods

14. Match the names of the dishes below with the ethnic food they represent. Then circle your favorite regional cuisine.

a. sushi

____Hánguócài (Cháoxiăncài) 韓國(朝鮮)菜/韩国(朝鲜)菜

b. chapatis/curry

____Mòxīgēcài 墨西哥菜/墨西哥菜

c. tacos/burritos

____Yuènáncài 越南菜/越南菜

d. pasta

____Měiguócài 美國菜/美国菜

e. green papaya salad

____Éguócài 俄國菜/俄国菜

f. pho beef noodle soup

____Rìběncài 日本菜/日本菜

g. gyros

____Tàiguócài 泰國菜/泰国菜

h. sauerkraut

____Zhōngguócài 中國菜/中国菜

i. kimchee

____Sūgéláncài 蘇格蘭菜/苏格兰菜

j. bouillabaisse

____Fēilùbīncài 菲律賓菜/菲律宾菜

k. borscht

____Móluògēcài 摩洛哥菜/摩洛哥菜

l. haggis

____Făguócài 法國菜/法国菜

m. chicken adobo

____Xīlàcài 希腊菜/希腊菜

n. couscous

____Déguócài 德國菜/德国菜

o. hot dogs

____Yìdàlìcài 意大利菜/意大利菜

p. steamed fish with ginger & green onion

____Yìndùcài 印度菜/印度菜

15. Write the names of three regional cuisines on a card. Next, walk around the room and find someone to go with you to a restaurant that serves that cuisine. If there is no appropriate restaurant available, find someone who will agree to cook with you! Report back to the class who you will go "cuisine sampling" with.

Lesson 4

Favorite sports

16. Underline the sports you have tried your hand at before. Then draw a circle around your five favorite sports. Try to remember the Chinese terms for those sports.

aerobics (zuò) yǒuyǎng yùndòng (做)有氧運動/有氧运动

badminton (dǎ) yǔmáoqiú (打)羽毛球

baseball (dǎ) bàngqiú (打)棒球

basketball (dǎ) lánqiú (打)籃球/篮球

bicycling (qí) zìxíngchē (騎/骑) 自行車/自行车

billiards (dǎ) táiqiú (打) 檯球/台球

bowling (dǎ) bǎolíngqiú (打) 保齡球/保龄球

boxing quánjī 拳擊/拳击

cross country yuèyěchángpǎo 越野長跑/越野长跑

fencing jījiànshù 擊劍術/击剑术

field hockey (dǎ) qūgùnqiú (打) 曲棍球

fishing diàoyú 釣魚/钓鱼

football (tī) Měishì zúqiú / (dǎ) gǎnlǎnqiú (踢)美式足球; (打) 橄欖球/橄榄球

golf (dǎ) gāo'ěrfūqiú (打) 高爾夫球/高尔夫球

gymnastics (zuò) tǐcāo (做) 體操/体操

hiking páshān 爬山

ice hockey (dǎ) bīngshàng qūgùnqiú (打) 冰上曲棍球

in-line skating huá hànbīng 滑旱冰

jogging pǎobù 跑步

kayaking (huá) dúmùzhōu (划)獨木舟/(划)独木舟

Unit A-1

martial arts (liàn) wǔshù (練/练) 武術/武朮

mountain/rock climbing pānyán yùndòng 攀岩運動/攀岩运动

racquetball (dǎ) huílì wǎngqiú (打) 回力網球/回力网球

rowing huáchuán 划船

sailing hánghǎi 航海/航海

scuba diving (or snorkeling) qiánshuǐ 潛水/潜水

skateboarding (wánr) huábǎn (玩) 滑板

skiing huáxuě 滑雪

snorkeling (or scuba diving) qiánshuǐ 潛水/潜水

snowboarding (wánr) huáxuěbǎn (玩) 滑雪板

soccer (tī) zúqiú (踢)足球

softball (dǎ) lěiqiú (打) 壘球/垒球

surfing chōnglàng 衝浪/冲浪

swimming yóuyǒng 游泳

table tennis (dǎ) pīngpāngqiú (打) 乒乓球

tennis (dǎ) wǎngqiú (打) 網球/网球

ultimate frisbee (rēng) fēipán (扔) 飛盤/飞盘

volleyball (dǎ) páiqiú (打) 排球

water polo (dǎ) shuǐqiú (打) 水球

weightlifting (liàn) jǔzhòng (練/练) 舉重/举重

windsurfing (wán) fānbǎn (玩) 帆板

wrestling shuāijiāo 摔跤

yoga (zuò) yújiā (做) 瑜珈

17. Write three sporting activities on a card. Next, walk around the room and find someone to do each activity with you. Report back to the class and tell who your partner for each activity will be. If no-one will do the sport with you, say you'll do it by yourself (*Wǒ zìjǐ yī ge rén qù ___*), or that you'll find someone outside of class to do it with you (*Wǒ dào wàimian qù zhǎo rén gēn wǒ ___*).

Lesson 4

Favorite movies

18. Match the PRC transliterations with the titles of the American movies. Then underline 3–4 favorites of the list given here.

a. Nǚ Wáng 女王

_____Little Miss Sunshine

b. Shēngsǐ Shísù 生死時速 / 生死时速

_____Forrest Gump

c. Zhòngxià Yè zhī Mèng 仲夏夜之夢 / 仲夏夜之梦 _____Sleepless in Seattle

d. Yīngguó Bìngrén 英國病人 / 英国病人

_____American Beauty

e. Měiguó Lìrén 美國麗人 / 美国丽人

_____The Queen

f. Yángguāng Xiǎo Měinǚ 陽光小美女 / 阳光小美女 _____True Lies

g. Zhěngjiù Dàbīng Lái-ēn
拯救大兵萊恩 / 拯救大兵莱恩

_____The Joy Luck Club

h. Ā-Gān Zhèng Zhuàn 阿甘正傳 / 阿甘正传

_____Speed

i. Xīyǎtú Bùmiányè 西雅圖不眠夜 /
西雅图不眠夜

_____Saving Private Ryan

j. Piàoliàng Nǚrén 漂亮女人

_____A Midsummer Night's Dream

k. Xǐfúhuì 喜福會 / 喜福会

_____The English Patient

l. Zhēnshí de Huǎngyán 真實的謊言 / 真实的谎言 _____Pretty Woman

19. Walk around the room and find someone to watch each movie on video/DVD with you. Report back to the class and tell who your companion for each movie will be.

Unit A-1

20. Now interview one or more of your classmates on the following topics: *place of origin, favorite foods, favorite sports, favorite movies*. Take notes so that you can report back to the class in some detail, if there is time.

21. Otherwise, note the ONE most interesting fact about your classmate. Write this fact (in Chinese) on a slip of paper, and hand this slip in to your teacher, who will shuffle the slips and then redistribute them one to a student, to be read out loud. As each fact is read, try to guess to which of your classmates it pertains. Sample "facts":

她每天早上六點鐘起來去跑步 / 她每天早上六点钟起来去跑步。

他從華盛頓州來的 / 他从华盛顿州来的。

°A　她是美國人，可是出生在韓國 / 她是美国人，可是出生在韩国。

Reading / Writing

21. Following is the response to a letter you wrote to a penfriend in Beijing, with more information. Read it, and write a response.

亲爱的笔友：

感谢你这么快就给我回信了。

我现在已开始准备写毕业论文了。我每天的日程不变，总是宿舍—图书馆—食堂—图书馆—宿舍。即使周末也是如此。食堂的饭很难吃，特别咸。我很想念我家乡的粤菜。听说美国的饭很好吃，但不健康，因为肉太多。是这样的吗？校园里新开了一个韩国餐馆，我去吃过。我发现韩国菜很好吃。你呢？你喜欢吃哪国菜？

我今年暑假想回广州。在那儿我可以游泳、打篮球和滑旱冰。其实在北京也可以做这些运动，但我的朋友都在广州，我喜欢和朋友一起运动。

你每天的日程安排是什么？紧张吗？你喜欢做什么体育运动？你喜欢旅游吗？除了你的家乡，你还去过美国的其他地方吗？

等你的回信。

陈今　02.6.7

Lesson 4

22. Excluding the opening salutation and the closing signature, this letter from Chén Jīn can be divided into five sections. Write a sentence in English to summarize each section.

Sec. 1 (1 line): _____

Sec. 2 (6 lines): _____

Sec. 3 (3 lines): _____

Sec. 4 (2 lines): _____

Sec. 5 (1 line): _____

Check your responses with the ones provided below.

1. Thanks for your response to my letter.
2. Here's a rundown of my daily activities. I hate the food. What food do you like?
3. I'm looking forward to going home on vacation.
4. What do you do every day?
5. I'll be waiting for your reply.

23. Respond to the following to provide specific information

Sec. 1. Chén Jīn writes that your response to her was (circle one) long / quick / nice.

Sec. 2.
a. She has started preparing her (circle one) exam / term paper / graduation essay.

b. Which of the following buildings does she frequent each day? Check as appropriate.

____ gym   ____library   ____dormitory   ____cinema   ____cafeteria   ____classroom

c. On weekends her life is (circle one) the same / different.

d. She finds the food in the cafeteria extremely (circle one) bland / spicy / greasy / salty.

e. She prefers the food of her hometown: (circle one) Guangdong / Shanghai / Sichuan.

f. She has heard that American food is not (fill in the blanks) _____ because it
   includes too much _____.

g. She states that she really likes the food of (circle one) Japan / Korea / Thailand.

h. At home on vacation, she can (check all that apply)

   ____ swim   ____ run   ____ play soccer
   ____ play basketball   ____ play Ping-Pong   ____ fly kites
   ____ go in-line skating ____ surf   ____ do yoga

Unit A-1

i. She's particularly pleased to be able to (check one) ____exercise with friends   ____sleep.

j. Which of the following does she ask about you? Check as appropriate.

____your daily schedule   ____who your friends are

____whether your schedule is busy   ____what you like to do in your leisure time

____what kinds of exercise you like   ____if you like to swim

____where you live   ____where else you've been in the U.S.

____if you've been overseas   ____what you like to eat

24. Fill in the blanks by guessing the missing information (characters, *pinyin*, or English) in the vocabulary list below, which is keyed to Chén Jīn's letter.

感謝 / 感谢 gǎnxiè _____

已 _____ *already*

開始 / 开始 kāishǐ _____

_____ zhǔnbèi *prepare, get ready*

畢業 / 毕业 _____ *graduate, graduation*

論文 / 论文 _____
    thesis, essay

日程 _____ *daily schedule*

_____ biàn *change*

總是 / 总是 zǒngshì _____

宿舍 _____ *dormitory*

圖書館 / 图书馆 túshūguǎn
    _____

食堂 _____ *cafeteria*

_____ jíshǐ *even, even if*

週末 / 周末 zhōumò *weekend*

如此 _____ *be like this*

特別 tèbié _____

鹹 / 咸 _____ *salty*

想念 _____ *miss, long for*

_____ jiāxiāng *hometown*

粵菜 Yuècài _____

聽説 / 听说 tīngshuō _____

_____ jiànkāng *health, healthy*

這樣的 / 这样的 _____
    this way

校園 / 校园 xiàoyuán _____

新開 / 新开 _____
    newly open(ed)

韓國 / 韩国 _____ *Korea, Korean*

餐館 / 餐馆 cānguǎn _____

_____ chīguo *have eaten*

發現 / 发现 _____ *discover*

_____ shǔjià *summer vacation*

廣州 / 广州 _____ *Canton, Guangzhou*

游泳 yóuyǒng _____

打籃球 / 打篮球 dǎ lánqiú
    _____

_____ huá hànbīng *in-line skate, rollerskate*

其實 / 其实 _____
    actually, in reality

Lesson 4

運動 / 运动　yùndòng ＿＿＿＿＿＿＿＿＿

＿＿＿＿＿＿＿＿＿　yīqǐ　together

安排　＿＿＿＿＿＿＿＿＿　organize

緊張 / 紧张　＿＿＿＿＿＿＿＿＿　tense, intense

體育 / 体育　＿＿＿＿＿＿＿＿＿　physical education

＿＿＿＿＿＿＿＿＿　chúle　except, besides

其他　qítā　＿＿＿＿＿＿＿＿＿

回信　huíxìn　＿＿＿＿＿＿＿＿＿

25. Following is the completed vocabulary list to help you decode Chén Jīn's letter.

感謝 / 感谢　gǎnxiè　thank

已　yǐ　already

開始 / 开始　kāishǐ　begin, start

準備 / 准备　zhǔnbèi　prepare, get ready

畢業 / 毕业　bìyè　graduate, graduation

論文 / 论文　lùnwén　thesis, essay

日程　rìchéng　daily schedule

變 / 变　biàn　change

總是 / 总是　zǒngshì　always

宿舍　sùshè　dormitory

圖書館 / 图书馆　túshūguǎn　library

食堂　shítáng　cafeteria

即使　jíshǐ　even, even if

週末 / 周末　zhōumò　weekend

如此　rúcǐ　be like this

特別　tèbié　extremely, especially

鹹 / 咸　xián　salty

想念　xiǎngniàn　miss, long for

家鄉 / 家乡　jiāxiāng　hometown

粵菜　Yuècài　Cantonese cuisine

聽說 / 听说　tīngshuō　hear it said

健康　jiànkāng　health, healthy

這樣的 / 这样的　zhè yàng de this way

校園 / 校园　xiàoyuán　campus

新開 / 新开　xīnkāi　newly open(ed)

韓國 / 韩国　Hánguó　Korea, Korean

餐館 / 餐馆　cānguǎn　restaurant

吃過 / 吃过　chīguo　have eaten

發現 / 发现　fāxiàn　discover

暑假　shǔjià　summer vacation

廣州 / 广州　Guǎngzhōu　Canton, Guangzhou

游泳　yóuyǒng　swim

打籃球 / 打篮球　dǎ lánqiú play basketball

滑旱冰　huá hànbīng　in-line skate, rollerskate

其實 / 其实　qíshí　actually, in reality

運動 / 运动　yùndòng　exercise

Unit A-1

一起　yīqǐ *together*

安排　ānpái *organize*

緊張／紧张　jǐnzhāng *tense, intense*

體育／体育　tǐyù *physical education*

除了　chúle *except, besides*

其他　qítā *other*

回信　huíxìn *return letter, reply*

26. Write a response to Chén Jīn's letter, telling her about your life on weekdays and weekends during the school year.

親愛的陳今：

　　感謝你的來信！你現在已經開始寫畢業論文了，一定很忙吧？我們學校跟你們不一樣，不必寫畢業論文。可是我還是很忙，因爲我的課很多，課外的活動也很多。我參加了中國會、少年足球隊、游泳隊。還有，因爲我需要錢，每個星期都在校園裡的書店工作二十個鐘頭。有的時候連吃飯的時間都沒有。可是我並不瘦！

　　我週末非常喜歡和朋友們在一起說說笑笑。有的時候我們跟你一樣，也去吃韓國菜。可是平常是，大家一起叫一個 pizza (中文怎麼說？)在宿舍裡吃。你喜歡吃 pizza 嗎？那是我最愛吃的東西。可惜吃了pizza 很容易發胖。

　　對我來說，寫中文很難。我寫了這麼多已經很累了。我下次再寫吧！

　　等你的回信。

　　　　　　你愛吃 pizza 的朋友

　　　　　　　　　白理
　　　　　　　　　02.9.18

Unit A-1

彭德：哎，你好！
馬玉萍：你好！
彭德：你叫甚麼名字？
馬玉萍：呃，我叫…我叫馬玉
萍。
余修明：呃，你今年多大了？
馬玉萍：呃，我今年三十二
了。
余修明：您是甚麼地方人？
馬玉萍：我是山東青島人。
彭德：你甚麼時候到這來
（的）？
馬玉萍：我去年過來的。對。
余修明：哦。你每天的日程是
甚麼？
噢，嗯，你做甚麼？
馬玉萍：我是來進修的，學
習。
彭德：你有沒有孩子？
馬玉萍：我有孩子。一個女
兒。
彭德：她幾歲？
馬玉萍：她已經九歲了。
余修明：你喜歡看電影嗎？
馬玉萍：我喜…我喜歡看電
影。
余修明：你最喜歡的電影是甚
麼？
馬玉萍：呃，我，現在比較喜
歡看《泰坦尼克號》。

彭德： 哎，你好！
馬玉萍：你好！
彭德：你叫什么名字？
馬玉萍：呃，我叫…我叫马玉
萍。
余修明：呃，你今年多大了？
馬玉萍：呃，我今年三十二
了。
余修明：您是什么地方人？
馬玉萍：我是山东青岛人。
彭德：你什么时候到这来
（的）？
馬玉萍：我去年过来的。对。
余修明：哦。你每天的日程是
什么？
噢，嗯，你做什么？
馬玉萍：我是来进修的，学
习。
彭德：你有没有孩子？
馬玉萍：我有孩子。一个女
儿。
彭德：她几岁？
馬玉萍：她已经九岁了。
余修明：你喜欢看电影吗？
馬玉萍：我喜…我喜欢看电
影。
余修明：你最喜欢的电影是什
么？
馬玉萍：呃，我，现在比较喜
欢看《泰坦尼克号》。

Lesson 4

Péng Dé: Ai, nǐ hǎo!

Mǎ Yùpíng: Nǐ hǎo!

Péng Dé: Nǐ jiào shénme míngzi?

Mǎ Yùpíng: E, wǒ jiào ... wǒ jiào Mǎ Yùpíng.

Yú Xiūmíng: E, nǐ jīnnián duō dà le?

Mǎ Yùpíng: E, wǒ jīnnián sānshíèr le.

Yú Xiūmíng: Nín shì shénme dìfang rén?

Mǎ Yùpíng: Wǒ shì Shāndōng Qīngdǎo rén.

Péng Dé: Nǐ shénme shíhòu dào zhè(r) lái (de)?

Mǎ Yùpíng: Wǒ qùnián guòlái de. Duì.

Yú Xiūmíng: O. Nǐ měitiān de rìchéng shì shénme?

O, ng, nǐ zuò shénme?

Mǎ Yùpíng: Wǒ shì lái jìnxiū de, xuéxí.

Péng Dé: Nǐ yǒu mei yǒu háizi?

Mǎ Yùpíng: Wǒ yǒu háizi. Yī ge nǚér.

Péng Dé: Tā jǐ suì?

Mǎ Yùpíng: Tā yǐjīng jiǔ suì le.

Yú Xiūmíng: Nǐ xǐhuan kàn diànyǐng ma?

Mǎ Yùpíng: Wǒ xǐ ... xǐhuan kàn diànyǐng.

Yú Xiūmíng: Nǐ zuì xǐhuan de diànyǐng shì shénme?

Mǎ Yùpíng: E, wǒ, xiànzài bǐjiào xǐhuan kàn *Tàitǎnníkè Hào*.

Todd Pavel: Oh, hello!

Ma Yuping: Hello.

Todd Pavel: What is your name?

Ma Yuping: Er, my name ... my name is Ma Yuping.

Robyn Yee: How old are you?

Ma Yuping: Er, I am 32 this year.

Robyn Yee: Where are you from?

Ma Yuping: I'm from Qingdao in Shandong Province.

Todd Pavel: When did you come here?

Ma Yuping: I came here last year ... right.

Robyn Yee: Er, what's your schedule every day?

Oh, er, what do you do?

Ma Yuping: I came here for advanced studies, to study.

Todd Pavel: Do you have kids?

Ma Yuping: I have a child, a daughter.

Todd Pavel: How old is she?

Ma Yuping: She is already 9 years old.

Robyn Yee: Do you like to see movies?

Ma Yuping: I like ... I like seeing movies.

Robyn Yee: What film do you like the best?

Ma Yuping: Er, I, now rather enjoyed watching *Titanic*.

Unit A-1

彭德：也喜歡看中國電影嗎？

馬玉萍：也很喜歡看中國電影。

余修明：你喜歡吃甚麼？

馬玉萍：我喜歡吃中國菜。

余修明：你最喜歡吃甚麼？

馬玉萍：我最喜歡吃川菜。

彭德：那你吃美國菜嗎？

馬玉萍：美國菜也可以。但是美國的西餐脂肪含量太高了。

彭德：嗯，對。

馬玉萍：因爲女士都喜歡苗條一點。

彭德：那你有沒有兄弟姐妹？

馬玉萍：我有一個哥哥，一個姐姐。

彭德：他們都住在山東嗎？

馬玉萍：他們都住在青島。

彭德：啊，青島。

馬玉萍：對。

余修明：你有空（的）時候做甚麼？喜歡做甚麼？

馬玉萍：我喜歡做運動。

余修明：呃，甚麼運動？

彭德：也喜欢看中国电影吗？

马玉萍：也很喜欢看中国电影。

余修明：你喜欢吃什么？

马玉萍：我喜欢吃中国菜。

余修明：你最喜欢吃什么？

马玉萍：我最喜欢吃川菜。

彭德：那你吃美国菜吗？

马玉萍：美国菜也可以。但是美国的西餐脂肪含量太高了。

彭德：嗯，对。

马玉萍：因为女士都喜欢苗条一点。

彭德：那你有没有兄弟姐妹？

马玉萍：我有一个哥哥，一个姐姐。

彭德：他们都住在山东吗？

马玉萍：他们都住在青岛。

彭德：啊，青岛。

马玉萍：对。

余修明：你有空（的）时候做什么？喜欢做什么？

马玉萍：我喜欢做运动。

余修明：呃，什么运动？

Lesson 4

Péng Dé: Yě xǐhuan kàn Zhōngguó
    diànyǐng ma?

Mǎ Yùpíng: Yě hěn xǐhuan kàn
    Zhōngguó diànyǐng.

Yú Xiūmíng: Nǐ xǐhuan chī shénme?

Mǎ Yùpíng: Wǒ xǐhuan chī Zhōngguócài.

Yú Xiūmíng: Nǐ zuì xǐhuan chī shénme?

Mǎ Yùpíng: Wǒ zuì xǐhuan chī
    Chuāncài.

Péng Dé: Nà nǐ chī Měiguócài ma?

Mǎ Yùpíng: Měiguócài yě kěyǐ. Dànshì
    Měiguó de xīcān zhīfáng hánliàng tài
    gāo le.

Péng Dé: Ng, duì.

Mǎ Yùpíng: Yīnwèi nǚshì dōu xǐhuan
    miáotiao yīdiǎn(r).

Péng Dé: Nà nǐ yǒu mei yǒu xiōngdì-
    jiěmèi?

Mǎ Yùpíng: Wǒ yǒu yī ge gēge, yī ge jiějie.

Péng Dé: Tāmen dōu zhùzài Shāngdōng ma?

Mǎ Yùpíng: Tāmen dōu zhùzài Qīngdǎo.

Péng Dé: A, Qīngdǎo.

Mǎ Yùpíng: Duì.

Yú Xiūmíng: Nǐ yǒu kòng(r) (de) shíhou
    zuò shénme? Xǐhuan zuò shénme?

Mǎ Yùpíng: Wǒ xǐhuan zuò yùndòng.

Yú Xiūmíng: E, shénme yùndòng?

Todd Pavel: Do you like watching Chinese
    movies too?

Ma Yuping: I also like watching Chinese
    movies very much.

Robyn Yee: What do you like to eat?

Ma Yuping: I like Chinese food.

Robyn Yee: What do you like to eat the
    most?

Ma Yuping: I like eating Sichuan food the
    most.

Todd Pavel: Do you like American food?

Ma Yuping: American food is fine too.
    But the fat content of Western food in
    America is too high.

Todd Pavel: Mmm, right.

Ma Yuping: Because all women like to be
    a bit slimmer.

Todd Pavel: Do you have any siblings, then?

Ma Yuping: I have one older brother and
    one older sister.

Todd Pavel: Do they all live in Shandong?

Ma Yuping: They all live in Qingdao.

Todd Pavel: Oh, Qingdao.

Ma Yuping: Right.

Robyn Yee: What do you do in your free
    time? What do you like to do?

Ma Yuping: I like to exercise.

Robyn Yee: Er, what (kind of) exercise?

Unit A-1

72

馬玉萍：嗯，比如說打打網
　　　球呀，跑步呀。
彭德：你想到美國去嗎？
馬玉萍：可以。如果有機會的
　　　話，我可以去。
彭德：去做甚麼？
馬玉萍：我去學習一下那兒
　　　的現代科技呀，甚麼
　　　環境呀，都是比較好
　　　的。
彭德：嗯。
馬玉萍：西方文化我還是 ...
　　　還是很好的。
彭德：好。
余修明：謝謝你。
馬玉萍：謝謝你。
彭德：再見。

马玉萍：嗯，比如说打打网
　　　球呀，跑步呀。
彭德：你想到美国去吗？
马玉萍：可以。如果有机会的
　　　话，我可以去。
彭德：去做什么？
马玉萍：我去学习一下那儿
　　　的现代科技呀，什么
　　　环境呀，都是比较好
　　　的。
彭德：嗯。
马玉萍：西方文化我还是 ...
　　　还是很好的。
彭德：好。
余修明：谢谢你。
马玉萍：谢谢你。
彭德：再见。

Lesson 4

Mǎ Yùpíng: Ng, bǐrúshuō dǎ dǎ wǎngqiú
          ya, pǎobù ya.
Péng Dé: Nǐ xiǎng dào Měiguó qù ma?

Mǎ Yùpíng: Kěyǐ. Rúguǒ yǒu jīhuì de
          huà, wǒ kěyǐ qù.
Péng Dé: Qù zuò shénme?
Mǎ Yùpíng: Wǒ qù xuéxí yīxia nà(r)
          de xiàndài kējì ya, shénme huánjìng
          ya, dōu shì bǐjiào hǎo de.

Péng Dé: Ng.
Mǎ Yùpíng: Xīfāng wénhuà wǒ háishi
          ... háishi hěn hǎo de.
Péng Dé: Hǎo.
Yú Xiūmíng: Xièxie nǐ.
Mǎ Yùpíng: Xièxie nǐ.
Péng Dé: Zàijiàn.

Ma Yuping: Mmm, for example, I play
          some tennis, and I jog.
Todd Pavel: Would you like to go to
          America?
Ma Yuping: Yes, if I have the chance I
          might go.
Todd Pavel: To do what?
Ma Yuping: I'd go study, oh, modern
          technology, or the environment or
          such, both (of those) are
          rather good.
Todd Pavel: Uh-huh.
Ma Yuping: Western culture I find
          rather ... it's still relatively good.
Todd Pavel: Okay.
Robyn Yee: Thank you.
Ma Yuping: Thank you.
Todd Pavel: Good-bye.

Unit A-1

Unit A-2: Making Friends (cont.)
Lesson 5: *A Seven-Way Chat*

Robyn, Todd, and James Yao (a Chinese-American graduate student) chat with seniors at the high school attached to Peking University.

Previewing Activity

1. You and other U.S. students are getting to know some Beijing high school students you have never met before. What might you ask them about? What might they ask you?
List five possible topics in each area, writing in either English or Chinese, as you wish.

Topics you would ask them about

_____

_____

_____

_____

_____

Topics they might ask you about

_____

_____

_____

_____

_____

First Viewing: Global Information

2. Check off the topics you predicted that were actually touched upon in the conversation.

3. Number the following by the order in which they came up in the conversation.

_____Where are you from?

_____How old are you?

_____I'm happy to meet you.

_____My name is ...

_____What were your strongest impressions of Beijing when you came?

_____Have you been to China before?

_____Where will you go to college next year?

_____What do you like to do in your free time?

_____Which college are you studying at?

_____What's your purpose in coming to China?

_____What do you want to be in the future?

Second Viewing: Specific Information

4. Write two facts about each of the people indicated, based on the conversation.

Person 1 _____   _____

Person 2 _____   _____

Person 3 _____   _____

Person 4 _____   _____

Person 5 _____   _____

Person 6 _____   _____

Person 7 _____   _____

Unit A-2

5. Number each of the utterances below according to the number of the person who said it.

```
        3        4        5
   2  Shū Huá  Ān Shūmǐn  James Yao   6
Zhōu Hǎixiá                        Robyn Yee

1
Huáng Shūhuá                          7
                                  Todd Pavel
```

_____I'm from China's Hebei (province).

_____I'm a Heilongjiang-er.

_____We're in the same class.

_____All three of us will go to Peking University.

_____I will go to Tsinghua University.

_____We'll graduate from college in four years.

_____Are you learning Chinese in order to better understand China?

_____I think YOU understand China (somewhat) better.

_____She lives in Hawaii. I live in San Francisco.

_____I already graduated.

_____She's in high school.

_____Which college did you graduate from?

_____I graduated from America's University of Chicago.

_____How did you happen to come together?

_____We came to film this ..., this ...

_____Teacher Ren used to be my teacher.

_____No, this is my first time.

_____Is it the first time for all of you?

_____When was your first time?

_____Are there changes, do you think?

_____Great changes, right?

_____Isn't that so. Eight years have gone by already.

_____The people here are particularly friendly.

_____The food's great.

_____You don't eat Chinese food often in the U.S., right?

_____You can get (Chinese food), but it's not as good as in Beijing.

_____Right, it's rather Westernized.

_____American-style Chinese food.

Lesson 5

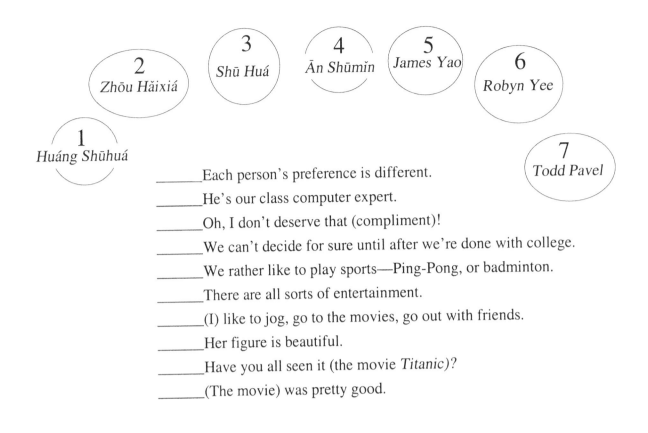

_____ Each person's preference is different.

_____ He's our class computer expert.

_____ Oh, I don't deserve that (compliment)!

_____ We can't decide for sure until after we're done with college.

_____ We rather like to play sports—Ping-Pong, or badminton.

_____ There are all sorts of entertainment.

_____ (I) like to jog, go to the movies, go out with friends.

_____ Her figure is beautiful.

_____ Have you all seen it (the movie *Titanic*)?

_____ (The movie) was pretty good.

Third Viewing: Linguistic Information

6. Match the person with the utterance and its English meaning.

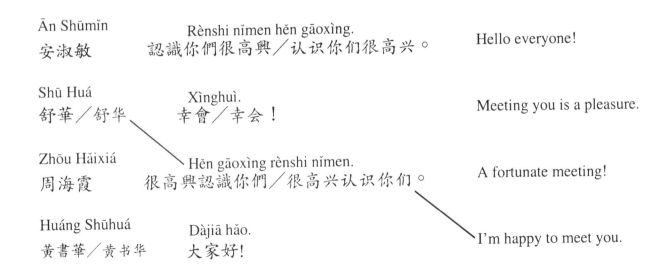

7. Match the questions on the left with the responses on the right.

a. Nǐ shì shénme dìfang rén?
你是甚麼地方人／
你是什么地方人？

b. Nǐ jīn nián duō dà le?
你今年多大了？

c. Nǐ zhīdào nǐ yào shàng něige dàxué ma?
你知道你要上哪個大學嗎／
你知道你要上哪个大学吗？

d. Běidà gēn Qīnghuá bǐ, něige bǐjiào hǎo?
北大和清華比，哪個比較好／
北大和清华比，哪个比较好？

e. Nǐ lái Zhōngguó de mùdì shì shénme?
你來中國的目的是甚麼／
你来中国的目的是什么？

_____Wǒ shì Mìxīgēn Dàxué.
我是密西根大學／我是密西根大学。

_____Wǒ lái xuéxi Hànyǔ.
我來學漢語／我来学汉语。

_____Wǒ shàng Běidà.
我上北大。

_____Wǒ yǐjīng zhīdào le.
我已經知道了／我已经知道了。

_____Yīyàng hǎo.
一樣好／一样好。

_____Wǒ zhǐ shì lái kànyikan.
我只是來看一看／我只是来看一看。

_____Dōu hěn bàng.
都很棒。

_____Wǒ xiǎng duō liáojiě Zhōngguó.
我想多了解中國／我想多了解中国。

_____Wǒ shì Běijīng de.
我是北京的。

_____Wǒ cái shíbā ne.
我才十八呢。

_____Wǒ lái zì Běijīng.
我來自北京／我来自北京。

_____Wǒ gāng mǎn èrshíyī.
我剛滿二十一／我刚满二十一。

_____Dōu yīyàng.
都一樣／都一样。

_____Wǒ shì Běijīng rén.
我是北京人。

_____Wǒ shíjiǔ suì.
我十九歲／我十九岁。

Lesson 5

8. Read the following excerpt.

1) Ān Shūmǐn: Nǐmen lái Zhōngguó de mùdi shì shénme? Lái kànyikan ma?

   安淑敏：   你們來中國的目的是甚麼？來看一看嗎？／
               你们来中国的目的是什么？来看一看吗？

2) Todd: Duì, kàn yi kan yě xuéxí Zhōngwén.

   彭德：   對，看一看，也學習中文／对，看一看，也学习中文。

3) Ān Shūmǐn: Xuéxí Zhōngwén.

   安淑敏：   學習中文／学习中文。

4) Todd: Duì.

   彭德：   對／对。

5) Ān Shūmǐn: Xuéxí Zhōngwén shì wèile gèng hǎo de liáojiě Zhōngguó ma?

   安淑敏：   學習中文是爲了更好的了解中國嗎？／
               学习中文是为了更好的了解中国吗？

6) Todd: Duì duì...yīnggāi...yīnggāi...nng...xuéxí Zhōngwén, ránhòu...

   彭德：   對對，應該，應該，呃...學習中文，然後...／
               对对，应该，应该，呃...学习中文，然后...

7)   nng...míngbai...míngbai Zhōngguó de qíngkuàng.

               呃...明白...明白中國的情況。／
               呃...明白...明白中国的情况。

8) Ān Shūmǐn: O.

   安淑敏：   哦。

9) Todd: Duì bu dui?

   彭德：   對不對／对不对？

•Write the *pinyin* for "purpose" (see line 1): _____

•Write the *pinyin* for two ways of saying "to understand" (see lines 5 and 7):

    _____,   _____

A common strategy used in conversation, especially when one of the participants does not speak the language fluently, is to restate what one hears and understands. In line 3, for example, An Shumin repeats Todd's statement that he is in China to "study Chinese." In lines 6 and 7, Todd, for his part, is valiantly trying to confirm the substance of An's question— "Yes, I am studying Chinese in order to understand China better"—using terms other than the ones she used. Can you help him out? Select your favorite among the statements below (they are all correct).

Duì, duì, xuéxí Zhōngwén...
對，對，學習中文／
对，对，学习中文

_____wèi le duō liǎojiě Zhōngguó.
爲了多了解中國／为了多了解中国。
_____wèi le gèng liǎojiě Zhōngguó.
爲了更了解中國／为了更了解中国。
_____wèi le lǐjiě Zhōngguó.
爲了理解中國／为了理解中国。

Unit A-2

Todd often asks "Duì bu dui?" (as in line 9) to confirm that what he has said is linguistically correct—"Did I say it right?" To make his intention clearer, he might have said any of the following. Check the one you prefer.

_____"Wǒ shuō de duì ma?" 我説得對嗎／我说得对吗？

_____"Kěyǐ zhème shuō ma?" 可以這麼説嗎／可以这么说吗？

_____"Wǒ shuō de huà nǐ néng tīngdǒng ma?"
我説的話你能聽懂嗎／我说的话你能听懂吗？

9. Read the following excerpt.

Shū Huá: Nǐmen jiā zài Xiàwēiyí ma?
           你們家在夏威夷嗎／你们家在夏威夷吗？

Todd: E, wǒmen... wǒmen dōu... wǒmen dōu... Tā (pointing to Robyn), tā zhù zài
           哦，我們，我們都，我們都 ... 她，她住在／
           哦，我们，我们都，我们都 ... 她，她住在

           Xiàwēiyí. Wǒ ne, wǒ zhù zài Jiùjīnshān.
           夏威夷。我呢，我住在舊金山／我呢，我住在旧金山。

James: Wǒ de fùmǔ zhù zài Xiàwēiyí.
           我的父母住在夏威夷。

Todd was trying to say "We all live in different places," in response to Shu Hua's question, but got no further than "Wǒmen dōu..." Can you complete his answer for him? Select one of the following statements (they are all correct).

Wǒmen dōu...   _____zhù Měiguó, kěshì bù dōu zhù zài Xiàwēiyí.
我們都／   住美國，可是不都住在夏威夷／
我们都   住美国，可是不都住在夏威夷。

                    _____zhù zài Měiguó bùtóng de dìfang.
                           住在美國不同的地方／
                           住在美国不同的地方。

                    _____zhù Měiguó bù yīyàng de dìfang.
                           住美國不一樣的地方／
                           住美国不一样的地方。

At the time, James was in the process of moving from New York City to Palo Alto. Rather than take the trouble to explain, he chose to answer "Yes," in a way, to Shu Hua's question: his *parents* live in Hawaii (even though he himself doesn't).

Lesson 5

10. Fill in the blanks in the dialogue below using *pinyin* and the English cues given.

Ān Shūmǐn: Nǐ zài dú shénme dàxué?

安淑敏：   你在讀什麼大學？/ 你在读什么大学？

Yáo Shǒuzhèng: E, wǒ yǐjīng_____le. *(graduated)*

姚守正：   呃，我已經畢業了。/ 呃，我已经毕业了。

(zhǐ zhe Yú Xiūmíng) 【指著余修明】

          E, ránhòu tā xiànzài zài dú _____. *(high school)*

          呃，然後她現在在讀高中/呃，然後她現在在讀高中。

(zhǐ zhe Péng Dé) 【指著彭德】

          Tā yě _____ bìyè le. *(already)*

          他也已經畢業了。/他也已经毕业了。

Shū Huá: Shénme dàxué bìyè?

舒華/舒华：   甚麼大學畢業？/ 什么大学毕业？

Yáo Shǒuzhèng: E, wǒ shì Měiguó Zhījiāgē bìyè de.

          呃，我是美國芝加哥畢業的。/

          呃，我是美国芝加哥毕业的。

Shū Huá: O, _____. Nǐ ne? *(The University of Chicago)*

          哦，芝加哥大學。你呢？/ 哦，芝加哥大学。你呢？

Péng Dé: Xiàwēiyí Dàxué.

彭德：   夏威夷大學。/ 夏威夷大学。

Zhōu Hǎixiá: Zěnme yòu còu dào yīkuàir le ne?

周海霞：   怎麼又湊到一塊兒了呢？/ 怎么又凑到一块儿了呢？

Péng Dé: A?

          啊？

Zhōu Hǎixiá: Nǐmen zěnme jù dào yīqǐ de?

          你們怎麼聚到一起的？/ 你们怎么聚到一起的？

Ān Shūmǐn: *Get together.* Zěnme jù dào yīkuàir de?

          Get together。怎麼聚到一塊兒的？/怎么聚到一块儿的？

Péng Dé: O, wǒmen ...

          哦，我們... /哦，我们...

Yáo Shǒuzhèng: Shì lái _____ zhège ... zhège ... *(film)*

          是來拍這個...這個... / 是来拍这个…这个…

Unit A-2

Ān Shūmǐn: _____. (program)

                   節目。/ 节目。

Yáo Shǒuzhèng: O, duì.

                   哦，對。/ 哦，对。

Shū Huá, Zhōu Hǎixiá: Zhè shì ge jiémù ma?

                   這是個節目嗎？/ 这是个节目吗？

Péng Dé: Rén lǎoshī yǐqián shì wǒ de _____. (teacher)*

                   任老師以前是我的老師。/ 任老师以前是我的老师。

Zhòng: O.

眾 / 众：   哦。

Ān Shūmǐn: Yǐqián láiguo Zhōngguó ma?

                   以前來過中國嗎？ / 以前来过中国吗？

Yáo Shǒuzhèng: O, méiyǒu. Zhè shì wǒ _____. (first time)

                   哦，沒有。這是我第一次。/ 哦，没有。这是我第一次。

Ān Shūmǐn: Dōu shì dì yī cì?

                   都是第一次？

Yú Xiūmíng: Dì yī cì.

余修明：   第一次。

Péng Dé: Dì èr cì ...

                   第二次 ... 。

Ān Shūmǐn, Shū Huá: Dì èr cì.

                   第二次。

Péng Dé: ... dào zhè(r) lái.

                   ... 到這來。/... 到这来。

Shū Huá: Shénme shíhou dì yī cì ya?

                   甚麼時候第一次呀?/ 什么时候第一次呀?

* "Rén lǎoshī" refers to the author of this book, Cynthia Ning, whose Chinese name is Rén Yǒuméi. The Chinese students wanted to know how three American students from such different places ended up together in Beijing. Todd gave part of the answer—that he was the former student of the author. The rest of the response should have been: James was working in Beijing at the time, and was recruited to help with the program because his father and the author are colleagues at the University of Hawaii, and Robyn Yee is the author's daughter. So the three American students were together to work on the program.

Lesson 5   83

Ān Shūmǐn, Shū Huá : Dào Běijīng lái?

到北京來？/到北京来？

Péng Dé: Jiǔlíng nián.

九零年。

Shū Huá, Zhōu Hǎixiá: O.

哦。

Zhōu Hǎixiá: Yǒu biànhuà ma, gǎnjué?

有變化嗎，感覺？/有变化吗，感觉？

Péng Dé: Hěn dà _____, duì bu duì? (change)

很大變化，對不對？/ 很大变化，对不对？

Ān Shūmǐn: Jiǔlíng nián. Kě bù, dào xiànzài yǐjīng bā nián guòqu le.

九零年。可不，到現在已經八年過去了。/

九零年。可不，到现在已经八年过去了。

Péng Dé: Duì.

對。/对。

Shū Huá: Dāngshí lái Běijīng duì shénme _____ zuì shēn ne? (impression)

當時來北京對什麼印象最深呢？/

当时来北京对什么印象最深呢？

Péng Dé: Zhèr de rén tèbié yǒushàn.

這兒的人特別友善。/ 这儿的人特别友善。

(zhòng xiào) 【眾笑/众笑】

Péng Dé: Duì bu duì?

對不對？/ 对不对？

Yáo Shǒuzhèng: Duì duì.

對對。/ 对对。

Péng Dé: Nǐmen ne?

你們呢？/ 你们呢？

Yáo Shǒuzhèng: Cài hǎochī.

菜好吃。/菜好吃。

(zhòng xiào) 【眾笑/众笑】

Unit A-2

11. Write three ways to say "get together" by filling in the blanks, and matching them to the character equivalents.

còu dào _____,   聚到一塊兒／聚到一块儿

jū dào _____,   凑到一塊兒／凑到一块儿

_____ dào yīkuàir   聚到一起

12. Please circle and number phrases in the extract below to correspond to the English phrases listed.

Ān Shūmǐn: Dào le, nèige, Měiguó, kěnéng Zhōngguó cài de fēngwèi
到了，那個，美國，可能中國菜的風味／
到了，那个，美国，可能中国菜的风味
yě jiù yǒu diǎnr biànhuà le.
也就有點兒變化了。／也就有点儿变化了。

Yáo Shǒuzhèng: Bǐjiào yánghuà.
比較洋化。／比较洋化。

Shū Huá: Měishì Zhōngcān.
美式中餐。

1. American-style Chinese food

2. the flavor of Chinese dishes

3. perhaps

4. by the time it gets to America

5. (it is) comparatively Westernized

6. changes somewhat

13. When his classmates call him the class "computer expert," Huáng Shūhuá demurs (as is polite and proper whenever one is given a compliment) by saying something like "Oh, but I don't deserve the honor!" Fill in the blanks and reorder the characters.

"Kě bù _____ _____ a!"

敢   啊   可   當／当   不

—————   —————   —————   —————   —————

What is a simpler way of saying the same thing? Fill in the blanks.

"Bù _____ _____!"

14. The Chinese students mention "all kinds of entertainments" (gè zhǒng yúlè 各種娛樂／各种娱乐). Check four from the list below that they name in the course of the conversation. Then match each item on the list with its English equivalent.

_____ kànkan xiǎoshuō 看看小説／看看小说		a. go dancing
_____ qù tiàowǔ 去跳舞		b. play electronic games
_____ dǎ pīngpāng qiú 打乒乓球		c. go out with friends
_____ wánr diànzǐ yóuxì 玩電子遊戲／玩电子游戏		d. listen to music
_____ gēn péngyou chūqù wánr 跟朋友出去玩		e. read a novel
_____ tīngting yīnyuè 聽聽音樂／听听音乐		f. play badminton
_____ dǎ yǔmáo qiú 打羽毛球		g. play Ping-Pong

15. Ān Shūmǐn says of Robyn, "Tā de tǐxíng hěn měi" 她的體形很美。／她的体形很美。 Guess what this means.

_____ She's got pretty hair.

_____ She's wearing a nice outfit.

_____ She's got a good figure.

_____ She's got a pleasant personality.

16. When Ān Shūmǐn says the movie *Titanic* was "pretty good," which TWO of the following expressions does she use?

_____ Hái kěyǐ. 還可以／还可以。

_____ Tǐng yǒu yìsi. 挺有意思。

_____ Tǐng hǎokàn de. 挺好看的。

Post-Viewing Activities

Speaking

17. Prepare descriptions of at least five sentences each about any TWO of the people in the conversation.

Example:
Ān Shūmǐn zhù zài Běijīng. Tā shì ge shíjiǔ suì de gāozhōngshēng, lái zì Héběi Shěng. Tā jīnnián shàng Běidà Fùshǔ Zhōngxué, míngnián yào shàng Běijīng Dàxué. Tā juéde Běidà hé Qīnghuá dōu shì hǎo xuéxiào. Tā xǐhuān xuéxí Yīngyǔ, yě xǐhuān yùndòng, tīng yīnyuè, kàn xiǎoshuō.

Unit A-2

Reading / Writing

18. Following is another installment in your correspondence with your penfriend in Beijing. Highlight what you can understand of it.

我的笔友：

你好！

我多么想现在就飞到美国去看你呀，可是我知道我必须得等到明年毕业、考取了美国大学的研究生才行。

我的一个好朋友前不久去了一趟美国。他是随父母一起去旅游的。他们去了佛罗里达和纽约。他最喜欢佛罗里达东海岸的白沙滩。当他开着汽车行驶在一望无际的白沙上时，感觉自己象鸟一样快乐与自由。佛罗里达给他印象最深的是那儿特别干净，气候也好，人也很友好。纽约给他的印象可没这么好了。人多、车多、建筑物也很拥挤。站在高楼林立的曼哈顿街道上，他感到自己是那么渺小，那么微不足道。"纽约使我感到压抑"他对我说。

你知道，每个人的审美观点是不同的。光听我的朋友描述美国是远远不够的。我必须要自己亲自去看看。

为了申请美国大学读研究生，我开始查阅美国各所大学的介绍。我最后把范围缩小在两所大学上：一是加州大学洛杉矶分校，另一个是佛罗里达大学。你去过这两个学校吗？你觉得它们的区别在哪儿？哪一个更好呢？

友　陈今

19. Excluding the opening salutations and the closing signature, this letter from Chén Jīn can be divided into four sections. Write a sentence in English to summarize each section.

Sec. 1 (2 lines):_____

Sec. 2 (7 lines): _____

Sec. 3 (2 lines): _____

Sec. 4 (4 lines): _____

Check your responses with the ones provided below.

4. What do you know about UCLA and the University of Florida?

3. People have different tastes.

2. My friend told me about his visit to Florida and New York.

1. I'd like to come to the U.S. right now but I can't.

20. Re-read the letter, and respond to the following.
Sec. 1. Chén Jīn says that she can't come to the U.S. until next year, and then only if two things happen. What are these two things? a. *She graduates.* b. _____

Sec. 2. Fill in the blanks with the facts taken from Chén Jīn's narrative.
Her friend went to the U.S. recently. He went with (whom?) _____, in order to (do what?) _____. They went to Florida and (where?)

_____.
He liked best the white beaches on (where?) _____.
When he went (by what means of transportation?)_____
on the endless white sand, he felt himself as free and (how did he feel?) _____
as a bird. His deepest impression of Florida is that it is (what?) _____, the
(what?) _____ is very good, and the (who?)_____ are very
friendly. The impression that New York made on him was not as good. (What are three reasons
his impression was not as good?) _____, _____, and
the buildings are crowded together. Standing on the streets of Manhattan, he felt himself to be so
tiny, so insignificant. "New York feels oppressive to me," he said.

Sec. 3. Number the following statements by the order in which they were made.
_____ I need to go see for myself.
_____ You know, each person's sense of aesthetics is different.
_____ Just listening to my friend describe the U.S. is by far not enough.

Sec. 4. Chén Jīn says, "In order to apply to be a graduate student at a U.S. university, I have begun to read introductions to many different U.S. universities. Finally, I have narrowed my scope to two institutions: one is UCLA and the other is the University of Florida." What three questions does she ask of you next?

a. _____

b. _____

c. _____

Unit A-2

21. Fill in the blanks by guessing the missing information (characters, *pinyin*, or English) in the vocabulary list below, which is keyed to Chén Jīn's letter.

多麼 / 多么 duōme _____

_____ bìxū děi *must need to*

等到 _____ *wait until*

考取了 _____

    be accepted by exam

才行 cái xíng _____

前不久 qián bù jiǔ _____

_____ yī tàng *one (measure for times, trips)*

隨 X 一起 / 随 X 一起

    _____

    following along with X

_____ lǚyóu *travel, tour*

佛羅里達 / 佛罗里达 Fóluólǐdá

    _____

紐約 / 纽约 Niǔyuē _____

_____ dōng hǎiàn *East Coast*

    _____

    báishātān *white sand beach*

當...時 / 当...时 _____

    while ..., during the time of ...

    _____

    kāizhe qìchē *driving a car*

一望無際 / 一望无际 _____

    boundless, stretching as far as the eye

    can see

白沙 báishā _____

感覺 / 感觉 gǎnjué _____

自己 zìjǐ _____

象鳥一樣 / 象鸟一样

    _____ *like a bird*

_____ kuàilè *happy*

_____ yǔ *and*

自由 _____ *free*

    _____

    yìnxiàng zuì shēn *the deepest impression*

特別 tèbié _____

_____ gānjìng *clean*

_____ qìhòu *climate*

友好 yǒuhǎo _____

_____ jiànzhùwù *building*

_____ yōngjǐ *crowded*

高樓林立 / 高楼林立

    _____

    tall buildings standing like trees in a

    forest

曼哈頓 Mànhādùn _____

街道 _____ *streets and avenues*

_____ miǎoxiǎo *paltry, tiny*

微不足道 wēi _____

    not worth mentioning

使 _____ *cause*

感到 _____ *feel, get the feeling*

_____ yāyì *oppressive*

審美觀點 / 审美观点

    shěnměi _____

    aesthetic point of view

光 _____ *only, just*

Lesson 5

_____ miáoshù *describe*

遠遠不夠 / 远远不够 yuǎnyuǎn bù gòu _____

親自 / 亲自 _____ *personally*

申請 / 申请 shēnqǐng _____

查閱 / 查阅 cháyuè _____

各所 _____ *different (measure for institutions)*

_____ jièshào *introduce*

把範圍縮小 / 把范围缩小 bǎ fànwéi suōxiǎo _____

加州大學洛杉磯分校 / 加州大学洛杉矶分校

　　Jiāzhōu Dàxué Luòshānjī fēnxiào _____

區別 / 区别 _____ *difference*

_____ gèng hǎo *better*

22. Following is the completed vocabulary list. Re-read Chén Jīn's letter, and see if you understand it better.

多麼 / 多么 duōme *how, how much*

必須得 / 必须得 bìxū děi *must need to*

等到 děng dào *wait until*

考取了 kǎoqǔ le *be accepted by exam*

才行 cái xíng *only that will do*

前不久 qián bù jiǔ *not long ago*

一趟 yī tàng *one (measure for times, trips)*

隨 X 一起 / 随 X 一起 suí X yī qǐ *following along with X*

旅遊 / 旅游 lǚyóu *travel, tour*

佛羅里達 / 佛罗里达 Fóluólǐdá *Florida*

紐約 / 纽约 Niǔyuē *New York*

東海岸 / 东海岸 dōng hǎiàn *East Coast*

白沙灘 / 白沙滩 báishātān *white sand beach*

當...時 / 当...时 dāng ... shí *while ..., during the time of ...*

開著汽車 / 开著汽车 kāizhe qìchē *driving a car*

一望無際 / 一望无际 yīwàng-wújì *boundless, as far as the eye can see*

白沙 báishā *white sand*

感覺 / 感觉 gǎnjué *feel*

自己 zìjǐ *oneself*

象鳥一樣 / 象鸟一样 xiàng niǎo yīyàng *like a bird*

快樂 / 快乐 kuàilè *happy*

與 / 与 yǔ *and*

自由 zìyóu *free*

印象最深 yìnxiàng zuì shēn *deepest impression*

特別 tèbié *especially*

乾淨 / 干净 gānjìng *clean*

氣候 / 气候 qìhòu *climate*

友好 yǒuhǎo *friendly*

Unit A-2

建筑物　jiànzhùwù building

擁擠／拥挤　yōngjǐ crowded

高樓林立／高楼林立　gāolóu-línlì tall buildings standing like trees in a forest

曼哈頓　Mànhādùn Manhattan

街道　jiēdào streets and avenues

渺小　miǎoxiǎo paltry, tiny

微不足道　wēibùzúdào not worth mentioning

使　shǐ cause

感到　gǎndào feel, get the feeling

壓抑／压抑　yāyì oppressive

審美觀點／审美观点　shěnměi guāndiǎn aesthetic point of view

光　guāng only, just

描述　miáoshù describe

遠遠不夠／远远不够　yuǎnyuǎn bù gòu by far not enough

親自／亲自　qīnzì personally

申請／申请　shēnqǐng apply for

查閱／查阅　cháyuè look up and read

各所　gè suǒ different (measure for institutions)

介紹／介绍　jièshào introduce

把範圍縮小／把范围缩小　bǎ fànwéi suōxiǎo narrow the scope

加州大學洛杉磯分校／加州大学洛杉矶分校　Jiāzhōu Dàxué Luòshānjī Fēnxiào University of California–Los Angeles

區別／区别　qūbié difference

更好　gèng hǎo better

23. Write a response to Chén Jīn. Provide some information about U.S. universities.

Sample response

趙明：

　　你好！很可惜你不能現在就來美國，我也不能現在就去中國。沒關係，我們以後一定會有機會見面。世界越來越小！

　　對不起，加州大學洛杉磯分校和佛羅里達大學我都不很熟悉。我只知道加州大學洛杉磯分校比佛羅里達大學大，學生多。兩所都是好學校。你可以兩邊都申請：哪裡給你的錢多你就去哪裡。好嗎？不用緊張，你先來再說。要是你不喜歡你上的學校，以後還可以換。美國大學很多，大大小小有三千多所。一定能找到適合你的一所。

　　友 馬莉亞

安淑敏：我叫安淑敏。認識你
　　　們很高興。

舒華：我叫舒華。很高興認
　　　識你們。

周海霞：我叫周海霞。大家
　　　好！

黃書華：黃書華。幸會！

【笑】

彭德：我叫彭德。

余修明：我叫余修明。

姚守正：姚守正。

彭德：你們都是甚麼地方人？

安淑敏：我是來自中國的河
　　　北。

舒華：呃，我是黑龍江人。

周海霞：呃，我是北京的。北
　　　京。

黃書華：我也是北京人。

【笑】

余修明：你們今年多大？

安淑敏：我今年十九歲。

舒華：嗯，我十八。

周海霞：十八。

黃書華：我也十八歲。

安淑敏：我叫安淑敏。认识你
　　　们很高兴。

舒华：我叫舒华。很高兴认
　　　识你们。

周海霞：我叫周海霞。大家
　　　好！

黄书华：黄书华。幸会！

【笑】

彭德：我叫彭德。

余修明：我叫余修明。

姚守正：姚守正。

彭德：你们都是什么地方人？

安淑敏：我是来自中国的河
　　　北。

舒华：呃，我是黑龙江人。

周海霞：呃，我是北京的。北
　　　京。

黄书华：我也是北京人。

【笑】

余修明：你们今年多大？

安淑敏：我今年十九岁。

舒华：嗯，我十八。

周海霞：十八。

黄书华：我也十八岁。

Lesson 5

Ān Shūmǐn: Wǒ jiào Ān Shūmǐn.
    Rènshi nǐmen hěn gāoxìng.
Shū Huá: Wǒ jiào Shū Huá. Hěn gāoxìng
    rènshi nǐmen.
Zhōu Hǎixiá: Wǒ jiào Zhōu Hǎixiá.
    Dàjiā hǎo!
Huáng Shūhuá: Huáng Shūhuá. Xìng huì!
(xiào)
Péng Dé: Wǒ jiào Péng Dé.
Yú Xiūmíng: Wǒ jiào Yú Xiūmíng.
Yáo Shǒuzhèng: Yáo Shǒuzhèng.
Péng Dé: Nǐmen dōu shì shénme dìfang rén?
Ān Shūmǐn: Wǒ shì láizì Zhōngguó de
    Héběi.
Shū Huá: E, wǒ shì Hēilóngjiāng rén.
Zhōu Hǎixiá: E, wǒ shì Běijīng de. Běijīng.
Huáng Shūhuá: Wǒ yě shì Běijīng rén.
(xiào)
Yú Xiūmíng: Nǐmen jīnnián duō dà?
Ān Shūmǐn: Wǒ jīnnián shíjiǔ suì.
Shū Huá: Ng, wǒ shíbā.
Zhōu Hǎixiá: Shíbā.
Huáng Shūhuá: Wǒ yě shíbā suì.

An Shumin: My name is An Shumin
    Meeting you is a pleasure.
Shu Hua: My name is Shu Hua. I'm happy
    to meet you.
Zhou Haixia: My name is Zhou Haixia,
    Hello, everybody.
Huang Shuhua: Huang Shuhua, a pleasure!
(laughter)
Todd Pavel: My name is Todd Pavel.
Robyn Yee: My name is Robyn Yee.
James Yao: James Yao.
Todd Pavel: Where are you all from?
An Shumin: I'm from China's Hebei
    province.
Shu Hua: Er, I'm from Heilongjiang.
Zhou Haixia: Er, I'm from Beijing. Beijing.
Huang Shuhua: I'm also from Beijing
(laughter)
Robyn Yee: How old are all of you?
An Shumin: I'm 19 years old this year.
Shu Hua: Er, 18.
Zhou Haixia: 18.
Huang Shuhua: I'm also 18.

Unit A-2

姚守正：你們明年都要上大學
　　　　嗎？

安淑敏：對。

周海霞：我們是一個班的。

姚守正：你們知道要上哪一個
　　　　大學嗎？

安淑敏：我們現在已經知道
　　　　了。

安淑敏、舒華【同時】：
　　　　我們三個都是北京大學。

舒華：他是清華大學。

黃書華【與舒華同時】：
　　　　我上清華大學。

彭德：那哪一個大學(是)更好？

安淑敏：一樣好。

舒華、周海霞、黃書華
【同時】：對，對對。

安淑敏：都很棒。

彭德【與安淑敏同時】：
　　　　一樣好嗎？

安淑敏：對，都很棒。

彭德：那你們什麼時候畢業？

安淑敏：四年以後大學畢業。
　　　　嗯。

彭德：噢。

姚守正：你们明年都要上大学
　　　　吗？

安淑敏：对。

周海霞：我们是一个班的。

姚守正：你们知道要上哪一个
　　　　大学吗？

安淑敏：我们现在已经知道
　　　　了。

安淑敏、舒华【同时】：
　　　　我们三个都是北京大学。

舒华：他是清华大学。

黄书华【与舒华同时】：
　　　　我上清华大学。

彭德：那哪一个大学(是)更好？

安淑敏：一样好。

舒华、周海霞、黄书华
　　　　【同时】：对，对对。

安淑敏：都很棒。

彭德【与安淑敏同时】：
　　　　一样好吗？

安淑敏：对，都很棒。

彭德：那你们什么时候毕业？

安淑敏：四年以后大学毕业。
　　　　嗯。

彭德：噢。

Yáo Shǒuzhèng: Nǐmen míngnián dōu yào
    shàng dàxué ma?
Ān Shūmǐn: Duì.
Zhōu Hǎixiá: Wǒmen shì yī ge bān de.
Yáo Shǒuzhèng: Nǐmen zhīdào yào shàng
    nǎ yī ge dàxué ma?
Ān Shūmǐn: Wǒmen xiànzài yǐjīng zhīdào
    le.
Ān Shūmǐn, Shū Huá (tóngshí):
    Wǒmen sānge dōu shì Běijīng Dàxué.
Shū Huá: Tā shì Qīnghuá Dàxué.
Huáng Shūhuá (yǔ Shū Huá tóngshí):
    Wǒ shàng Qīnghuá Dàxué.
Péng Dé: Nà nǎ yī ge dàxué (shì) gèng hǎo?
Ān Shūmǐn: Yīyàng hǎo.
Shū Huá, Zhōu Hǎixia, Huáng Shūhuá
    (tóngshí): Duì, duì duì.
Ān Shūmǐn: Dōu hěn bàng.
Péng Dé (yǔ Ān Shūmǐn tóngshí):
    Yīyàng hǎo ma?
Ān Shūmǐn: Duì, dōu hěn bàng.
Péng Dé: Nà nǐmen shénme shíhou bìyè?

Ān Shūmǐn: Sì nián yǐhòu dàxué bìyè.
    Ng.
Péng Dé: O.

James Yao: Are you all going to college
    next year?
An Shumin: Yes.
Zhou Haixia: We are all in the same class.
James Yao: Do you all know what schools
    you are going to?
An Shumin: We already know, now.

An Shumin/Shu Hua: We three will be at
    Peking University.
Shu Hua: He's Tsinghua University.
Huang Shuhua: (with Shu Hua) I'll go to
    Tsinghua University.
Todd Pavel: Which one is better?
An Shumin: They are equally good.
Shu Hua/Zhou Haixia/Huang Shuhua:
    Right, right, right.
An Shumin: Both schools are great.
Todd Pavel: (with An Shumin)
    Are they equally good?
An Shumin: Right, both are great.
Todd Pavel: Then when will you all
    graduate?
An Shumin: In four years, we'll
    graduate from college. Uh-huh.
Todd Pavel: Oh.

Unit A-2

安淑敏：　你們來中國的目的是甚麼？來看一看嗎？

彭德：對，看一看，也學習中文。

安淑敏：學習中文？

彭德：對。

安淑敏：學習中文是爲了更好的了解中國嗎？

彭德：對對，應該，應該，呃…學習中文，然後…呃…明白…明白中國的情況。

安淑敏：　哦。

彭　德：　對不對？

安淑敏【對姚守正】：
　　我想你更了解中國。

舒華：你們家在夏威夷嗎？

彭德：哦，我們…我們都…我們都…，她，她住在夏威夷。我呢，我住在舊金山。

安淑敏、舒華：哦。

姚守正：　我的父母住在夏威夷。

安淑敏、舒華：哦。

安淑敏：　你在讀甚麼大學？

姚守正：　呃，我已經畢業了。

安淑敏：你们来中国的目的是甚么？来看一看吗？

彭德：对，看一看，也学习中文。

安淑敏：学习中文？

彭德：对。

安淑敏：学习中文是为了更好的了解中国吗？

彭德：对对，应该，应该，呃…学习中文，然后…呃…明白…明白中国的情况。

安淑敏：　哦。

彭　德：　对不对？

安淑敏【对姚守正】：
　　我想你更了解中国。

舒华：你们家在夏威夷吗？

彭德：哦，我们…我们都…我们都…，她，她住在夏威夷。我呢，我住在旧金山。

安淑敏、舒华：哦。

姚守正：我的父母住在夏威夷。

安淑敏、舒华：哦。

安淑敏：你在读什么大学？

姚守正：呃，我已经毕业了。

Ān Shūmǐn: Nǐmen lái Zhōngguó de
    mùdì shì shénme? Lái kàn yi kàn ma?

Péng Dé: Duì, kàn yi kàn, yě xuéxí
    Zhōngwén.

Ān Shūmǐn: Xuéxí Zhōngwén?

Péng Dé: Duì.

Ān Shūmǐn: Xuéxí Zhōngwén shì wèile
    gèng hǎo de liǎojiě Zhōngguó ma?

Péng Dé: Duì duì, yīnggāi, yīnggāi,
    e... xuéxí Zhōngwén, ránhòu ... e...
    míngbai ... míngbai Zhōngguó de
    qíngkuàng.

Ān Shūmǐn: O.

Péng Dé: Duì bu duì?

Ān Shūmǐn (duì Yáo Shǒuzhèng):
    Wǒ xiǎng nǐ gèng liǎojiě Zhōngguó.

Shū Huá: Nǐmen jiā zài Xiàwēiyí ma?

Péng Dé: O, wǒmen ... wǒmen dōu
    ... wǒmen dōu ... tā, tā zhùzài
    Xiàwēiyí. Wǒ ne, wǒ zhùzài
    Jiùjīnshān.

Ān Shūmǐn, Shū Huá: O.

Yáo Shǒuzhèng: Wǒ de fùmǔ zhùzài
    Xiàwēiyí.

Ān Shūmǐn, Shū Huá: O.

Ān Shūmǐn: Nǐ zài dú shénme dàxué?

Yáo Shǒuzhèng: E, wǒ yǐjīng bìyè le.

An Shumin: What was your purpose in
    coming to China? To look around?

Todd Pavel: Yes, to see China and also
    learn Chinese.

An Shumin: Learn Chinese?

Todd Pavel: That's right.

An Shumin: Are you learning Chinese
    so that you can better understand
    China?

Todd Pavel: Yes, we should, should,
    er ... learn Chinese, then er, understand
    ... understand China's situation.

An Shumin: Oh.

Todd Pavel: Is that right?

An Shumin: (to James Yao) I think you
    understand China better.

Shu Hua: Is your home in Hawaii?

Todd Pavel: Oh, we ... we all ... we all,
    she, she lives in Hawaii, and I, I live in
    San Francisco.

An Shumin/Shu Hua: Oh.

James Yao: My parents live in Hawaii.

An Shumin/Shu Hua: Oh.

An Shumin: Which university do you
    attend?

James Yao: Er, I've already graduated.

Unit A-2

【指著余修明】呃，然後她現在在讀高中。

【指著彭德】他也已經畢業了。

彭德：對，對。

舒華：甚麼大學畢業?

姚守正：呃，我是美國芝加哥大學畢業的。

舒華：哦，芝加哥大學。你呢?

彭德：夏威夷大學。

周海霞：你們怎麼又湊到一塊兒了呢?

彭德：啊?

周海霞：你們怎麼聚到一起的?

安淑敏：*Get together.* 怎麼聚到一塊兒的?

彭德：哦，我們 ...

姚守正：是來拍這個 ... 這個 ...

安淑敏：節目。

姚守正：哦，對。

舒華、周海霞：這是個節目嗎?

彭德：任老師以前是我的老師。

Lesson 5

(zhǐ zhe Yú Xiūmíng)

　E, ránhòu tā xiànzài zài dú gāozhōng.

(zhǐ zhe Péng Dé)

　Tā yě yǐjīng bìyè le.

Péng Dé:　Duì, duì.

Shū Huá:　Shénme dàxué bìyè?

Yáo Shǒuzhèng:　E, wǒ shì Měiguó Zhījiāgē
　　Dàxué bìyè de.

Shū Huá:　O, Zhījiāgē Dàxué. Nǐ ne?

Péng Dé:　Xiàwēiyí Dàxué.

Zhōu Hǎixiá:　Nǐmen zěnme yòu còu dào
　　yīkuài(r) le ne?

Péng Dé:　A?

Zhōu Hǎixiá:　Nǐmen zěnme jù dào yīqǐ de?

Ān Shūmǐn:　*Get together.* Zěnme jù dào
　　yīkuài(r) de?

Péng Dé:　O, wǒmen ...

Yáo Shǒuzhèng:　Shì lái pāi zhège ... zhège
　　...

Ān Shūmǐn:　Jiémù.

Yáo Shǒuzhéng:　O, duì.

Shū Huá, Zhōu Hǎixiá:
　　Zhè shì ge jiémù ma?

Péng Dé:　Rèn lǎoshī yǐqián shì wǒ de
　　lǎoshī.

(points at Robyn)

　Er, and she is going to high school
　right now.

(points at Todd)

　He's also already graduated.

Todd Pavel:　Right, right.

Shu Hua: Which college did you graduate
　　from?

James Yao: Er, I graduated from the
　　University of Chicago in the U.S.

Shu Hua:　Oh, the University of
　　Chicago. How about you?

Todd Pavel:　The University of Hawaii.

Zhou Haixia: How did you all meet up?

Todd Pavel:　Huh?

Zhou Haixia:　How did you come
　　together?

An Shumin:　"Get together." How did
　　you all meet up?

Todd Pavel:　Er, we ...

James Yao: We came to film this ...
this ...

An Shumin:　Program.

James Yao: Er, right.

Shu Hua, Zhou Haixia:　Is this a program?

Todd Pavel:　Professor Ning was my
　　teacher.

Unit A-2

眾：哦。	众：哦。
安淑敏：以前來過中國嗎？	安淑敏：以前来过中国吗？
姚守正：哦，沒有。這是我第一次。	姚守正：哦，没有。这是我第一次。
安淑敏：都是第一次？	安淑敏：都是第一次？
余修明：第一次。	余修明：第一次。
彭德：第二次 ...	彭德：第二次 ...
安淑敏、舒華：第二次。	安淑敏、舒华：第二次。
彭德：...到這來。	彭德：...到这来。
舒華：甚麼時候第一次呀？	舒华：什么时候第一次呀？
安淑敏【與舒華同時】：到北京來？	安淑敏【与舒华同时】：到北京来？
彭德：九零年。	彭德：九零年。
舒華、周海霞：哦。	舒华、周海霞：哦。
周海霞：有變化麼，感覺？	周海霞：有变化么，感觉？
彭德：很大變化，對不對？	彭德：很大变化，对不对？
安淑敏：九零年。可不，到現在已經八年過去了。	安淑敏：九零年。可不，到现在已经八年过去了。
彭德：對。	彭德：对。
舒華：當時來北京對甚麼印象最深呢？	舒华：当时来北京对什么印象最深呢？
彭德：這兒的人特別友善。	彭德：这儿的人特别友善。
【眾笑】	【众笑】
彭德：對不對？	彭德：对不对？
姚守正：對對。	姚守正：对对。
彭德：你們呢？	彭德：你们呢？

Lesson 5

Zhòng: O.

Ān Shūmǐn: Yǐqián láiguo Zhōngguó ma?

Yáo Shǒuzhèng: O, méiyǒu. Zhè shì wǒ dì
    yī cì.

Ān Shūmǐn: Dōu shì dì yī cì?

Yú Xiūmíng: Dì yī cì.

Péng Dé: Dì èr cì ...

Ān Shūmǐn, Shū Huá: Dì èr cì.

Péng Dé: ... dào zhè(r) lái.

Shù Huá: Shénme shíhou dì yī cì ya?

Ān Shūmǐn (yǔ Shū Huá tóngshí):
    Dào Běijīng lái?

Péng Dé: Jiǔlíng nián.

Shū Huá, Zhōu Hǎixiá: O.

Zhōu Hǎixiá: Yǒu biànhuà me, gǎnjué?

Péng Dé: Hěn dà biànhuà, duì bu duì?

Ān Shūmǐn: Jiǔlíng nián. Kě bù, dào
    xiànzài yǐjīng bānián guòqu le.

Péng Dé: Duì.

Shū Huá: Dāngshí lái Běijīng duì shénme
    yìnxiàng zuì shēn ne?

Péng Dé: Zhèr de rén tèbié yǒushàn.

(zhòng xiào)

Péng Dé: Duì bu duì?

Yáo Shǒuzhèng: Duì duì.

Péng Dé: Nǐmen ne?

All four: Oh.

An Shumin: Have you been to China
    before?

James Yao: Oh, no. This is my first
    time.

An Shumin: The first time for all of you?

Robyn Yee: It's my first time.

Todd Pavel: It's my second time ...

An Shumin/Shu Hua: Your second time ...

Todd Pavel: ... coming here.

Shu Hua: When was the first time?

An Shumin: (with Shu Hua)
    To Beijing?

Todd Pavel: In 1990.

Shu Hua/ Zhou Haixia: Oh.

Zhou Haixia: Has anything changed, do
    you feel?

Todd Pavel: It has changed a lot, right?

An Shumin: 1990. Absolutely, eight
    years have gone by now.

Todd Pavel: Uh-huh.

Shu Hua: At that time, what impressed you
    the most about Beijing?

Todd Pavel: The people here are so friendly.

(all laugh)

Todd Pavel: Right?

James Yao: Right, right.

Todd Pavel: What do you (two) think?

Unit A-2

姚守正：菜好吃。【眾笑】

舒華：在美國不常吃中國菜吧?

姚守正：吃得到。可是沒有北京好吃。

安淑敏：到了，那個，美國，可能中國菜的風味也就有點兒變化了。

姚守正：對，對。比較洋化。

舒華：美式中餐。

姚守正：嘿嘿！

彭德：你們喜歡學習甚麼?

安淑敏：喜歡甚麼?

彭德：學習甚麼?

安淑敏：學習 ... 呃 ... 英語。

舒華【與安淑敏同時】：每個人的愛好都不一樣。

安淑敏：計算機。

姚守正、彭德【同時】：計算機是嗎?

彭德：電腦。

安淑敏：對。

【指著黃書華】他是我們班的電腦高手。

周海霞：對，電腦高手。

姚守正：菜好吃。【众笑】

舒华：在美国不常吃中国菜吧?

姚守正：吃得到。可是没有北京好吃。

安淑敏：到了，那个，美国，可能中国菜的风味也就有点儿变化了。

姚守正：对，对。比较洋化。

舒华：美式中餐。

姚守正：嘿嘿！

彭德：你们喜欢学习什么?

安淑敏：喜欢什么?

彭德：学习什么?

安淑敏：学习 ... 呃 ... 英语。

舒华【与安淑敏同时】：每个人的爱好都不一样。

安淑敏：计算机。

姚守正、彭德【同时】：计算机是吗?

彭德：电脑 。

安淑敏：对。

【指著黄书华】他是我们班的电脑高手。

周海霞：对，电脑高手。

Lesson 5

Yáo Shǒuzhèng: Cài hǎo chī.

(zhòng xiào)

Shū Huá: Zài Měiguó bù cháng chī Zhōngguócài ba?

Yáo Shǒuzhéng: Chī de dào. Kěshì méiyǒu Běijīng hǎochī.

Ān Shūmǐn: Dào le, nèige, Měiguó, kěnéng Zhōngguócài de fēngwèi(r) yě jiù yǒu diǎnr biànhuà le.

Yáo Shǒuzhèng: Duì, duì. Bǐjiào yánghuà.

Shū Huá: Měishì Zhōngcān.

Yáo Shǒuzhèng: Hei hei!

Péng Dé: Nǐmen xǐhuan xuéxí shénme?

Ān Shūmǐn: Xǐhuan shénme?

Péng Dé: Xuéxí shénme?

Ān Shūmǐn: Xuéxí ... e... Yīngyǔ.

Shū Huá *(yǔ Ān Shūmǐn tóngshí)*: Měige rén de àihào dōu bù yīyàng.

Ān Shūmǐn: Jìsuànjī.

Yáo Shǒuzhèng, Péng Dé *(tóng shí)*: Jìsuànjī shì ma?

Péng Dé: Diànnǎo.

Ān Shūmǐn: Duì.

(zhǐ zhe Huáng Shūhuá)
Tā shì wǒmen bān de diànnǎo gāoshǒu.

Zhōu Hǎixiá: Duì, diànnǎo gāoshǒu.

James Yao: The food is delicious.

(all laugh)

Shu Hua: In America, you don't eat Chinese food often, do you?

Yao Shouzheng: We can get it, but it's not as good as in Beijing.

An Shumin: After it gets to, er, America, perhaps the flavor of Chinese food will change a little.

James Yao: Yes, yes. It becomes relatively westernized.

Shu Hua: American-style Chinese food.

James Yao: Uh-huh.

Todd Pavel: What do you like to study?

An Shumin: What do we like?

Todd Pavel: What do you study?

An Shumin: We study ... er ... English.

Shu Hua *(with An Shumin)* :
Everybody's preference is different.

An Shumin: Computers.

James Yao, Todd Pavel *(together)*:
Computers?

Todd Pavel: "Electric brains."

An Shumin: Right.

(points at Huang Shuhua)
He is the class computer expert.

Zhou Haixia: Right, the computer expert.

黃書華： 唏，不敢當啊！

余修明： 你們將來要做甚麼？

安淑敏： 將來要做甚麼 ... 現在
好象還沒有定下來呢。
（還沒有）完全定下來。

周海霞： 慢慢發展吧。

黃書華： 等上完大學才能基本
上確定呢。反正我估計我
就是去搞計算機了。

彭德：那你們有空的時候喜
歡做甚麼？

安淑敏： 做運動。

舒華：對，我們是比較喜歡運
動。打球，乒乓球，羽毛
球。

安淑敏：或者聽聽音樂，看看
小說。

周海霞：對。

安淑敏：各種娛樂都有。

姚守正：聽甚麼種音樂？

安淑敏、舒華【同時】：
呃，pop music, pop music.

姚守正：美國的？西方的？還
是…

安淑敏：都有，嗯。

黄书华： 唏，不敢当啊！

余修明： 你们将来要做什么？

安淑敏： 将来要做什么 ... 现在
好象还没有定下来呢。
（还没有）完全定下来。

周海霞： 慢慢发展吧。

黄书华： 等上完大学才能基本
上确定呢。反正我估计我
就是去搞计算机了。

彭德：那你们有空的时候喜
欢做什么？

安淑敏： 做运动。

舒华：对，我们是比较喜欢运
动。打球，乒乓球，羽毛
球。

安淑敏：或者听听音乐，看看
小说。

周海霞：对。

安淑敏：各种娱乐都有。

姚守正：听什么种音乐？

安淑敏、舒华【同时】：
呃，pop music, pop music.

姚守正：美国的？西方的？还
是…

安淑敏：都有，嗯。

Lesson 5

Huáng Shūhuá: Yo, bù gǎn dāng a!

Yú Xiūmíng: Nǐmen jiānglái yào zuò
    shénme?

Ān Shūmǐn: Jiānglái yào zuò shénme ...
    xiànzài hǎoxiàng hái méiyǒu
    dìngxiàlái ne. (Hái méiyǒu) wánquán
    dìngxiàlái.

Zhōu Hǎixiá: Mànmàn fāzhǎn ba.

Huáng Shūhuá: Děng shàng wán dàxué
    cáinéng jīběnshàng quèdìng ne.
    Fǎnzhèng wǒ gūjì wǒ jiù shì qù gǎo
    jìsuànjī le.

Péng Dé: Nà nǐmen yǒu kòng(r) de
    shíhou xǐhuan zuò shénme?

Ān Shūmǐn: Zuò yùndòng.

Shū Huá: Duì, wǒmen shì bǐjiào xǐhuan
    yùndòng. Dǎqiú, pīngpāngqiú,
    yǔmáoqiú.

Ān Shūmǐn: Huòzhě tīngting yīnyuè,
    kànkan xiǎoshuō.

Zhōu Hǎixiá: Duì.

Ān Shūmǐn: Gèzhǒng yúlè dōuyǒu.

Yáo Shǒuzhèng: Tīng shénme zhǒng
    yīnyuè?

Ān Shūmǐn, Shū Huá *(tóngshí)*:
    E, pop music, pop music.

Yáo Shǒuzhèng: Měiguó de? Xīfāng de?
    Háishì ...

Huang Shuhua: Ho, you flatter me!

Robyn Yee: What are you all going to
    become in the future?

An Shumin: Become in the future ... right
    now it seems we haven't decided yet.
    We haven't quite decided (yet).

Zhou Haixia: We'll develop in time.

Huang Shuhua: We can't basically decide
    until after we finish college. In any
    case, I suspect I'll go work with
    computers.

Todd Pavel: Well, what do you do in your
    spare time?

An Shumin: Exercise.

Shu Hua: Yes, we rather like to exercise.
    Play ball—Ping-Pong, badminton.

An Shumin: Or listen to music, or read
    novels.

Zhou Haixia: Uh-huh.

An Shumin: We have all kinds of
    entertainment.

James Yao: What kind of music do you
    listen to?

An Shumin/Shu Hua *(together)*:
    Er, pop music. Pop music.

James Yao: American music? Western
    music? Or ...

Unit A-2

周海霞：都有。

安淑敏：對，都有。嗯，你們
　　　　呢？課外活動幹嘛呢？

姚守正：也是喜歡打球、聽音
　　　　樂、看電影。

安淑敏：出去旅行嗎？

姚守正：啊，對，喜歡旅行。

余修明：嗯，喜歡跑步、看電
　　　　影。嗯，跟朋友出去。

安淑敏：她的體形很美。

【笑】

彭德：對。那我喜歡看電
　　　影，也看書。

周海霞：對。

彭德：對。

安淑敏：啊，看電影，看
　　　　《泰坦尼克》。

彭德：你們都看過了嗎？

眾：看過了。

姚守正：覺得好看嗎？

安淑敏：還可以。

【笑】挺好看的。

周海霞：都有。

安淑敏：对，都有。嗯，你们
　　　　呢？课外活动干嘛呢？

姚守正：也是喜欢打球、听音
　　　　乐、看电影。

安淑敏：出去旅行吗？

姚守正：啊，对，喜欢旅行。

余修明：嗯，喜欢跑步、看电
　　　　影。嗯，跟朋友出去。

安淑敏：她的体形很美。

【笑】

彭德：对。那我喜欢看电
　　　影，也看书。

周海霞：对。

彭德：对。

安淑敏：啊，看电影，看
　　　　《泰坦尼克》。

彭德：你们都看过了吗？

众：看过了。

姚守正：觉得好看吗？

安淑敏：还可以。

【笑】挺好看的。

Ān Shūmín: Dōu yǒu, ng.

Zhōu Hǎixiá: Dōu yǒu.

Ān Shūmín: Duì, dōu yǒu. Ng, nǐmen ne?
Kèwài huódòng gàn má ne?

Yáo Shǒuzhèng: Yě shì xǐhuan dǎqiú, tīng
yīnyuè, kàn diànyǐng.

Ān Shūmín: Chūqù lǚxíng ma?

Yáo Shǒuzhèng: À, duì, xǐhuan lǚxíng.

Yú Xiūmíng: Ng, xǐhuan pǎobù, kàn
diànyǐng. Ng, gēn péngyǒu chūqù.

Ān Shūmín: Tā de tǐxíng hěn měi.

(Xiào)

Péng Dé: Duì. Nà wǒ xǐhuan kàn
diànyǐng, yě kàn shū.

Zhōu Hǎixiá: Duì.

Péng Dé: Duì.

Ān Shūmǐn: A, kàn diànyǐng, kàn
Tàitǎnníkè (hào).

Péng Dé: Nǐmen dōu kànguo le ma?

Zhòng: Kànguò le.

Yáo Shǒuzhèng: Juéde hǎo kàn ma?

Ān Shūmǐn: Hái kěyǐ.

(Xiào) Tǐng hǎokàn de.

An Shumin: All of that. Uh-huh.

Zhou Haixia: All of that.

An Shumin: Uh-huh, all of that.
Mmm, how about you? What do you
do for extracurricular activity?

James Yao: I also like to play ball,
listen to music, and watch movies.

An Shumin: Do you go traveling?

James Yao: Ah, yes, I like traveling.

Yu Xiuming: Er, I like jogging and
watching movies ... er, going out with
my friends.

An Shumin: She has a beautiful build.

(laughter)

Todd Pavel: Uh-huh. Well, I like
watching movies, and I read books.

Shu Hua: Uh-huh.

Todd Pavel: Right.

An Shumin: Er, watching movies,
watching *Titanic*.

Todd Pavel: Have you all seen that?

All: Yes, we've seen it.

James Yao: Did you like it?

An Shumin: It was okay.

(laughter) It was pretty good.

Unit A-2

Unit A-2: Making Friends (cont.)

Lesson 6: *Introductory Comments by Two Boys*

Two sociable junior high boys on bicycles introduce themselves to our camera crew.

Previewing Activity

1. In this desultory conversation, a number of questions were asked of the boys. Write in Chinese (using 漢字，*pinyin*, or a combination) at least one sentence in response to each question, which you think might have been a likely answer.

☐	What are you eating?
☐	Where do you live?
☐	What do you do after class?
☐	Tell us about your bikes.
☐	Where are you from?

First Viewing: Global Information

2. Number the questions in the order in which they were asked, by writing in the boxes above.

3. For your predictions, highlight or circle the ones which approximate what the boys did reply.

Second Viewing: Specific Information

4. Match the person with the name:

Boy on the right of the screen   Xú Zhèngyǔ

Boy on the left of the screen   Lǔ Áng

5. Where are they from? Answer: _____

6. What do they say they like to do after class? Check as appropriate.

[ ] go swimming

[ ] hang around in the classroom

[ ] go home

[ ] ride their bikes

[ ] chat with classmates

[ ] arm wrestle

7. Where do they live? Circle the correct choice in each of the two sentences below.

Xú Zhèngyǔ
Lǔ Áng   lives at Liùdàokǒu, which is   13
                                                 30   minutes away by bike.

Xú Zhèngyǔ
Lǔ Áng   lives at Tsinghua University, which is   13
                                                         30   minutes away by bike.

8. What do they say about their bikes? For each of the statements below, identify the boy who made it—write 1 for Xú Zhèngyǔ and 2 for Lǔ Áng.

[ ] It was bought recently.

[ ] My mom came back from Japan and bought it for me.

[ ] It was bought when school started.

[ ] The chain keeps falling off; it's hard to ride.

[ ] I ride it to school every day.

[ ] I don't like it, but it was cheap, so I have to ride it.

[ ] It's easy to ride, and I like its color.

Unit A-2

9. Lǚ Áng talks about the bottle of water he is holding. Fill in the blanks in English.

"This is the bottle we must carry every day, (to hold) the water that we drink. Every _____ we fill it up, and then we go to school. Then between classes or during _____ we have water to drink, so that we don't need to _____."

10. What is the flavor of the ice pop Xú Zhèngyǔ is eating? Circle one choice:

      vanilla   lychee   coconut   yogurt   apple

11. Where did he buy the ice pop? Answer: _____

Third Viewing: Linguistic Information

12. Todd opens the interview by telling the boys to eat their popsicles as they talk. Fill in the blanks in the *pinyin:*

"Yì _____ jiǎng yì _____ chī."
一邊講一邊吃 ／ 一边讲一边吃

Make up another statement in Chinese about two things you can do at the same time.

_____

13. Todd asks, "Nǐmen xiàkè de shíhou xǐhuān zuò shénme?"
"你們下課的時候喜歡做甚麼？" ／ "你们下课的时候喜欢做什么？"
which means something like, "What do you like to do when class lets out?"

Xú Zhèngyǔ's response is, "Xiàkè...zài jiàoshì dāi zhe"
"下課…在教室待著" ／ "下课…在教室待著"
which means, "When class lets out ... (I) hang around the classroom."

If Todd had meant not "just at the time when class ends" but generally "after class" or "after school," which of the following do you think he could have said? Circle two choices.

                xiàkè yǐhòu
                下課以後 ／ 下课以后

"Nǐmen   fàngxué yǐhòu   xǐhuān zuò shénme?"
                放學以後 ／ 放学以后

                fàngxué de shíhou
                放學的時候 ／ 放学的时候

Lesson 6

14. Below are some verbal phrases that the boys use. Match them with their English equivalents.

_____zài jiàoshì dāizhe a. drink water

_____hé tóngxué yīqǐ liáoliáotiānr b. ride a bicycle

_____bāi shǒuwànr c. put water inside

_____qí zìxíngchē d. arm wrestle

_____dài píngzi e. hang around the classroom

_____hē shuǐ f. be eating a lychee ice

_____bǎ shuǐ cún zài lǐbiānr g. chat with classmates

_____zài chī lìzhībīng h. bring a bottle

15. Now match the English with both the traditional and the simplified character equivalents.

___ ___drink water 1.帶瓶子 a.在教室里呆著

___ ___ride a bicycle 2.騎自行車 b.和同学一起聊聊天

___ ___put the water inside 3.在教室裡呆著 c.掰手腕

___ ___arm wrestle 4.把水存在裡邊 d.騎自行车

___ ___hang around the classroom 5.在吃荔枝冰 e.带瓶子

___ ___be eating a lychee ice 6.掰手腕 f.喝水

___ ___chat with classmates 7.喝水 g.把水存在里边

___ ___bring a bottle 8.和同學一起聊聊天 h.在吃荔枝冰

Note: "zài" indicates a progressive—someone is in the process of doing something. E.g.:

Tā zài shuìjiào (他在睡覺 ／他在睡觉) = He is sleeping.

16. Write the following progressive forms, using either *pinyin* or characters:

He is drinking water. _____

She is riding a bike. _____

Unit A-2

Post-Viewing Activities

Speaking

17. Make up a brief description (4–6 sentences) about what <u>you</u> generally do after school.
Following is some vocabulary for your reference.

work	gōngzuò	工作
go shopping (for food, etc.)	qù cǎigòu	去採購／去采购
go window shopping	qù guàngjiē	去逛街
run/jog	pǎobù	跑步／跑步
work out	duànliàn shēntǐ	鍛煉身體／锻炼身体
cook dinner	zuò wǎnfàn	做晚飯／做晚饭
meet friends	huì péngyou	會朋友／会朋友
read a book	kànshū	看書／看书
read the newspaper	kànbào	看報／看报
read a magazine	kàn zázhì	看雜誌／看杂志
do homework	zuò gōngkè	做功課／做功课
watch television	kàn diànshì	看電視／看电视
watch a video	kàn lùxiàng	看錄像／看录像
play computer games	wán diànzǐ yóuxì	玩電子遊戲／玩电子游戏
read e-mail	kàn diànzǐ yóujiàn	看電子郵件／看电子邮件
surf the Web	shàng wǎng	上網／上网
nap	dǎ dǔnr, shuì wǔjiào	打盹兒／打盹儿，睡午覺／睡午觉

(for your notes—write pinyin, characters, or a combination)

Lesson 6

17. *Sample statement:*

Xīngqīyī, sān, wǔ wǒ xià le kè yǐhòu děi qù gōngzuò. Wǒ zài gòuwùzhōngxīn de yī ge cāntīng lǐ dāng fúwùyuán. Xīngqīèr hé sì, wǒ yìbān huíjiā zuò gōngkè, kàn diànzi yóujiàn, huò shàng wǎng. Zhōumò wǒ xǐhuān huì péngyǒu, chūqu sànsànbù, huòzhě zài jiālǐ wánr diànzǐ yóuxì.

Cultural activity

Lǚ Áng introduces himself by describing his name as the "Lǚ 吕" written with two "mouth 口" radicals, and the "Áng" from the word "ángyáng 昂揚 / 昂扬," meaning "to be proud." Such "identifications" of names are necessary and very common in conversation.

18. See if you can decipher the characters for Mr. Wáng Dàozhōng's name, based on the "identifiers" below: Write the characters here: _____ _____ _____

Family name: "Sān héng Wáng" (the "Wáng" written with three horizontal strokes)
Personal name: "Zhīdào de dào, Zhōngguó de zhōng" (the "dao" of the term meaning "to know," and the "zhong" of the word meaning "China")

19. With the help of your teacher, a native speaker, or any reference materials you can find, write out similar "identifications" below for each of the characters in your Chinese name, if you have one. Memorize these identifications, and if you wish, share them with your classmates. See if you can learn some of the identifications of their names as well.

Your family name: _____

Description: _____

The first character of your personal name: _____

Description: _____

The second character of your personal name (if there is one): _____

Description: _____

Unit A-2

Reading / Writing

20. Rewrite your notes from the previous section into a well-organized statement about your after-school activities, using characters as much as possible.

```

```

21. Did 1) 呂昂 / 吕昂 or 2) 徐正宇 make each of the statements below, about their bicycles?

☐ 這輛自行車我剛買不久，是我媽媽從日本回來給我買的 /
這辆自行车我刚买不久，是我妈妈从日本回来给我买的。

☐ 我每天上學下學都騎它。我覺得挺好騎的，而且它的顏色我
也比較喜歡 / 我每天上学下学都骑它。我觉得挺好骑的，而
且它的颜色我也比较喜欢。

☐ 這輛自行車呢，是開學的時候買的，就是鏈子老掉，不好騎
/ 这辆自行车呢，是开学的时候买的，就是链子老掉，不好骑。

☐ 我是不太喜歡騎，但是由於價錢便宜，我就只能騎了 / 我是
不太喜欢骑，但是由于价钱便宜，我就只能骑了。

Answers

18. *Characters for Mr. Wáng Dàozhōng's name:* 王道中

20. *Sample statement in character format (both traditional and simplified):*

星期一、三、五我下了課以後得去工作。我在購物中心的一個餐廳裏當服務員。星期二和四，我一般回家做功課、看電子郵件，或上網。週末我喜歡會朋友，出去散散步，或者在家裏玩電子遊戲。

星期一、三、五我下了課以后得去工作。我在购物中心的一个餐厅里当服务员。星期二和四，我一般回家做功课、看电子邮件，或上网。周末我喜欢会朋友，出去散散步，或者在家里玩电子游戏。

Unit A-2

彭德： 一邊 ... 一邊講一邊吃。

徐正宇、呂昂：好的，沒關係。

彭德： 你叫甚麼名字？

徐正宇：我叫徐正宇。

呂昂： 我叫呂昂，呂昂，雙口呂，昂揚的昂。

彭德： 你們是甚麼地方人？

徐正宇：我們是北京人。

呂昂： 對。

彭德： 你們下課的時候喜歡做甚麼？

徐正宇：下課…在教室裡呆著。

呂昂： 有時候和同學一起，那，聊聊天。還特別流行那種掰手腕。

彭德： 你們，你們都是北京人，對不對？

徐正宇、呂昂：對。

彭德： 你們住在哪裡？

呂昂： 我住在六道口。

徐正宇：我住在清華。

彭德： 離這兒遠不遠？

呂昂： 離這兒騎車半個小時。

徐正宇：離這兒騎車十三分鐘。

彭德： 一边 ... 一边讲一边吃。

徐正宇、吕昂：好的，没关系。

彭德： 你叫什么名字？

徐正宇：我叫徐正宇。

吕昂： 我叫吕昂，吕昂，双口吕，昂扬的昂。

彭德： 你们是什么地方人？

徐正宇：我们是北京人。

吕昂： 对。

彭德： 你们下课的时候喜欢做什么？

徐正宇：下课…在教室里呆著。

吕昂： 有时候和同学一起，那，聊聊天。还特别流行那种掰手腕。

彭德： 你们，你们都是北京人，对不对？

徐正宇、吕昂：对。

彭德： 你们住在哪里？

吕昂： 我住在六道口。

徐正宇：我住在清华。

彭德： 离这儿远不远？

吕昂： 离这儿骑车半个小时。

徐正宇：离这儿骑车十三分钟。

Lesson 6

Péng Dé: Yībiān... yībian jiǎng yībiān chī.

Xú Zhèngyǔ, Lǔ Áng:
                 Hǎo de, méi guānxi.

Péng Dé: Nǐ jiào shénme míngzi?

Xú Zhèngyǔ: Wǒ jiào Xú Zhèngyǔ.

Lǔ Áng: Wǒ jiào Lǔ Áng, Lǔ Áng, shuāng
                 kǒu lǔ, ángyáng de áng.

Péng Dé: Nǐmen shì shénme dìfang rén?

Xú Zhèngyǔ: Wǒmen shì Běijīng rén.

Lǔ Áng: Duì.

Péng Dé: Nǐmen xiàkè de shíhou xǐhuan
                 zuò shénme?

Xú Zhèngyǔ: Xiàkè ... zài jiàoshì dāizhe.

Lǔ Áng: Yǒushíhou, hé tóngxué yīqǐ, nà,
                 liáoliaotiānr. Hái tèbié liúxíng nà
                 zhǒng bāi shǒuwànr.

Péng Dé: Nǐmen, nǐmen dōu shì Běijīng
                 rén, duì bu duì?

Xú Zhèngyǔ, Lǔ Áng: Duì.

Péng Dé: Nǐmen zhù zài nǎli?

Lǔ Áng: Wǒ zhù zài Liùdàokǒu.

Xú Zhèngyǔ: Wǒ zhù zài Qīnghuá.

Péng Dé: Lí zhèr yuǎn bu yuǎn?

Lǔ Áng: Lí zhèr qíchē bàn ge xiǎoshí.

Xú Zhèngyǔ: Lí zhèr qíchē shísān fēnzhōng.

Todd Pavel: You can talk and eat at the
                 same time.

Xu Zhengyu, Lu Ang: Okay, no problem.

Todd Pavel: What's your name?

Xu Zhengyu: My name's Xu Zhengyu.

Lü Ang: My name's Lü Ang, Lü Ang; it's the
             "Lü" written with the two "mouth"
             radicals and the "Ang" from the word
             meaning "to be proud."

Todd Pavel: Where are you guys from?

Xu Zhengyu: We're both from Beijing.

Lü Ang: That's right.

Todd Pavel: When class lets out, what do
                 you guys like to do?

Xu Zhengyu: When class is over ... we stay
                 in the classroom.

Lü Ang: Sometimes we sit around and talk
             with our classmates. And that arm
             wrestling is very popular.

Todd Pavel: You guys are both from Beijing,
                 right?

Xu Zhengyu, Lü Ang: That's right.

Todd Pavel: Where do you guys live?

Lü Ang: I live in Liudaokou.

Xu Zhengyu: I live in Qinghua.

Todd Pavel: Is that far from here?

Lü Ang: About a half hour by bike.

Xu Zhengyu: About 13 minutes by bike.

Unit A-2

呂昂：　不用説那麼精確。

女：請你們…了解（講）
　　一下你們的自行車好嗎?

徐正宇、呂昂：嗯?

女：了解（講）一下你們
　　的自行車。

呂昂：　哎，好的。

徐正宇：你先説吧。

呂昂：　甚麼意思呀?

徐正宇：問你呀！

女：自行車，買的? 或者
　　是 …

徐正宇：你先來吧。

呂昂：　你先來，你先來。

女：喜歡你們的自行車嗎?

徐正宇、呂昂：好的，嗯，好
　　的。

徐正宇：這輛自行車，呃，甚
　　麼時候買的?

呂昂：　別講那麼具體。

徐正宇：哦，對，這輛自行車
　　呢是開學的時候買的，就
　　是鏈子老掉，不好騎。我
　　…我是不太喜歡騎，但是
　　由於這個…價錢便宜，我就
　　只能騎了。就沒甚麼了。

呂昂：　不用说那么精确。

女：请你们…了解（讲）
　　一下你们的自行车好吗?

徐正宇、呂昂：嗯?

女：了解（讲）一下你们
　　的自行车。

呂昂：　哎，好的。

徐正宇：你先说吧。

呂昂：　什么意思呀?

徐正宇：问你呀！

女：自行车，买的? 或者
　　是 …

徐正宇：你先来吧。

呂昂：　你先来，你先来。

女：喜欢你们的自行车吗?

徐正宇、呂昂：好的，嗯，好
　　的。

徐正宇：这辆自行车，呃，什
　　么时候买的?

呂昂：　别讲那么具体。

徐正宇：哦，对，这辆自行车
　　呢是开学的时候买的，就
　　是链子老掉，不好骑。我
　　…我是不太喜欢骑，但是
　　由于这个…价钱便宜，我就
　　只能骑了。就没什么了。

Lesson 6

Lǔ Áng: Bù yòng shuō nàme jīngquè.

Nǔ: Qǐng nǐmen ... liǎojiě (jiǎng)
           yīxià nǐmen de zìxíngchē hǎo ma?

Xú Zhèngyǔ, Lǔ Áng: En?

Nǔ: Liǎojiě (jiǎng) yīxià nǐmen de
           zìxíngchē.

Lǔ Áng: Ai, hǎo de.

Xú Zhèngyǔ: Nǐ xiān shuō ba.

Lǔ Áng: Shénme yìsi ya?

Lǔ Áng: Wèn nǐ ya!

Nǔ: Zìxíngchē, mǎi de? Huòzhě shi ...

Xú Zhèngyǔ: Nǐ xiān lái ba.

Lǔ Áng: Nǐ xiān lái, nǐ xiān lái.

Nǔ: Xǐhuan nǐmen de zìxíngchē ma?

Xú Zhèngyǔ, Lǔ Áng: Hǎo de, en, hǎo de.

Xú Zhèngyǔ: Zhèliàng zìxíngchē, e, shénme
           shíhou mǎi de?

Lǔ Áng: Bié jiǎng nàme jùtǐ.

Xú Zhèngyǔ: E, duì, zhèliàng zìxíngchē ne
           shì kāixué de shíhou mǎi de, jiùshì
           liànzi lǎo diào, bù hǎo qí. Wǒ ... wǒ
           shì bù tài xǐhuan qí, dànshì yóuyú
           zhège ... jiàqian piányi, wǒ jiù zhǐ
           néng qí le. Jiù méi shénme le.

Lü Ang: You don't need to be so accurate.

Woman: Could you guys (talk) ... I'd like to
           find out about your bikes, okay?

Xu Zhengyu, Lü Ang: Eh?

Woman: Let us know (tell us) about your
           bikes.

Lü Ang: Oh, okay.

Xu Zhengyu (to Lü Ang): You go first.

Lü Ang: What does she mean?

Xu Zhengyu: She asked you!

Woman: Your bikes, did you buy them? Or ...

Xu Zhengyu: You go first.

Lü Ang: You go first! You go first!

Woman: Do you guys like your bikes?

Xu Zhengyu, Lü Ang: Okay, er, we
           understand.

Xu Zhengyu: As for this bike, um, when did
           I buy it?

Lü Ang: Don't talk in such detail.

Xu Zhengyu: Um, okay, my bike ... I got it
           when school started, it's just that the
           chain keeps falling off. It's not easy to
           ride. I ... I don't really like riding it, but
           because the ... price was low, I have no
           choice but to ride it. And that's about it.

Unit A-2   120

呂昂： 這輛自行車我剛買不
久，是我媽媽從日本回來
給我買的。我每天上學下
學都騎它。我覺得挺好騎
的，而且它的顏色我也比
較喜歡。

呂昂： 這是我們每天必帶的瓶
子，是我們喝水用的。每
天我們早上，每天我們早
上把水存在這裏邊，然後
再到學校。課間或者，那
個，午休的時候就可以喝
水，不用在這買了。

彭德： 你在吃甚麼？

徐正宇：啊？我在吃…叫甚麼
來著？哦，對，荔枝冰。

女：荔枝冰是不是一種冰激凌？

徐正宇：冰棍兒。

彭德： 好吃嗎？

徐正宇：味道不錯。

彭德： 在哪裏買的？

徐正宇：學校的小賣部。

呂昂： 这辆自行车我刚买不
久，是我妈妈从日本回来
给我买的。我每天上学下
学都骑它。我觉得挺好骑
的，而且它的颜色我也比
较喜欢。

呂昂： 这是我们每天必带的瓶
子，是我们喝水用的。每
天我们早上，每天我们早
上把水存在这里边，然后
再到学校。课间或者，那
个，午休的时候就可以喝
水，不用在这买了。

彭德： 你在吃什么？

徐正宇：啊？我在吃…叫什么
来著？哦，对，荔枝冰。

女：荔枝冰是不是一种冰激凌？

徐正宇：冰棍儿。

彭德： 好吃吗？

徐正宇：味道不错。

彭德： 在哪里买的？

徐正宇：学校的小卖部。

Lesson 6

Lǔ Áng: Zhè liàng zìxíngchē wǒ gāng
          mǎi bù jiǔ, shì wǒ māma cóng Rìběn
          huílai gěi wǒ mǎi de. Wǒ měi tiān
          shàngxué xiàxué dōu qí tā. Wǒ juéde
          tǐng hǎo qí de, érqiě tā de yánsè wǒ yě
          bǐjiào xǐhuan.

Lǔ Áng: Zhè shì wǒmen měi tiān bì dài
          de píngzi, shì wǒmen hē shuǐ yòng de.
          Měi tiān wǒmen zǎoshang, měi tiān
          wǒmen zǎoshang bǎ shuǐ cúnzai
          zhèlǐbian, ránhòu zài dào xuéxiào.
          Kèjiān huòzhě, nèige, wǔxiū de shíhou
          jiù kěyǐ hē shuǐ, bù yòng zài zhèr mǎi
          le.

Péng Dé: Nǐ zài chī shénme?

Xú Zhèngyǔ: A? Wǒ zài chī ... jiào shénme
          lái zhe? E, duì, lìzhībīng.

Nǚ: Lìzhībīng shì bu shì yī zhǒng
          bīngjīlíng?

Xú Zhèngyǔ: Bīnggùnr.

Péng Dé: Hǎo chī ma?

Xú Zhèngyǔ: Wèidào bùcuò.

Péng Dé: Zài nǎli mǎi de?

Xú Zhèngyǔ: Xuéxiào de xiǎomàibù.

Lü Ang: My bike I just got not too long ago.
       My mother bought it for me after she got
       back from Japan. Every day I ride it to
       and from school. I think it rides really
       well. I also rather like the color.

Lü Ang: This is the bottle we bring every day
       to school. It holds the water we drink.
       Every day we fill it up in the morning
       and then bring it to school. We drink it
       between classes or during our afternoon
       break. Then we don't have to buy
       any here.

Todd Pavel: What are you eating?

Xu Zhengyu: Uh? I'm eating ... what do you
          call these? Ah, yeah, lychee ices.

Woman: Are lychee ices a kind of ice cream?

Xu Zhengyu: Ice pops.

Todd Pavel: Does it taste good?

Xu Zhengyu: The flavor's not bad.

Todd Pavel: Where did you buy them?

Xu Zheng: At the school snack bar.

Unit A-2

Unit A-2: Making Friends (cont.)

Lesson 7: *Advice on Making Friends*

Dr. Hǎo Píng, Vice President of Peking University (also known as Beijing University, or Běidà for short), offers advice on how to go about making friends in China.

Previewing Activity

1. List (in English) three suggestions you think he might make about how to make friends.

Suggestions (English)

a. _____

b. _____

c. _____

Write the Chinese equivalents (in *pinyin* and/or characters) of these suggestions, then check your responses with your classmates.

a. _____

b. _____

c. _____

First Viewing: Global Information

2. Check off any of the suggestions you listed above that Dr. Hao actually did mention.

3. Which of the following statements do you think best summarizes the gist of what Dr. Hao is saying?

_____ The friends you make will determine the quality of your stay in China.

_____ Be outgoing; feel free to speak to people you do not know.

_____ Choose friends of the same background as you.

_____ Focus on meeting Chinese young people; don't stick to Americans.

Second Viewing: Specific Information

4. Number the following statements in the order in which Dr. Hao makes them.

_____ "Try not to make friends with people whose backgrounds you don't know."

_____ "It's important to make friends."

_____ "In Chinese we say, you 'speak the same language.'"

_____ "Many Chinese people will be friendly to you, and will want to be your friends."

_____ "Their backgrounds are the same as yours—you're all students, all in school."

_____ "I recommend that you make friends with your classmates here at Beida."

Third Viewing: Linguistic Information

5. Fill in the blanks in the *pinyin* glossary for the English terms below.

make friends	_____ péngyou
be friendly to you	duì nǐ hěn _____hǎo
extremely important	fēicháng _____
I recommend	wǒ _____yì
in this circle	zhèige _____ lǐ
this circle on campus	zhèige _____yuán quān lǐ
their backgrounds	tāmen de _____jǐng
in Chinese we say	Zhōngguó huà _____
to have a common language	yǒu gòngtóng _____
age is about the same	nián_____ yě chūbuduō yīyàng _____
to be lots of help	yǒu hěn duō de bāng_____
do your best to not ...	jìn_____ bù yào
young people in society	shèhuì shàng de nián_____ rén
don't know their backgrounds	duì tāmen de _____ bù liǎojiě
don't know their occupations	duì tāmen de zhíyè bù _____
get along well	xiāng_____ de hǎo

Unit A-2

6. Match the traditional and simplified character phrases to their English equivalents.

___ ___*make friends*	a.這個圈裡	1. 他们的背景
___ ___*be friendly to you*	b.有很多的幫助	2. 年龄也差不多一样大
___ ___*extremely important*	c.對你們很友好	3. 有很多的帮助
___ ___*I recommend*	d.相處得好	4. 中国话叫
___ ___*in this circle*	e.對他們的背景不了解	5. 相处得好
___ ___*this circle on campus*	f.我建議	6. 社会上的年轻人
___ ___*their backgrounds*	g.有共同語言	7. 交朋友
___ ___*in Chinese we say*	h.盡量不要	8. 非常重要
___ ___*to have a common language*	i.年齡也差不多一樣大	9. 对他们的职业不了解
___ ___*age is about the same*	j.交朋友	10. 我建议
___ ___*to be lots of help*	k.他們的背景	11. 这个圈里
___ ___*do your best to not ...*	l.非常重要	12. 有共同语言
___ ___*young people in society*	m.社會上的年輕人	13. 尽量不要
___ ___*don't know their backgrounds*	n.對他們的職業不了解	14. 对他们的背景不了解
___ ___*don't know their occupations*	o.中國話叫	15. 对你们很友好
___ ___*get along well*	p.這個校園圈	16. 这个校园圈

Lesson 7

Post-Viewing Activities

Speaking

7. Pretend you need to report the gist of what Dr. Hao says to some Chinese friends. Prepare (and dictate to a classmate to record in *pinyin* and/or characters) a three- to five-sentence summary of his remarks. Take some notes below.

8. Take a stand agreeing or disagreeing with what Dr. Hao suggests, and give a reason. Select one of the six choices given below (feel free to modify it, or make up your own in the space provided), and communicate it to your classmates.

"Wǒ tóngyì.
我同意。

_____ Yīyàng de bèijǐng hěn zhòngyào."
一樣的背景很重要。／一样的背景很重要。

_____ Gòngtóng yǔyán hěn zhòngyào."
共同語言很重要。／共同语言很重要。

_____ Gēn tóngxué jiāo péngyou zuì fāngbian."
跟同學交朋友最方便。／跟同学交朋友最方便。

"Wǒ bù tóngyì.
我不同意。

_____ Gēn yīyàng de bèijǐng de rén jiāo péngyou hěn wúliáo."
跟一樣的背景的人交朋友很無聊。／
跟一样的背景的人交朋友很无聊。

_____ Lǎo zài dàxué quān lǐ zǒu hěn wúliáo."
老在大學圈裏走很無聊。／老在大学圈里走很无聊。

_____ Wǒ yuànyi dào shèhuì shàng qù zhǎo xīn de péngyou."
我願意到社會上去找新的朋友。／我愿意到社会上去找新的朋友。

Unit A-2

7.

郝平老師說交朋友很重要。有共同語言也
很重要。他建議在大學圈裏交朋友。

他說有很多同學跟我們一樣,想交朋友。他說
交朋友很重要,可是他建議最好不要和背景不
了解的人交朋友。

8.

我不同意,因爲我覺得老在大學圈裏走很無
聊。我喜歡到社會上找新朋友。我想多了解
和我不同的人的看法。

我同意,因爲我覺得跟同學交朋友最方便。共
同語言也很重要。我跟外面的人沒有話說。

Lesson 7

Reading / Writing

9. Skim through the following letter from a Chinese penfriend, and highlight what you can understand of it.

我的朋友：

　　最近忙嗎？功課多不多？

　　我前兩天在課上新結識了兩個朋友。我們都是中文系的學生，很談得來。

　　說到交朋友，我認為朋友就是能一起分享快樂與煩惱的人。比如，當我遇到了不順心的事，我就去找朋友聊天，把心裏的不愉快講出來，然後聽聽朋友的意見。如果一個人沒有朋友，那麼他有甚麼煩惱也只能憋在心裏。這樣活著多累呀！

　　我的朋友一般都是我的同學。我們有很多共同感興趣的話題。我很少在校外交朋友。學校外面的人看起來很複雜，他們感興趣的東西也和我不一樣。對他們來說，房子、孩子和職稱是最重要的事。

　　你願意跟我講講你的朋友嗎？你交朋友的標準是甚麼呢？你覺得在交朋友這個問題上中美兩種文化有甚麼不同嗎？我聽一個去過美國的朋友說，在美國，在一起玩的就是朋友，但知心朋友卻很難有，因為沒有人有時間、有興趣聽你訴說自己的煩惱，是嗎？

　　　　　　　　　　　　你在中國的朋友　　鄭秋

Unit A-2

128

10. This letter can be divided into five sections, excluding the opening salutation and closing signature. Write a sentence in English to summarize each section.

Sec. 1 (1 line):_____

Sec. 2 (2 lines):_____

Sec. 3 (5 lines):_____

Sec. 4 (4 lines):_____

Sec. 5 (5 lines):_____

Check your responses with the ones provided below.

5. What does friendship mean to you?
4. This is why my friends are all my schoolmates.
3. This is my definition of a friend.
2. I made two new friends.
1. Have you been busy?

11. Re-read the letter, and respond to the following.

Sec. 1. Fill in the blank. Zhèng Qiū asks if you have a lot of _____.

Sec. 2. Where did she make two new friends? Circle one:

   at a dinner / in class / at a friend's house / on the sports field

Sec. 3. Fill in the blanks in the discussion: "A friend is someone with whom you can share _____ and _____."

What does she do when things do not go her way? Select all that apply:
   _____ go find a friend to talk with
   _____ sleep off the frustration
   _____ write in a journal
   _____ ask for advice

Under what circumstances does she say one would have to keep one's feelings hidden or repressed? Select one: When one
   _____ is ashamed.
   _____ is depressed.
   _____ has no one to talk with.

Life under these circumstances, Zhèng Qiū writes, would be very (select one):
   _____ tiresome;   _____ difficult;   _____ confusing.

Lesson 7

Sec. 4. Zhèng Qiū's friends are mostly her (fill in the blank) _____, because they (select one)

_____ spend time together at school.

_____ have common interests in after-school activities.

_____ like to talk about the same things.

She does not have many friends outside of school, because "outsiders" (check all that apply)

_____ seem very complex.

_____ spend too much money.

_____ don't have the same interests as she does.

_____ care too much about home, children, and job titles.

_____ care too much about clothes and appearances.

Sec. 5. Zhèng Qiū asks you about friends and friendship. To what do her questions pertain? Check all that apply.

_____ How to meet people.

_____ What you look for in friends.

_____ The benefits of friendship.

_____ Cultural differences between U.S. and Chinese notions of friendship.

_____ The U.S. notion of friendship.

_____ Same-sex vs. opposite-sex friendships.

12. Fill in the blanks by guessing the missing information (characters, *pinyin*, or English) in the vocabulary list below, which is keyed to Zhèng Qiū's letter.

_____ / 结识 jiéshí *get to know (someone)*

中文系 _____ *Chinese department*

談得來 / 谈得来 tándelái _____

交朋友 jiāo péngyou _____

認為 / 认为 _____ *think, believe*

_____ fēnxiǎng *share*

快樂 / 快乐 _____ *joy, happiness*

與 / 与 yǔ _____

_____ / 烦恼 fánnǎo *worry, frustration*

比如 bǐrú _____

當 / 当 _____ *when, while*

_____ yùdao *run into, encounter*

_____ / 不顺心 bù shùnxīn *unsatisfactory, displeasing*

聊天 liáotiānr _____

不愉快 _____ *unhappy, unhappiness*

講出來 / 讲出来 _____ *express, tell*

然後 / 然后 ránhòu _____

意見 / 意见 _____ *opinion*

如果 rúguǒ _____

有甚麼X也只能Y / 有什么X也只能 Y yǒu shénme X yě _____ Y *no matter how much X one has, one can still only Y*

Unit A-2

_____ / 憋在心里
biē zài xīnli *repress feelings*

活著多累 _____
what a chore to be alive

一般 _____
generally, normally

共同 gòngtóng _____

感興趣 / 感兴趣 _____
find interesting

話題 / 话题 _____
topic of conversation

_____ / 复杂 fùzá
complex, complicated

_____ / 职称 zhíchēng
professional or technical job title

重要 zhòngyào _____

願意 / 愿意 _____
be willing

_____ / 标准 biāozhǔn
standard, standards

兩種文化 / 两种文化
_____ *two cultures*

不同 _____
different, difference

_____ dàn *but, however*

知心朋友 _____
intimate or bosom friend

卻 / 却 què _____

訴說 / 诉说 _____
relate, tell

自己 zìjǐ _____

13. Following is the completed vocabulary list. Re-read the letter, and see if you can understand more, now.

結識 / 结识 jiéshí *get to know (someone)*

中文系 Zhōngwén xì *Chinese department*

談得來 / 谈得来 tándelái *get along well*

交朋友 jiāo péngyou *make friends, be friends*

認爲 / 认为 rènwéi *think, believe*

分享 fēnxiǎng *share*

快樂 / 快乐 kuàilè *joy, happiness*

與 / 与 yǔ *and*

煩惱 / 烦恼 fánnǎo *worry, frustration*

比如 bǐrú *for example*

當 / 当 dāng *when, while*

遇到 yùdao *run into, encounter*

不順心 / 不顺心 bù shùnxīn *unsatisfactory, displeasing*

聊天 liáotiānr *chat, converse*

不愉快 bù yúkuài *unhappy, unhappiness*

講出來 / 讲出来 jiǎngchulai *express, tell*

然後 / 然后 ránhòu *then, thereafter*

意見 / 意见 yìjiàn *opinion*

如果 rúguǒ *if*

有甚麼 X 也只能 Y /
　　有什么 X 也只能 Y
yǒu shénme X yě zhǐ néng Y
no matter how much X one has, one can still only Y

憋在心裏 / 憋在心里 biē zài xīnli
repress feelings

活著多累 huózhe duō lèi
what a chore to be alive

一般 yībān *generally, normally*

Lesson 7

共同　gòngtóng *common, shared*

感興趣 / 感兴趣　gǎn xìngqu
　　find interesting

話題 / 话题　huàtí *topic of conversation*

複雜 / 复杂　fùzá *complex, complicated*

職稱 / 职称　zhíchēng *professional or technical job title*

重要　zhòngyào *important*

願意 / 愿意　yuànyì *be willing*

標準 / 标准　biāozhǔn *standard, standards*

兩種文化 / 两种文化　liǎng zhǒng wénhuà *two cultures*

不同　bù tóng *different, difference*

但　dàn *but, however*

知心朋友　zhīxīn péngyou *intimate or bosom friend*

卻 / 却　què *but, on the other hand*

訴說 / 诉说　sùshuō *relate, tell*

自己　zìjǐ *oneself*

14. Write a response to Zhèng Qiū's letter.

Unit A-2

*Sample (edited) statements by American students
(on the meaning of friendship)*

一起吃飯、看電視、談心的人就是朋友。

常常在一起玩兒的人就是朋友。

跟你说心里话，听你讲你心里的事的人就是朋友。

我认为中美两种文化中，朋友跟朋友之间的关系不太一样。美国人，特别是男人，平常不跟朋友谈心里的不愉快。自己的烦恼是自己的事情。跟朋友在一起的时候应当高兴高兴。

我覺得在中美文化中，交朋友的標準沒有甚麼不同。一般都是找談得來和相處得好的人做朋友。

我喜欢骑摩托车。愿意跟我一起骑摩托车的人就是我的朋友。

【北京大學副校長郝平博士談話】

同學們到北京來讀書，或者到北大來讀書。

那麼周圍的好多中國人對你們都很友好，都想和你們交朋友。

那麼交朋友非常重要，交甚麼樣的朋友也很重要。

怎麼去交朋友？

我建議大家呢，一定，首先，要交朋友是交，呃，北大的同學，這個圈 ... 這個校園圈裏的北大學生。

因爲他們都住在校園。呃，他們的背景和你們的背景都一樣，都是學生，都在讀書。

中國話叫有共同語言。

年齡也差不多一樣大。

【北京大学副校长郝平博士谈话】

同学们到北京来读书，或者到北大来读书。

那么周围的好多中国人对你们都很友好，都想和你们交朋友。

那么交朋友非常重要，交什么样的朋友也很重要。

怎么去交朋友？

我建议大家呢，一定，首先，要交朋友是交，呃，北大的同学，这个圈 ... 这个校园圈里的北大学生。

因为他们都住在校园。呃，他们的背景和你们的背景都一样，都是学生，都在读书。

中国话叫有共同语言。

年龄也差不多一样大。

Unit A-2

[Běijīng Dàxué fùxiàozhǎng Háo Píng bóshì tánhuà]

(Dr. Hao Ping, Vice President of Peking University, offers advice.)

Tóngxuémen dào Běijīng lái dúshū, huòzhě dào Běidà lái dúshū.

You might come to Beijing, or even to Peking University, to study.

Nàme zhōuwéi de hǎoduō Zhōngguórén duì nǐmen dōu hěn yǒuhǎo, dōu xiǎng hé nǐmen jiāo péngyou.

In that case many Chinese people around you will be very friendly to you, and will want to be your friends.

Nàme jiāo péngyou fēicháng zhòngyào, jiāo shénmeyàng de péngyou yě hěn zhòngyào.

And making friends is very important, (and) what kind of friends you make is important as well.

Zěnme qù jiāo péngyou?

How should you go about making friends?

Wǒ jiànyì dàjiā ne, yīdìng, shǒuxiān, yào jiāo péngyou shì jiāo, e, Běidà detóngxué, zhège quān ... zhège xiàoyuán quān lǐ de Běidà xuéshēng.

I suggest that you all, first, in making friends, look to your classmates at Beida, in this circle ... this circle on campus made up of Beida students.

Yīnwèi tāmen dōu zhù zai xiàoyuán. E, tāmen de bèijǐng hé nǐmen de bèijǐng dōu yīyàng, dōu shì xuéshēng, dōu zài dúshū.

Because they all live on campus. Uhm, their backgrounds are the same as yours, you're all students, all obtaining an education.

Zhōngguóhuà jiào, yǒu gòngtóng yǔyán.

In Chinese, we would say, you have a common language.

Niánlíng yě chàbuduō yīyàng dà.

And your ages are about the same.

Lesson 7

他們都會對你們很友好，也會對你們學習漢語有很多的幫助。

盡量不要和社會上的一些、你對他們的背景不了解、對他們的職業不了解的、這樣的年輕人交朋友。

因爲對他們不了解，你就很難和他們能相處得好。

所以我建議呢，一定要和大學生交朋友。

他们都会对你们很友好，也会对你们学习汉语有很多的帮助。

尽量不要和社会上的一些、你对他们的背景不了解、对他们的职业不了解的、这样的年轻人交朋友。

因为对他们不了解，你就很难和他们能相处得好。

所以我建议呢，一定要和大学生交朋友。

Tāmen dōu huì duì nǐmen hěn yǒuhǎo, yě huì duì nǐmen xuéxí Hànyǔ yǒu hěn duō de bāngzhù.

Jìnliàng bù yào hé shèhuì shàng de yīxiē, nǐ duì tàmen de bèijǐng bù liǎojiě, duì tāmen de zhíyè bù liǎojiě de, zhèyàng de niánqīng rén jiāo péngyou.

Yīnwèi duì tāmen bù liǎojiě, nǐ jiù hěn nán hé tāmen néng xiāngchǔ de hǎo. Suǒyǐ wǒ jiànyì ne, yīdìng yào hé dàxuéshēng jiāo péngyou.

They will be very friendly to you, and very useful to you for learning Chinese.

As much as possible, don't make friends with people out in society, young people whose backgrounds you don't know, whose occupations you are unclear about.

Since you won't know who they are, really, it'll be difficult to get along well with them. Therefore, I suggest, you must choose college students for your friends.

Unit A-2

Unit B: Making Plans to Get Together

Lesson 8:

Making an Appointment Face-to-Face

James Yao and Ān Shūmǐn make plans to see a movie together.

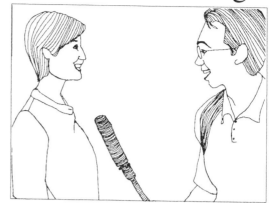

Previewing Activity

1. Which of the following topics given in English do you think James and Shūmǐn will discuss in the course of making their plans? Underline or circle six that you consider most likely.

1. Which day to go	___ 到哪兒去看 / 到哪儿去看
2. Whether to see a Chinese or an English movie	___ 電影開始前做甚麼 / 电影开始前做什么
	___ 電影的情節（是甚麼）/ 电影的情节（是什么）
3. What genre of movie to see	
4. Which specific movie to see	___ 看哪部電影 / 看哪部电影
5. The plot of the film	___ 穿甚麼 / 穿什么
6. The actors of the film	___ 得帶多少錢 / 得带多少钱
7. Where to see it	___ 幾點去看 / 几点去看
8. What time to see it	___ 大概會幾點到家 / 大概会几点到家
9. Who else to go with	___ 到電影院怎麼走 / 到电影院怎么走
10. What to wear	___ 想看哪類的電影 / 想看哪类的电影
11. How to get there	___ 去看中文還是英文的電影 / 去看中文还是英文的电影
12. What to do before the movie	___ 還有誰去 / 还有谁去
13. What to do after the movie	___ 電影完了以後做甚麼 / 电影完了以后做什么
14. How much money to bring	___ 哪天去
15. When they'll get home	___ 電影的演員（是誰）/ 电影的演员（是谁）

2. For each of the topics you have selected, what <u>question</u> would elicit the necessary information? Match the Chinese on the right with the English on the left.

First Viewing: Global Information

3. Which of the topics 1–15 were actually discussed? List below, then circle the ones you'd predicted.

Topics # _____, _____, _____, _____, _____, _____.

4. For each of the topics you've identified, circle "James" or "Shūmǐn" depending on who first brought it up.

Topic #_____: James   Shūmǐn   Hard to say

Topic #_____: James   Shūmǐn   Hard to say

Topic #_____: James   Shūmǐn   Hard to say

Topic #_____: James   Shūmǐn   Hard to say

Topic #_____: James   Shūmǐn   Hard to say

Topic #_____: James   Shūmǐn   Hard to say

Second Viewing: Specific Information

5. When they first meet, Shūmǐn compliments James on his (circle one):

appearance / punctuality / progress in Chinese / fluency in English

6. Fill in the information requested below.

Day they will go to the movies: _____

Type of movie James proposes (circle one):

action thriller / comedy / drama / love story / horror film

Type of movie Shūmǐn proposes (circle two):

action thriller / comedy / drama / love story / horror film

Name of the movie they will see: _Lóng Chéng Shíyuè (Dragon Town Story)_

Language of the movie (circle one): Chinese / English / other

Name of the theatre: _Hǎidiàn Jùyuàn_

Time the movie begins: _____

Time Shūmǐn and James will meet: _____

Place Shūmǐn and James will meet: _____

Unit B

Third Viewing: Linguistic Information

7. Shūmǐn pays the following compliment to James (fill in the blank):

"Wǒ fāxiàn nǐ de Yīngyǔ ... nǐ de Hànyǔ shuōde _____ liúlì le."

我發現你的英語 ... 你的漢語說得越來越流利了。／
我发现你的英语 ... 你的汉语说得越来越流利了。

(*"I find your English ... your Chinese is becoming more and more fluent."*)

8. Very properly, James denies the compliment by saying:

"_____, _____, _____." ("No, no, no.")

9. What are the questions asked to elicit the following information?

a. Whether James is free this afternoon.

_____

b. Whether Shūmǐn would like to see a movie.

_____

c. What kind of move James enjoys.

_____

d. Whether the movie is contemporary or historical.

_____

e. Whether James and Shūmǐn should go see the movie together:

_____

f. What time the movie begins.

_____

g. Whether they should meet for coffee first.

_____

h. Where they should meet.

_____

Lesson 8

10. Match the traditional and simplified character versions of the questions below, and number the traditional character questions according to the English ones in Exercise 9.

_____ 電影甚麼時候開始播映？

是现代的电影呢，
还是古代的？

_____ 是現代的電影呢，
還是古代的？

我们在哪儿见面？

_____ 你想去看電影嗎？

你喜欢看什么样的电影呢？

_____ 我們在哪兒見面？

我们看电影之前要不要
先去喝一点咖啡？

_____ 我們一塊兒去看好不好？

电影什么时候开始播映？

_____ 你喜歡看甚麼樣的電影呢？

你今天下午有什么事情吗？

_____ 你今天下午有甚麼事情嗎？

你想去看电影吗？

_____ 我們看電影之前要不要
先去喝一點咖啡？

我们一块儿去看好不好？

11. Note: James asks, "Wŏmen wŭ diăn bàn yàobuyao jiànmiàn?" This is an odd way of posing the question, since generally the point of the inquiry follows "yàobuyao" immediately. Since he has "jiànmiàn" after "yàobuyao," it sounds as if he wants to know, "What shall we do at five-thirty today? Meet? Or do something else?" when actually he intends to ask, "When shall we meet? At five-thirty, or some other time?" Re-order James' question below, so that it asks, "Shall we meet at five-thirty?"

| 我們 / 我们 | 五點半 / 五点半 | 要不要 | 見面 / 见面？ |

1 ___ ___ ___

12. How else might you ask the same question? Write _pinyin_ and/or characters.

_____

Unit B

13. Match the English, *pinyin,* and characters for the film terms below:

àiqíng piān	documentary	故事片
shēnghuó piān	action thriller	生活片
xǐjù piān	feature film	動作片 / 动作片
gùshì piān	love story	好萊塢大片 / 好莱坞大片
jìlù piān	horror film	記錄片 / 记录片
kǒngbù piān	comedy	愛情片 / 爱情片
dòngzuò piān	life drama	恐怖片
Hǎoláiwū dàpiān	Hollywood blockbuster	喜劇片 / 喜剧片

14. Match the English and Chinese expressions below. Note: Some of the Chinese expressions match to more than one English expression.

_____ Yǒu shénme shì ma?
有甚麼事嗎 / 有什么事吗？

_____ Hǎo zhǔyì!
好主意！

_____ Shénme yàng de diànyǐng?
甚麼樣的電影 / 什么样的电影？

_____ Yǒu diǎnr tài wéinán wǒ le.
有點兒太爲難我了 / 有点儿太为难我了。

_____ Nà bù cuò a.
那不錯啊 / 那不错啊。

_____ Zuì jìn zài fàngyìng.
最近在放映。

_____ Kěnéng shì.
可能是。

_____ Jiù zhèyàng dìng le.
就這樣定了 / 就这样定了。

a. Is something happening?

b. That's a bit hard to take.

c. Perhaps.

d. That's settled, then.

e. It's been showing recently.

f. Good idea!

g. What kind of movie?

e. That'd be a little too hard on me.

f. That's not bad!

g. Possibly.

h. Do you need something?

Lesson 8

Post-Viewing Activities

Speaking

15. Make a list of three movies showing around town that you would like to see. Note the times and places they are playing, and days when you are available to go see them.

Speak to your classmates one at a time; find someone to go to each of the movies with. For each appointment, note <u>date</u>, <u>time</u>, <u>place</u>, where you are <u>meeting</u>, and whether or not you want to <u>do something</u> before or after the movie.

16. After you have made all your appointments, prepare a brief oral report to the class, noting the details of each of your appointments.

(Three movies you would like to see; times & places; days when you are available)

-
-
-

(Person with whom you will see each movie; date/ time/ place; will you do something before or after the movie?)

-
-
-

Unit B

Reading / Writing

17. Following are the PRC titles of six of the American movies mentioned previously, in Lesson 4. Write the English titles of these movies.

a. 拯救大兵萊恩 / 拯救大兵萊恩 _____

b. 陽光小美女 / 阳光小美女 _____

c. 英國病人 / 英国病人 _____

d. 阿甘正傳 / 阿甘正传 _____

e. 西雅圖不眠夜 / 西雅图不眠夜 _____

f. 女王 _____

18. Brief descriptions of each of these movies are provided below. Match them with their titles by writing the letters (a–f) in the boxes provided. Scan the descriptions to extract whatever meaning you can; don't try to understand all the terms there!

☐ 杰克是一個窮畫家。在從英國開往美國的新船上，他認識了英國貴族少女羅絲。兩人一見鐘情。可是在穿過大西洋時，那條船撞上了冰山 / 杰克是一个穷画家。在从英国开往美国的新船上，他认识了英国贵族少女罗丝。二人一见钟情。可是在穿过大西洋时，那条船撞上了冰山。

☐ 二戰中，美國軍官約翰‧米勒帶領一隻八人的小隊到敵人控制區尋找士兵詹姆斯‧萊恩。影片以逼真的畫面再現了戰爭的殘酷與無情 / 二战中，美国军官约翰‧米勒带领一只八人的小队到敌人控制区寻找列兵詹姆斯‧莱恩。影片以逼真的画面再现了战争的残酷与无情。

Lesson 8   143

☐ 在二戰時期，一個神秘的陌生人被從一架燃燒著的飛機中救出來。他的臉被燒得面目全非，記憶也由於這場大火而喪失。美國盟軍以爲他是英國人／在二战时期，一个神秘的陌生人被从一架燃烧著的飞机中救出来。他的脸被烧得面目全非，记忆也由于这场大火而丧失。美国盟军以为他是英国人。

☐ 一個年輕的女人從收音機裡聽到一個男人講述他對死去的妻子的思念，她就愛上了這個男人。最後，在一個小孩兒的安排下，他們兩個人終於在紐約帝國大廈的樓頂相遇了／一个年轻的女人从收音机里听到一个男人讲述他对死去的妻子的思念，她就爱上了这个男人。最后，在一个小孩儿的安排下，他们两个人终於在纽约帝国大厦的楼顶相遇了。

☐ 一個商人發現了重新孵恐龍的方法。於是，他在一個海島上建了一個恐龍世界。就在這個公園即將對外開放時，公園的電腦系統出現了問題，吃人的恐龍跑了出來／一个商人发现了重新孵恐龙的方法。於是，他在一个海岛上建了一个恐龙世界。就在这个公园即将对外开放时，公园的电脑系统出现了问题，吃人的恐龙跑了出来。

☐ 因爲這部電影的男主角腦子反應比較慢，大家都覺得他很笨。但他無論做甚麼都很執著，不輕易放棄。他參加過越戰，也訪問過中國，可是他一輩子忘不了他小時候的好友珍妮／因为这部电影的男主角脑子反应比较慢，大家都觉得他很笨。但他无论做什么都很执著，不轻易放弃。他参加过越战，也访问过中国，可是他一辈子忘不了他小时候的好友珍妮。

Unit B 144

19. Read the following note from your roommate. Highlight what you can understand.

我今天刚考完试，想轻松一下。我们今晚去看电影好不好？

这一阵儿似乎好看的电影很多。有国产片，也有进口片；有关于古代的，也有讲现代的。不知你喜欢看什么类型的电影：动作片、恐怖片、喜剧片还是爱情片？我比较喜欢美国片，节奏很快，不象有的国产片总令我打瞌睡。

我的一个朋友前不久去看了一部美国电影，她十分喜欢并且推荐我也去看。她说这是一部很感人的爱情片，看到结尾时，她甚至哭了。既然她说得这么好，我们也就去看看，怎么样？正好离学校最近的那个电影院正在放映这部片子。晚上八点开始。当然，如果你对爱情片不感兴趣，我们也可以看别的。

请留个便条告诉我你的决定。

你的同屋

20. The note from your roommate can be divided into four sections. Write a sentence in English to summarize each section.

Sec. 1 (2 lines):_____

Sec. 2 (4 lines):_____

Sec. 3 (6 lines):_____

Sec. 4 (1 line):_____

Lesson 8

21. Check your responses with the ones provided below.

22. Why does your roommate want to see a movie tonight? Choose one selection:

_____ To accompany an out-of-town visitor.

_____ To relax after an exam.

_____ To check out the new theater.

23. Your roommate suggests that there are four major types of movies. Fill in the blanks:

domestic
_____

_____ <-------------|-------------> _____*contemporary*_____

_____

24. He or she then lists four genres of movies. Which are these? Select from the list below.

_____ comedy   _____ horror   _____ science fiction / fantasy

_____ action thriller   _____ drama   _____ romance

25. Your roommate prefers American movies because of their (select one):

_____ special effects   _____ storyline   _____ pacing   _____ stars

26. Your roommate's friend recommended an American (select one):

_____ action thriller   _____ comedy   _____ love story

27. He or she said the ending was particularly (select one) _____ shocking _____ moving.

28. Your roommate suggests a time and place to see this movie. What are they?

Place: _____ Time: _____

29. Fill in the blanks by guessing the missing information (simplified characters, *pinyin*, or English) in the vocabulary list below.

Unit B

考完試 / 考完试 _____ finish an examination

輕鬆 / _____ qīngsōng relax

這一陣兒 / _____ zhèi yī zhènr this period of time

_____ sìhū seemingly, seems as if

國產 / 国产 guóchǎn _____

片（子） _____ movie, film

進口 / 进口 _____ imported

關於 / 关于 guānyú _____

_____ gǔdài historical, about the past

現代 / 现代 _____ contemporary, about the present

類型 / 类型 lèixíng _____

動作 / _____ dòngzuò action

恐怖 kǒngbù _____

喜劇 / 喜剧 xǐjù _____

愛情 / 爱情 àiqíng _____

比較 / 比较 _____ compare, comparatively

節奏 / 节奏 jiézòu _____

總 / 总 _____ always

_____ lìng make, cause

_____ dǎ kēshuì nod off, doze

十分 _____ 100 percent, completely

並且 / _____ bìngqiě moreover

推荐 tuījiàn _____

感人 _____ be touching, moving

結尾 / _____ jiéwěi end, ending, conclusion

時 / _____ shí time (simplification of shíhòu)

甚至 _____ even to the point of, so much so that

_____ kū cry, tear up

_____ jìrán as long as, now that, since

_____ zhènghǎo fortunately, opportunely

正在 _____ be in the process of

Lesson 8

放映　fàngyìng _____

_____　bù *(measure word for films)*

當然 / 当然 _____　*of course, naturally*

如果　rúguǒ _____

別的 _____　*other, another*

_____　liú *to leave behind*

便條 / 便条 _____　*a note*

決定 / 决定　juédìng _____

30. Following is the completed vocabulary list. Re-read the note, and see if you can understand more, now.

考完試 / 考完试　kǎowánshì *finish an examination*

輕鬆 / 轻松　qīngsōng *relax*

這一陣兒 / 这一阵儿　zhèi yī zhènr *this period of time*

似乎　sìhū *seemingly, seems as if*

國產 / 国产　guóchǎn *domestically produced*

片（子）　piān(zi) *movie, film*

進口 / 进口　jìnkǒu *imported*

關於 / 关于　guānyú *about, concerning*

古代　gǔdài *historical, about the past*

現代 / 现代　xiàndài *contemporary, about the present*

類型 / 类型　lèixíng *type, category*

動作 / 动作　dòngzuò *action*

恐怖　kǒngbù *horror, terror*

喜劇 / 喜剧　xìjù *comedy*

愛情 / 爱情　àiqíng *love, romance*

比較 / 比较　bǐjiào *compare, comparatively*

節奏 / 节奏　jiézòu *rhythm, pace*

總 / 总　zǒng *always*

令　lìng *make, cause*

打瞌睡　dǎ kēshui *nod off, doze*

十分　shífēn *100 percent, completely*

Unit B

並且 / 并且　bìngqiě *moreover*

推荐　tuījiàn *recommend*

感人　gǎnrén *be touching, moving*

結尾 / 结尾　jiéwěi *end, ending, conclusion*

時 / 时　shí *time (simplification of shíhòu)*

甚至　shènzhì *even to the point of, so much so that*

哭　kū *cry, tear up*

既然　jìrán *as long as, now that, since*

正好　zhènghǎo *fortunately, opportunely*

正在　zhèngzài *be in the process of*

放映　fàngyìng *to show, to screen*

部　bù *(measure word for films)*

當然 / 当然　dāngrán *of course, naturally*

如果　rúguǒ *if*

別的　biéde *other, another*

留　liú *to leave behind*

便條 / 便条　biàntiáo *a note*

決定 / 决定　juédìng *decide*

31. Write a response to your roommate.

Sample responses (edited)

好主意！到離學校最近的電影院去看吧。我們可以走路去。七點半從宿舍出發吧。

对不起。我对爱情片不太感兴趣。我们去看动作片好不好？我们可以七点半在 Ward 16 电影院门口见面。请你打我手机 384-9595 确认一下。

我們去看你說的那部電影吧。我也對愛情片有興趣。我們七點三十分在屋裏見面，好嗎?

你說的電影我已經看過了。我覺得不怎麼樣，不太好看。要是你還是想看的話，你可以找小李。他也想看。

Unit B

【安淑敏與姚守正對話】

淑敏：守正，你好！

守正：哎！淑敏，你好！

淑敏：哎，我發現你的英語
　　　…你的漢語說得越來越流利
　　　了。

守正：哦，沒有，沒有，沒有。
【笑】

淑敏：今天下午有甚麼事情嗎？

守正：呃，沒事。你想…呃…去
　　　看電影嗎？

淑敏：哎呀，好主意呀！
【笑】

守正：呃。

淑敏：你喜歡看甚麼樣的電影呢
　　　？

守正：我喜歡看恐怖片。你呢？

淑敏：啊？恐怖片？我…有點太
　　　爲難我了。

守正：那你想看甚麼東西？

淑敏：呃，我想呢，生活片不錯
　　　啊。

守正：生活片？哦…

淑敏：啊，對，最近我們…好像
　　　海淀劇院在放映那個《龍城十
　　　月》。

【安淑敏与姚守正对话】

淑敏：守正，你好！

守正：哎！淑敏，你好！

淑敏：哎，我发现你的英语
　　　…你的汉语说得越来越流利
　　　了。

守正：哦，没有，没有，没有。
【笑】

淑敏：今天下午有什么事情吗？

守正：呃，没事。你想…呃…去
　　　看电影吗？

淑敏：哎呀，好主意呀！
【笑】

守正：呃。

淑敏：你喜欢看什么样的电影呢
　　　？

守正：我喜欢看恐怖片。你呢？

淑敏：啊？恐怖片？我…有点太
　　　为难我了。

守正：那你想看什么东西？

淑敏：呃，我想呢，生活片不错
　　　啊。

守正：生活片？哦…

淑敏：啊，对，最近我们…好像
　　　海淀剧院在放映那个《龙城十
　　　月》。

Lesson 8

[Ān Shūmǐn yǔ Yáo Shǒuzhèng duìhuà]

Shūmǐn: Shǒuzhèng, nǐ hǎo!

Shǒuzhèng: Ai! Shūmǐn, nǐ hǎo!

Shūmǐn: Ai, wǒ fāxiàn nǐ de
Yīngyǔ ... nǐde Hànyǔ shuōde
yuèláiyuè liúlì le.

Shǒuzhèng: O, méiyǒu, méiyǒu, méiyǒu.

(Xiào)

Shūmǐn: Jīntiān xiàwǔ yǒu shénme
shìqing ma?

Shǒuzhèng: E, méishì. Nǐ xiǎng ...
e... qù kàn diànyǐng ma?

Shūmǐn: Aiya, hǎo zhǔyì ya!

(Xiào)

Shǒuzhèng: E.

Shūmǐn: Nǐ xǐhuan kàn shénmeyàng
de diànyǐng ne?

Shǒuzhèng: Wǒ xǐhuan kàn kǒngbù
piān. Nǐ ne?

Shūmǐn: A? Kǒngbù piān? Wǒ ...
yǒu diǎn(r) tài wéinán wǒ le.

Shǒuzhèng: Nà nǐ xiǎng kàn shénme
dōngxi?

Shūmǐn: E, wǒ xiǎng ne, shēnghuó
piān bùcuò a.

Shǒuzhèng: Shēnghuó piān? O...

Shūmǐn: A, duì, zuìjìn wǒmen ...
hǎoxiàng Hǎidiàn Jùyuàn zài fàng nàge
Lóngchéng Shíyuè.

(An Shumin speaks with James Yao.)

Shumin: Shouzheng, hello!

James: Hey! Shumin, hello!

Shumin: Ah, I see your English ... your
Chinese is becoming more and more
fluent.

James: Oh, no, no, not really.

[Laughter]

Shumin: Are you doing anything this
afternoon?

James: Nothing special. Do you.... er...
want to go see a movie?

Shumin: Yeah, that's a good idea!

[Laughter]

James: Uh-huh.

Shumin: What kind of movies do you like
to see?

James: I like watching horror films.
What about you?

Shumin: Huh? Horror films? I, er ...
Those are a little too hard on me.

James: Then, what kind of movie do you
want to see?

Shumin: Um, I think real life dramas are
pretty good.

James: Real life dramas?

Shumin: Yeah, recently we ... I think that
the Haidian Theater is showing
Dragon Town Story.

Unit B

守正：《龍城 ...

淑敏：... 十月》。它是，它是國語片。喜歡去看嗎？

守正：呃，你可以再說一說（嗎）？

淑敏：《龍城十月》。

守正：呃，是甚麼種（類的）故事 ... 一個生活片？

淑敏：呃，是一個 ... 可能是個愛情片。

守正：噢，愛情片。

淑敏：嗯。

守正：是現代的愛情片呢，還是古 ... 古代的？

淑敏：嗯，是近代的愛情片，是發生在那個抗日戰爭的時候的愛情片。有興趣嗎？

守正：有。好。

淑敏：我們一塊兒去看好不好？

守正：好，我們去看。

淑敏：我們甚麼時候（去）？
　　　呃，今天下午 ... 它是七點開始播映*。

守正：《龙城 ...

淑敏：... 十月》。它是，它是国语片。喜欢去看吗？

守正：呃，你可以再说一说（吗）？

淑敏：《龙城十月》。

守正：呃，是什么种（类的）故事 ... 一个生活片？

淑敏：呃，是一个 ... 可能是个爱情片。

守正：噢，爱情片。

淑敏：嗯。

守正：是现代的爱情片呢，还是古 ... 古代的？

淑敏：嗯，是近代的爱情片，是发生在那个抗日战争的时候的爱情片。有兴趣吗？

守正：有。好。

淑敏：我们一块儿去看好不好？

守正：好，我们去看。

淑敏：我们什么时候（去）？
　　　呃，今天下午 ... 它是七点开始播映*。

*Should be 放映 fàngyìng, "to show or project a film." 播映 bōyìng means "to broadcast on TV."

Lesson 8

Shǒuzhèng: *Lóngchéng ...*

Shūmǐn: ... *Shíyuè.* Tā shì, tā shì Guóyǔ piān. Xǐhuan qù kàn ma?

Shǒuzhèng: E, nǐ kěyǐ zài shuō yì shuō (ma)?

Shūmǐn: *Lóngchéng Shíyuè.*

Shǒuzhèng: E, shì shénme zhǒng(lèi de) gùshi ... yī ge shēnghuó piān?

Shūmǐn: E, shì yī ge ... kěnéng shì ge àiqíng piān.

Shǒuzhèng: O, àiqíng piān.

Shūmǐn: Ng.

Shǒuzhèng: Shì xiàndài de àiqíng piān ne, háishì gǔ ... gǔdài de?

Shūmǐn: Ng, shì jìndài de àiqíng piān, shì fāshēng zài nàge Kàngrì Zhànzhēng de shíhou de àiqíng piān. Yǒu xìngqù ma?

Shǒuzhèng: Yǒu. Hǎo.

Shūmǐn: Wǒmen yīkuàir qù kàn hǎo bu hǎo?

Shǒuzhèng: Hǎo, wǒmen qù kàn.

Shūmǐn: Wǒmen shénme shíhòu (qù)? E, jīntiān xiàwǔ ... tā shì qīdiǎn kāishǐ bōyìng*.

James: *Dragon Town...*

Shumin: ... *Story* (literally: *in October).* It's in Mandarin. Would you like to go?

James: Could you say that again?

Shumin: *Dragon Town Story.*

James: Er, what kind of story is... it's a real life drama?

Shumin: Er, it's a ... maybe it's a love story.

James: Ah, a love story.

Shumin: Uh-huh.

James: Is it a modern love story, or a his- ... historical story?

Shumin: It's a contemporary film that takes place during the War of Resistance against Japan (WWII). Are you interested?

James: Yeah. Okay.

Shumin: Then, shall we go together?

James: Okay, let's go.

Shumin: When shall we go? Er, this evening ... it starts at 7:00.

---

*Should be 放映 *fàngyìng,* "to show or project a film."

播映 *bōyìng* means "to broadcast on TV."

Unit B   154

守正：那我們看電影之前要不
要先去喝一點 ... 喝一點咖
啡，還是（別的）甚麼的？

淑敏：哦，那好，我們 ... 呃 ...

守正：那我們五點半要不要見
面？

淑敏：行行。海淀劇院旁邊有
個"當肯。"

守正：噢，好。

淑敏：我們可以去"當肯"，
呃，去 ... 六點半到"當
肯"，哦，五點半吧，五點
半，到"當肯"見面。然後
呢，我們吃點東西，然後就
去海淀劇院看電影。

守正：好。

淑敏：好不好？好。

守正：非常好。

淑敏：就這樣定下來了。

守正：哎，好。

淑敏：好。

守正：哎，再見。

守正：那我们看电影之前要不
要先去喝一点 ... 喝一点咖
啡，还是（别的）什么的？

淑敏：哦，那好，我们 ... 呃 ...

守正：那我们五点半要不要见
面？

淑敏：行行。海淀剧院旁边有
个"当肯。"

守正：噢，好。

淑敏：我们可以去"当肯"，
呃，去 ... 六点半到"当
肯"，哦，五点半吧，五点
半，到"当肯"见面。然后
呢，我们吃点东西，然后就
去海淀剧院看电影。

守正：好。

淑敏：好不好？好。

守正：非常好。

淑敏：就这样定下来了。

守正：哎，好。

淑敏：好。

守正：哎，再见。

Shǒuzhèng: Nà wǒmen kàn diànyǐng
          zhīqián yào bu yào xiān qù hē yīdiǎn(r)
          ... hē yīdiǎn(r) kāfēi, háishì (bié de)
          shénme de?

Shūmǐn: O, nà hǎo, wǒmen ... e ...

Shǒuzhèng: Nà wǒmen wǔdiǎn bàn yào
          bu yao jiànmiàn?

Shūmǐn: Xíngxíng. Hǎidiàn Jùyuàn
          pángbiān yǒuge Dāngkěn.

Shǒuzhèng: O, hǎo.

Shūmǐn: Wǒmen kěyǐ qù Dāngkěn,
          e, qù ... liùdiǎnbàn dào Dāngkěn, o,
          wǔdiǎnbàn ba, wǔdiǎnbàn, dào
          Dāngkěn jiànmiàn. Ránhòu ne, wǒmen
          chī diǎnr dōngxi, ránhòu jiùqù Hǎidiàn
          Jùyuàn kàn diànyǐng.

Shǒuzhèng: Hǎo.

Shūmǐn: Hǎo bu hǎo? Hǎo.

Shǒuzhèng: Fēichánghǎo.

Shūmǐn: Jiù zhèyàng dìngxialai le.

Shǒuzhèng: Ai, hǎo.

Shūmǐn: Hǎo.

Shǒuzhèng: Ai, zàijiàn.

James: Then before we see the movie
        do you want to get something to drink
        first ... some coffee, or something
        else?

Shumin: Ah, that sounds good. We ... er ...

James: At 5:30, do you want to meet?

Shumin: Okay. Right next door to The
         Haidian Theater there's a Dunkin
         Donuts.

James: Ah, good.

Shumin: We could go to Dunkin Donuts,
         er ... go to Dunkin Donuts ... at 6:30,
         um ... or how about 5:30, let's meet at
         Dunkin Donuts. Then we can have
         something to eat, and then go to the
         Haidian Theater and see the movie.

James: Okay.

Shumin: How's that? Good.

James: Great.

Shumin: Then it's settled.

James: Ah, good.

Shumin: Okay.

James: Okay, bye.

Unit B

Unit B: Making Plans to Get Together

Lesson 9:

Making an Appointment on the Telephone

Hú Jī calls Péng Qióng to make a date to see a movie.

Previewing Activity

1. Following are some hypothetical steps a telephone invitation to see a movie might involve. Check which ones you think you will find in this segment.

_____ a. Greetings

_____ b. Establish identity of caller/callee

_____ c. Make some small talk (How have you been recently?)

_____ d. Suggest a movie

_____ e. Suggest a date and time

_____ f. Suggest an alternate movie

_____ g. Suggest an alternate date and time

_____ h. Rejection—make conciliatory remarks

_____ i. Acceptance—confirm the arrangements

_____ j. Make some more small talk

_____ k. Say good-bye

First Viewing: Global Information

2. Which of the steps a–k were actually taken? List below, then circle the ones you'd predicted.

Steps # _____, _____, _____, _____, _____, _____.

Second Viewing: Specific Information

3. Hú Jī gives a reason why he is suggesting that they go to see a movie. What is it?

_____

4. Fill in the information requested below:

Name of movie (select one): _____Zhūluójì Gōngyuán (*Jurassic Park*)

_____Jiǎfāng Yǐfāng (*Side A, Side B*)

_____Júdòu (*Judou*)

Name of theater: _____

Location of theater (select one):

_____Downtown

_____On campus

_____Nearby, off-campus

Time of meeting: _____

Third Viewing: Linguistic Information

5. After the first exchange of greetings, Péng Qióng still does not know who the caller is. Rather than asking, "Nǐ shì shéi?" 你是誰？ which would have been abrupt and impolite, she uses a more polite question. What is it?

_____

6. When she finds out it is her good friend Hú Jì on the line, she is immediately curious about his reason for calling. What does she ask?

_____

7. Hú Jì couches his invitation to see a movie in some indirect language, to soften it. Write the English equivalent of what he says:

"Dú le yī ge xīngqī de shū, wǒ juéde jīntiān wǎnshang kěyǐ qù kàn diànyǐng."
讀了一個星期的書，我覺得今天晚上可以去看電影。

8. Péng Qióng accepts his suggestion. What does she say?

_____

Unit B

9. If she had chosen to decline, she might have said one of the following. Select the one you prefer:

_____ "Aiya, yòu shì kàn diànyǐng. Wǒmen bù néng zuò yīdiǎr bié de ma?"

唉呀，又是看電影。我們不能做一點兒別的嗎？

("Movies? Again? Can't we do something different?")

_____ "Nà nǐ qù kàn ba. Wǒ xiǎng wǒ háishi bù qù le."

那你去看吧。我想我還是不去了。

("Why don't you go then. I think I'd rather not go.")

_____ "Nǐ zhǎo [mǒumǒu rén] gēn nǐ yīqǐ qù kàn ba. Tā bǐjiào xǐhuan kàn diànyǐng. Wǒ jiù bù qù le."

你找（某某人）跟你一起去看吧。他比較喜歡看電影。我就不去了。

("Why don't you ask [so and so] to go with you. He or she likes movies more, and then I'll not go.")

10. Hú Jì and Péng Qióng use three descriptors for the film they are about to see. Match the English with the Chinese.

hěn bù cuò 很不錯 / 很不错   rather popular ("comparatively hot")

bǐjiào rèmén 比較熱門 / 比较热门   rather well-known

bǐjiào yǒumíng 比較有名 / 比较有名   pretty good

11. The Haidian Juyuan, they find, is "rather suitable." What is the expression in Chinese?

_____

12. Hú Jì confirms the appointment by saying, "Nà jiù jīntiān wǎnshang de qīdiǎn."
Péng Qióng confirms even more thoroughly by stating date, time, and place.
What does she say?

_____

13. They close their conversation by saying, "So that's set, then." What is the Chinese equivalent?

_____

Lesson 9

<u>Post-Viewing Activities</u>

Speaking

14. Role-play the following conversation.

A: (call B on the telephone)	B: (answer the telephone)
A: Ask to speak to B.	B: Respond that you are he or she.
A: Make some small talk.	B: Respond.
A: Suggest seeing a movie.	B: Agree. Ask which movie.
A: Suggest a movie.	B: Agree. Ask what time.
A: Suggest a time and a theater.	B: Agree. Ask how you are to get there.
A: Suggest a mode of transportation.	B: Agree. Suggest a meeting place.
A: Agree. Confirm the arrangements.	B: Repeat the arrangements.
A: Confirm the repetition.	B: Say good-bye.
A: Say good-bye.	

Unit B

Reading / Writing

15. Highlight what you can understand of the following note from your roommate from Taiwan.

今天上午吳明打電話給我。我們想明天一起去看電影。你有興趣和我們一塊兒去嗎？

吳明說她想看《造訪吸血鬼》*，因爲她對恐怖片特別感興趣，而且她特別喜歡那個電影裏的男主角。我印象裏你好象不太喜歡恐怖片。如果你不想看《造訪吸血鬼》，我們也可以去看其他的。現在有一部叫《勇敢的心》**的片子，據說不錯。你來決定吧！

另外，我們去哪裏看呢？如果去校外的影院，那麼我們可以吃完晚飯後走著去。如果去城裏那個新建的影院，就需要你開車。新建的那個影院音響效果很好，空調也不是冷得要死，但就是遠了一點。

等我今晚回來後，把你的決定告訴我吧。

鄭　威

*Interview with the Vampire (starring Tom Cruise)
**Braveheart (starring Mel Gibson)

16. Skim the note and try to determine why Zhèng Wēi is writing you. Check one:

_____ To invite you to go see a movie.
_____ To ask you to go to a movie and dinner.
_____ To request that you recommend a good movie.

Lesson 9

161

17. Write a sentence summarizing each of the four paragraphs in the note:

Para. 1: _____

Para. 2: _____

Para. 3: _____

Para. 4: _____

Check your responses with the ones provided below.

18. Re-read the note, and respond to the following:

Para. 1
Could you tell that Wú Míng is a person's name? Check one of the following.

_____ I could tell because "dǎ diànhuà" is a verb, and what precedes it must be the person doing the verb.

_____ I know the character "Wú" as a common last name, and "Míng" is a common first name.

_____ "Wú Míng" appears at the beginning of the second paragraph preceding "shuō"; what precedes "shuō" generally indicates "who" is speaking.

_____ I could tell another way. (Please share your strategy with your classmates!)

_____ I didn't know Wú Míng was a person's name, but I do now!

Para. 2
a. Wú Míng gives two reasons for wanting to see "Interview with the Vampire." What are they? Check as appropriate. She likes

_____ Nicole Kidman; _____ horror movies; _____ vampire movies; _____ Tom Cruise

b. Why does Zhèng Wēi recommend a second movie? Select one:

Because he knows

_____ you've seen "Interview with the Vampire" already.

_____ you are dying to see something with Mel Gibson in it.

_____ you don't like horror movies.

Unit B

c. How does Zhèng Wēi propose to decide between the two films? Check one:

____ you decide;   ____ go to the earlier showing;   ____ let Wú Míng decide

Para. 3

a. Zhèng Wēi suggests two theaters. Where are they located? Check two.

____ just off-campus; ____ on campus; ____ downtown; ____ at the shopping mall

b. He also suggests that there are two ways you could get to the theater. What are they? Select two:

____ take the bus; ____ bicycle; ____ walk; ____ by car; ____ call a taxicab; ____ by subway

c. What are the advantages of the first theater he names? Select all that apply:

____ Tickets are cheap.   ____ The theater is beautiful.   ____ It's nearby.

d. What are the advantages of the second theater he names? Select all that apply.

____ It's nearby.   ____ It's new.   ____ The sound system is great.

____ The air-conditioning is comfortable.   ____ It's not too expensive.

19. Fill in the blanks by guessing the missing information (characters, *pinyin*, or English) in the vocabulary list below.

_____ / 造访 zàofǎng *call upon, pay a visit to*

吸血鬼 xīxuèguǐ _____ (literally: *suck-blood-demon*)

恐怖片 kǒngbùpiān _____

特别 _____ *especially, particularly*

而且 érqiě _____

男主角 nán zhǔjué _____

_____ yìnxiàng *impression*

好象 _____ *appear to be, apparently*

其他 _____ *other*

勇敢 yǒnggǎn _____

Lesson 9

片子 piānzi _____

_____ / 据说 jùshuō *it is said, according to rumor*

决定 / 决定 juédìng _____

另外 _____ *in addition*

校外 _____ *off-campus*

影院 _____ *movie theater*

走著去 zǒuzhe qù _____

新建 _____ *newly built*

_____ xūyào *need, require*

_____ / 音响 yīnxiǎng *sound, acoustic*

效果 _____ *effect, result*

空調 / 空调 kōngtiáo _____

_____ lěngde yàosǐ *freezing (literally: so cold that you die)*

_____ / X 了一点 X le yīdianr *a little too X (where X is an adjective such as "far," "big," "expensive")*

20. Following is the completed vocabulary list to help decode Zhèng Wēi's note. Re-read the note, and see how much more you can understand now.

造訪 / 造访 zàofǎng *call upon, pay a visit to*

吸血鬼 xīxuèguǐ *vampire (literally: suck-blood-demon)*

恐怖片 kǒngbùpiān *horror film*

特别 tèbié *especially, particularly*

而且 érqiě *moreover*

男主角 nán zhǔjué *male lead*

印象 yìnxiàng *impression*

好象 hǎoxiàng *appear to be, apparently*

其他 qítā *other*

勇敢 yǒnggǎn *brave*

片子 piānzi *film*

據说 / 据说 jùshuō *it is said, according to rumor*

Unit B

決定 / 决定　juédìng *decide*

另外　lìngwài *in addition*

校外　xiàowài *off-campus*

影院　yǐngyuàn *movie theater*

走著去　zǒuzhe qù *go on foot*

新建　xīn jiàn *newly built*

需要　xūyào *need, require*

音響 / 音响　yīnxiǎng *sound, acoustic*

效果　xiàoguǒ *effect, result*

空調 / 空调　kōngtiáo *air-conditioning*

冷得要死　lěngde yàosǐ *freezing (literally: so cold that you die)*

X 了一點 / X 了一点　X le yīdianr *a little too X (where X is an adjective such as "far," "big," "expensive")*

21. Write a brief response to Zhèng Wēi's note.

鄭威：

　　我想跟你們一塊兒去看那部恐怖片。我覺的新電影院比較好。我可以開車。我們六點從這兒出發吧。

　　對不起，我很累，先去睡覺了。

　　　　　　　方華

鄭威：

　　一塊兒去看電影是個好主意！我當然想去。看甚麼電影都行，我無所謂。反正我下午都在家。我也可以開車，沒問題！

　　　　　　　小李

Unit B

166

Transcript of video segment

【彭瓊與胡基對話】
【撥電話號，鈴聲】

彭瓊： 喂，你好！喂，你好！

胡基： 喂，你好，彭瓊嗎？

彭瓊： 啊，對，你好！

胡基： 哎，你好！

彭瓊： 請問你是哪位？

胡基： 哎，我是胡基。

彭瓊： 噢，胡基。嗯，有甚麼事嗎？

胡基： 今天星（期）…是週末，請問你今天有空嗎？

彭瓊： 嗯，我今天有空。

胡基： 讀了一個星期的書了，我覺得今天晚上可以去看電影。

彭瓊： 嗯，好主意！那看甚麼電影呢？

胡基： 聽說最近在放一個比較有名…呃…比較熱門的電影，叫《甲方乙方》。你有興趣嗎？

彭瓊： 我聽說過這部電影，聽說很不錯。好吧，那咱們一起去看吧！

胡基： 你覺得哪地方比較合適？

彭瓊： 嗯…

【彭琼与胡基对话】
【拨电话号，铃声】

彭琼： 喂，你好！喂，你好！

胡基： 喂，你好，彭琼吗？

彭琼： 啊，对，你好！

胡基： 哎，你好！

彭琼： 请问你是哪位？

胡基： 哎，我是胡基。

彭琼： 噢，胡基。嗯，有什么事吗？

胡基： 今天星（期）…是周末，请问你今天有空吗？

彭琼： 嗯，我今天有空。

胡基： 读了一个星期的书了，我觉得今天晚上可以去看电影。

彭琼： 嗯，好主意！那看什么电影呢？

胡基： 听说最近在放一个比较有名…呃…比较热门的电影，叫《甲方乙方》。你有兴趣吗？

彭琼： 我听说过这部电影，听说很不错。好吧，那咱们一起去看吧！

胡基： 你觉得哪地方比较合适？

彭琼： 嗯…

Lesson 9

[*Péng Qióng yǔ Hú Jī duìhuà*]

[*Bō diànhuàhào, língshēng*]

Péng Qióng: Wèi, nǐ hǎo! Wèi, nǐ hǎo!

Hú Jī: Wèi, nǐ hǎo, Péng Qióng ma?

Péng Qióng: A, duì, nǐ hǎo!

Hú Jī: Ai, nǐ hǎo!

Péng Qióng: Qǐngwèn nǐ shì nǎwèi?

Hú Jī: Ai, wǒ shì Hú Jī.

Péng Qióng: O, Hú Jī. Ng, yǒu shénme shì ma?

Hú Jī: Jīntiān Xīng(qī) ... shì zhōumò, qǐngwèn nǐ jīntiān yǒukòng ma?

Péng Qióng: Ng, wǒ jīntiān yǒukòng.

Hú Jī: Dú le yī ge xīngqī de shū le, wǒ juéde jīntiān wǎnshang kěyǐ qù kàn diànyǐng.

Péng Qióng: Ng, hǎo zhǔyì! Nà kàn shénme diànyǐng ne?

Hú Jī: Tīngshuō zuìjìn zài fàng yī ge bǐjiào yǒumíng ... e ... bǐjiào rèmén(r) de diànyǐng, jiào *Jiǎfāng Yǐfāng*. Nǐ yǒu xìngqù ma?

Péng Qióng: Wǒ tīngshuōguo zhè bù diànyǐng, tīngshuō hěn bùcuò. Hǎoba, nà zánmen yīqǐ qù kàn ba!

Hú Jī: Nǐ juéde nǎ dìfang bǐjiào héshì?

Péng Qióng: Ng ...

[*Peng Qiong talks with Hu Ji*]

[*Dialing; ringing at the other end*]

Peng Qiong: Hello! Hello!

Hu Ji: Hello. Is this Peng Qiong?

Peng Qiong: Er, it is. Hello!

Hu Ji: Right, hi!

Peng Qiong: May I ask who is calling?

Hu Ji: Oh, this is Hu Ji.

Peng Qiong: Ah, Hu Ji. Mmm, what's going on?

Hu Ji: Today is Sat- ... the weekend, are you free today?

Peng Qiong: Uh-huh, I'm free today.

Hu Ji: Well, we've studied all week, I thought tonight we could go see a movie.

Peng Qiong: Uh-huh, good idea. What movie shall we see, then?

Hu Ji: I heard that there's a rather famous ... a rather popular movie called *Side A, Side B* playing right now. Are you interested?

Peng Qiong: I've heard of that movie, that it's pretty good. Fine, then let's go together!

Hu Ji: Where do you think the best place is?

Peng Qiong: Mmmm ...

Unit B

胡基： 在北大附近有不少電影
院。

彭瓊： 嗯，我想找一個是不是
離北大比較近的地方看電
影比較合適。

胡基： 那海淀劇院怎麼樣？

彭瓊： 嗯，好的。好主意！好
嗎？

胡基： 好嗎？

彭瓊： 嗯。

胡基： 那就今天晚上的七點。

彭瓊： 今天晚上七點鐘在海淀
劇院見面。

胡基： 好。

彭瓊： 好嗎？

胡基： 好。

彭瓊： 好。那就這樣？

胡基： 欸！那就這樣。

彭瓊： 再見！

胡基： 欸！好，再見！

胡基： 在北大附近有不少电影
院。

彭琼： 嗯，我想找一个是不是
离北大比较近的地方看电
影比较合适。

胡基： 那海淀剧院怎么样？

彭琼： 嗯，好的。好主意！好
吗？

胡基： 好吗？

彭琼： 嗯。

胡基： 那就今天晚上的七点。

彭琼： 今天晚上七点钟在海淀
剧院见面。

胡基： 好。

彭琼： 好吗？

胡基： 好。

彭琼： 好。那就这样？

胡基： 欸！那就这样。

彭琼： 再见！

胡基： 欸！好，再见！

Lesson 9

Hú Jī: Zài Běidà fùjìn yǒu bù shǎo
        diànyǐngyuàn.

Péng Qióng: Ng, wǒ xiǎng zhǎo yī ge
            shì bu shì lí Běidà bǐjiào jìn de dìfang
            kàn diànyǐng bǐjiào héshì.

Hú Jī: Nà Hǎidiàn Jùyuàn zěnmeyàng?

Péng Qióng: Ng, hǎode. Hǎo zhǔyì!
            Hǎoma?

Hú Jī: Hǎoma?

Péng Qióng: Ng.

Hú Jī: Nà jiù jīntiān wǎnshang de qīdiǎn.

Péng Qióng: Jīntiān wǎnshang
            qīdiǎnzhōng zài Hǎidiàn Jùyuàn
            jiànmiàn.

Hú Jī: Hǎo.

Péng Qióng: Hǎo ma?

Hú Jī: Hǎo.

Péng Qióng: Hǎo. Nà jiù zhèyàng?

Hú Jī: Ei! Nà jiù zhèyàng.

Péng Qióng: Zàijiàn!

Hú Jī: Ei! Hǎo, zàijiàn!

Hu Ji: Around Beida there are a lot of
        theaters.

Peng Qiong: I'm thinking it'd be best to
            find a place relatively near Beida.

Hu Ji: What about the Haidian
        Theater, then?

Peng Qiong: Yeah! That's a good idea.
            Okay, then?

Hu Ji: All right?

Peng Qiong: Uh-huh.

Hu Ji: Tonight at 7:00, then.

Peng Qiong: Tonight we'll meet at the
            Haidian Theater at 7:00.

Hu Ji: Okay.

Peng Qiong: Is that all right?

Hu Ji: Yeah.

Peng Qiong: Good. Then it's settled?

Hu Ji: Yup! It's settled.

Peng Qiong: Bye.

Hu Ji: Uh-huh. Right, bye.

Unit B

Unit B: Making Plans to Get Together

Lesson 10:

A Follow-up Call

*Péng Qióng calls Hú Jī
about their movie date.*

Previewing Activity

1. If you have an appointment with someone and they call you shortly before it, what do you expect they might be calling about? Check the one you think is the most likely.

_____ 1. Confirm time, date, place

_____ 2. Change time, date, place, or purpose of meeting

_____ 3. Cancel the appointment

_____ 4. Obtain more information

2. Match the utterances below with the purposes listed above. Circle one of the four options for each.

a. *1 2 3 4*   "Wèi! Wǒmen shì jǐdiǎn jiànmiàn a?"

b. *1 2 3 4*   "Wǒmen shì yīqǐ guòqu háishi zài nèi biān jiànmiàn?"

c. *1 2 3 4*   "Zhēn duìbuqǐ, wǒ jīntiān bù néng qù kàn diànyǐng. Gǎi tiān xíng ma?"

d. *1 2 3 4*   "Wéi? Hú Jī ... nǐ shuō cuò le! Diànyǐng shì liùdiǎn de, bù shì qīdiǎn de! Wǒmen zǎo diǎn qù ba!"

e. *1 2 3 4*   "Diànyǐngyuàn lǐtou huì lěng ma?"

f. *1 2 3 4*   "Hú Jī a, hěn bàoqiàn ... wǒ bù néng qù le."

g. *1 2 3 4*   "Wǒ tīngshuō nèi bù diànyǐng méi yìsi ... zánmen bié qù kàn le! Huàn yī bù diànyǐng ba."

First Viewing: Global Information

3. For which of the purposes suggested above was Péng Qióng actually calling?

Circle one: *1   2   3   4*

Second Viewing: Specific Information

4. Péng Qióng describes a complication to her original plan to see a movie with Hú Jī that evening. What is it?

_____

5. What is the solution she proposes?

_____

6. When and where do they agree to meet?

_____

7. Hú Jī closes the conversation with an admonition. What is it?

_____

Third Viewing: Linguistic Information

8. Hú Jī responds to Péng Qióng's greeting. Match the English to the Chinese, then circle what he says.

Zěnmeyàng?   *What's up?*
怎麼樣／怎么样？

Yǒu shì ma?   *Are you calling me for a reason?*
有事嗎／有事吗？

Nǐ zhǎo wǒ yǒu shì ma?   *How are things?*
你找我有事嗎／你找我有事吗？

9. Péng Qióng apologizes twice in the conversation, using a phrase which has the same meaning as "Zhēn duìbuqǐ." Reorder the *pinyin* to match the characters:

qiàn fēi bào cháng   非常抱歉 (literally: "extremely feel apologetic")

—— —— —— ——

10. Péng Qióng says, "I suddenly remembered, tonight I have a friend coming to see me." Fill in the blanks in the *pinyin* for this statement.

Wǒ tūrán xiǎng_____lai le, jīntiān wǎnshang wǒ _____ yī ge péngyou yào lái _____ wǒ.

11. This explains why she cannot make the movie date as planned. Fill in the blank below.

"Kǒngpà wǒ, ng, wǒ jīntiān bù néng qù kàn diànyǐng _____."

"*I'm afraid I, er, I can't go see the movie tonight.*"

Unit B

12. Write the Chinese for the following exchange:

Péng Qióng: *"Can we change to another time, then?"* <u>*Nà zánmen*</u>   ?

Hú Jī: *"Well, what time should we make it?"* _____?

13. "Zánmen" 咱們 is a Beijing colloquialism that includes the person being addressed. What is a synonym for this term, except that it <u>might</u> not include the person being addressed?

_____

14. Match the English and the Chinese below:

Nǐ míngtiān yǒu shì ma?
你明天有事嗎／你明天有事吗？

How about tomorrow?

Nǐ míngtiān yǒu kòng ma?
你明天有空嗎／你明天有空吗？

Are you busy tomorrow?

Míngtiān zěnmeyàng?
明天怎麼樣／明天怎么样？

Are you free tomorrow?

15. Hú Jī says he is free all day, the next day. Following are four ways he could have said that; check what he did say.

_____Wǒ míngtiān yī zhěng tiān dōu méi shì.
我明天一整天都沒事。

_____Míngtiān wǒ quántiān dōu méi shì.
明天我全天都沒事。

_____Wǒ míngtiān quántiān dōu yǒu kòng.
我明天全天都有空。

_____Míngtiān wǒ yītiān dōu yǒu kòng.
明天我一天都有空。

16. Péng Qióng eventually reconfirms their new appointment by stating the day, time, and place they will meet. Reorder the elements below based on what she says.

jiǔdiǎnzhōng / zài Hǎidiàn Jùyuàn / jiànmiàn / shàngwǔ / míngtiān / hǎo ma?
九點鐘   在海淀劇院   見面   上午   明天   好嗎？

___   ___   ___   ___   ___

17. They close with one of the expressions below. Check it, and then match all the Chinese expressions with their English equivalents.

_____Shì zhèyàng de ... 是這樣的 ...

How about doing this ...

_____Nà jiù zhèyàng ... 那就這樣 ...

That's it, then ...

_____Zhèyàng ba ... 這樣吧 ...

It's like this ...

Lesson 10

Post-Viewing Activities

Speaking:

18. Guided dialogue

Student A	Student B
•Say hello. Ask to speak to B.	•Identify yourself.
•Greet B. Identify yourself.	•Greet A.
•Confirm that you had an appointment to see a movie together—specify date and time (make them up).	•Confirm A's information about date and time; confirm which movie you were going to see (make it up).
•Explain the problem—something has come up and you can't keep the appointment.	•Ask what you should do then. Suggest a different day.
•Apologize; say that day won't work either. Suggest another day.	•Ask what time A would like to meet on that day.
•Suggest a time.	•Apologize; explain why that time won't work. Suggest a different time.
•Agree to that time.	•Confirm the day and time, and confirm the place you will be meeting.
•Ask to be reminded which movie you will be seeing.	•Remind A of the movie you will be seeing. Say a sentence or two about what the movie is about.
•Agree to the arrangements. Confirm date, time, place, and name of the movie. Take your leave of B.	•Take your leave of A.

Unit B

Reading / Writing

19. Your name is Wang. Your friend Zhang leaves you and your friend Chen this note. Read it as best you can:

小王、小陈：

　　最近有一个俄国舞蹈团到我们这里演出芭蕾舞剧《天鹅湖》。我记得你们两个对舞蹈很感兴趣。大家一起去看，怎么样？他们的演出时间是这个星期的三、四、五晚上七点。我星期三晚上有课，所以我希望星期四或星期五去，不知你们两个的时间如何？

友　　小张

20. Xiao Chen has written the following response. Highlight what you can read of it.

小张：

　　我看到了你留的条子。我很想去看。不过，我星期五晚上要去机场送一个朋友。他的飞机晚上八点半起飞，但我跟他约好了晚上六点送他去飞机场。我不知道能不能在七点以前赶回来。如果小王有时间的话，我们可不可以星期四晚上去看？

友：小陈

Lesson 10

21. Note 1
a. You might have deduced that Xiǎo Zhāng is inviting you somewhere. Where? Check one.

_____ The movies   _____ A play   _____ A ball game   _____ A ballet performance

b. When is Xiǎo Zhāng available to attend the event? Fill in the two days/times:

_____ and _____

22. Note 2
a. Would Xiǎo Chén like to go with you and Xiǎo Zhāng?

Check one. _____ yes   _____ no

b. When is Xiǎo Chén available to attend the event? Fill in the day: _____

Why isn't Xiǎo Chén available on the other day? Summarize the reason in English:

_____

23. Fill in the blanks by guessing the missing information (characters, *pinyin*, or English) in the vocabulary list below.

俄國 / 俄国 Éguó _____

_____ / 舞蹈团 wǔdǎotuán *dance troupe*

演出 yǎnchū _____

芭蕾舞劇 / 芭蕾舞剧 bāléiwǔjù _____

_____ / 天鹅湖 Tiāné Hú *Swan Lake*

記得 / 记得 _____ *remember*

不知 _____ *I wonder*

如何 _____ *how (it is)*

****

_____ liú *leave behind*

條子 / 条子 _____ *a note*

_____ sòng *take to, send off*

飛機 / 飞机 _____ *airplane*

起飛 / 起飞 _____ *take off*

Unit B   176

但 _____ but

_____ / 约好了 yuēhǎole *fixed an appointment*

飛機場 / 飞机场 fēijīchǎng _____

_____ / 赶 gǎn *hurry, rush*

如果X的話 / 如果X的话 _____ *if X is the case*

24. Following is the completed vocabulary list, turned on its side to discourage you from peeking before you are done with the exercise above! Re-read the two notes, using the list as a guide.

俄國 / 俄国 Éguó *Russia*

舞蹈團 / 舞蹈团 wǔdǎotuán *dance troupe*

演出 yǎnchū *perform*

芭蕾舞劇 / 芭蕾舞剧 bālěijù *ballet*

天鵝湖 / 天鹅湖 Tiāné Hú *Swan Lake*

記得 / 记得 jìde *remember*

不知 bùzhī *I wonder*

如何 rúhé *how (it is)*

****

留 liú *leave behind*

條子 / 条子 tiáozi *a note*

送 sòng *take to, send off*

飛機 / 飞机 fēijī *airplane*

起飛 / 起飞 qǐfēi *take off*

但 dàn *but*

約好了 / 约好了 yuēhǎole *fixed an appointment*

飛機場 / 飞机场 fēijīchǎng *airport*

趕 / 赶 gǎn *hurry, rush*

如果X的話 / 如果X的话 rúguǒ X de huà *if X is the case*

25. Write a response to both your friends.

_____

Lesson 10

Sample responses (edited)

我星期四不能去。我
星期五要考试。星期
五晚上行吗?

好! 没有問題。
我星期四有空。
我們什麼時候見面?

星期四晚上去看,没问题! 那我们
几点、在什么地方见面呢?

Unit B

178

【彭瓊與胡基對話】
【撥號。電話鈴】

胡基： 你好！

彭瓊： 喂，你好！請問是胡基嗎？

胡基： 對，是我。

彭瓊： 哎，你好！我是彭瓊。

胡基： 哎，怎麼樣？

彭瓊： 哎，你好！是這樣的，非常抱歉，我突然間想起來了，今天晚上我有一個朋友要來找我。

胡基： 你今天有事是嗎？

彭瓊： 所以 ... 對，恐怕今天我 ... 呃，我們今天不能去看電影了。那咱們改一個時間好嗎？

胡基： 那改甚麼時候呢？

彭瓊： 嗯，你覺得明天怎麼樣？

胡基： 明天…

彭瓊： 嗯。

胡基： 你看你明天甚麼時候有空？我明天全天都有空。

彭瓊： 嗯，好的。那咱們明天上午去看電影。

【彭琼与胡基对话】
【拨号。电话铃】

胡基： 你好！

彭琼： 喂，你好！请问是胡基吗？

胡基： 对，是我。

彭琼： 哎，你好！我是彭琼。

胡基： 哎，怎么样？

彭琼： 哎，你好！是这样的，非常抱歉，我突然间想起来了，今天晚上我有一个朋友要来找我。

胡基： 你今天有事是吗？

彭琼： 所以 ... 对，恐怕今天我 ... 呃，我们今天不能去看电影了。那咱们改一个时间好吗？

胡基： 那改什么时候呢？

彭琼： 嗯，你觉得明天怎么样？

胡基： 明天…

彭琼： 嗯。

胡基： 你看你明天什么时候有空？我明天全天都有空。

彭琼： 嗯，好的。那咱们明天上午去看电影。

Lesson 10

179

[Péng Qióng yǔ Hú Jī duìhuà]

[Bō hào. Diànhuàlíng]

Hú Jī: Nǐ hǎo!

Péng Qióng: Wèi, nǐ hǎo! Qǐngwèn shì
     Hú Jī ma?

Hú Jī: Duì, shì wǒ.

Péng Qióng: Ai, nǐ hǎo! Wǒ shì Péng
     Qióng.

Hú Jī: Ai, zěnmeyàng?

Péng Qióng: Ai, nǐhǎo!
     Shì zhèyàng de, fēicháng bàoqiàn, wǒ
     tūránjìUan xiǎngqǐlai le, jīntiān
     wǎnshang wǒ yǒu yī ge péngyou yào lái
     zhǎo wǒ.

Hú Jī: Nǐ jīntiān yǒu shì shì ma?

Péng Qióng: Suǒyǐ ... duì, kǒngpà jīntiān
     wǒ ... e, wǒmen jīntiān bùnéng qù kàn
     diànyǐng le. Nà zánmen gǎi yī ge
     shíjiān hǎo ma?

Hú Jī: Nà gǎi shénme shíhou ne?

Péng Qióng: Ng, nǐ juéde míngtiān
     zěnmeyàng?

Hú Jī: Míngtiān ...

Péng Qióng: Ng.

Hú Jī: Nǐ kàn nǐ míngtiān shénme
     shíhou yǒukòng? Wǒ míngtiān
     quántiān dōu yǒukòng.

Péng Qióng: Ng, hǎo de. Nà zánmen
     míngtiān shàngwǔ qù kàn diànyǐng.

[Peng Qiong speaks with Hu Ji.]

[Dialing. Ringing.]

Hu Ji: Hello.

Peng Qiong: Hello. May I ask if this is
     Hu Ji?

Hu Ji: Yes, that's me.

Peng Qiong: Ah, hello. This is Peng
     Qiong.

Hu Ji: Hey, how's it going?

Peng Qiong: Ah, hi!
     It's like this, I'm so sorry, but I sud-
     denly realized that a friend of mine is
     coming over tonight to visit me.

Hu Ji: Oh, you're busy tonight?

Peng Qiong: So ... yeah, I'm afraid I
     am ... ah, tonight we can't go to the
     movies together. Can we reschedule,
     then?

Hu Ji: When should we reschedule for, then?

Peng Qiong: Er, what do you think about
     tomorrow?

Hu Ji: Tomorrow ...

Peng Qiong: Uh-huh.

Hu Ji: When are you free tomorrow?
     Tomorrow I'm free all day long.

Peng Qiong: Okay. Then let's go to the
     movie tomorrow morning.

Unit B

胡基：　明天上午。

彭瓊：　好嗎？

胡基：　還是在海淀劇院嗎？

彭瓊：　嗯，海淀劇院。

胡基：　海淀劇院。

彭瓊：　對。

胡基：　上午幾點？

彭瓊：　明天上午幾點鐘 ...

胡基：　上午九點鐘。

彭瓊：　明天上午九點鐘在海
　　　　淀劇院見面，好嗎？

胡基：　好，好的。

彭瓊：　好，那就這樣。

胡基：　希望沒有別的事情。

彭瓊：　嗯，非常抱歉。

胡基【與彭瓊同時】：　好，
　　　　再見！

彭瓊：　就這樣。再見！

胡基【與彭瓊同時】：　好，
　　　　再見！

胡基：　明天上午。

彭琼：　好吗？

胡基：　还是在海淀剧院吗？

彭琼：　嗯，海淀剧院。

胡基：　海淀剧院。

彭琼：　对。

胡基：　上午几点？

彭琼：　明天上午几点钟 ...

胡基：　上午九点钟。

彭琼：　明天上午九点钟在海
　　　　淀剧院见面，好吗？

胡基：　好，好的。

彭琼：　好，那就这样。

胡基：　希望没有别的事情。

彭琼：　嗯，非常抱歉。

胡基【与彭琼同时】：　好，
　　　　再见！

彭琼：　就这样。再见！

胡基【与彭琼同时】：　好，
　　　　再见！

Lesson 10

Hú Jī: Míngtiān shàngwǔ.

Péng Qióng: Hǎo ma?

Hú Jī: Hái shì zài Hǎidiàn Jùyuàn ma?

Péng Qióng: Ng, Hǎidiàn Jùyuàn.

Hú Jī: Hǎidiàn Jùyuàn.

Péng Qióng: Duì.

Hú Jī: Shàngwǔ jǐdiǎn?

Péng Qióng: Míngtiān shàngwǔ
    jǐdiǎnzhōng ...

Hú Jī: Shàngwǔ jiǔdiǎnzhōng.

Péng Qióng: Míngtiān shàngwǔ
    jiǔdiǎnzhōng zài Hǎidiàn Jùyuàn
    jiànmiàn, hǎoma?

Hú Jī: Hǎo, hǎode.

Péng Qióng: Hǎo, nàjiù zhèyàng.

Hú Jī: Xīwàng méiyǒu biéde shìqing.

Péng Qióng: Ng, fēicháng bàoqiàn.

Hú Jī (yǔ Péng Qióng tóngshí):
    Hǎo, zàijiàn!

Péng Qióng: Jiù zhèyàng. Zàijiàn!

Hú Jī (yǔ Péng Qióng tóngshí):
    Hǎo, zàijiàn!

Hu Ji: Tomorrow morning.

Peng Qiong: Okay?

Hu Ji: Still at the Haidian Theater?

Peng Qiong: Uh-huh, the Haidian
    Theater.

Hu Ji: The Haidian Theater.

Peng Qiong: Yeah.

Hu Ji: What time?

Peng Qiong: What time tomorrow
    morning ...

Hu Ji: At 9:00 in the morning.

Peng Qiong: We can meet at 9:00 at
    the Haidian Theater tomorrow
    morning, okay?

Hu Ji: Yeah, good.

Peng Qiong: Okay, then it's settled.

Hu Ji: I hope that nothing else comes
    up.

Peng Qiong: Uh-huh, I'm so sorry.

Hu Ji (with Peng Qiong):
    Okay, bye!

Peng Qiong: That's it, then. Bye!

Hu Ji (with Peng Qiong):
    Okay, bye!

Unit B

Unit B: Making Plans to Get Together

Lesson 11:
Advice on Refusing an Invitation

Dr. Hao gives advice on how to refuse invitations.

Previewing Activity

1. Check which ideas you think he will mention.

____ Be direct. Don't beat around the bush.

____ Be indirect. Don't hurt the other person's feelings.

____ Always give a reason why you are refusing.

____ Don't feel you have to give a reason why you are refusing.

____ Always suggest an alternative to the activity proposed.

____ Don't feel compelled to suggest an alternative.

____ Put off deciding; say you can't say "yes" or "no" at the moment.

First Viewings: Global Information

2. Which of the ideas listed above did Dr. Hao actually discuss? Check the appropriate boxes above, right.

Second Viewings: Specific Information

3. *Answer the questions or fill in the blanks below in English.*

A. Hǎo Píng suggests that visitors will receive many invitations—to do what? _____

B. He suggests that you NOT say, "_____," because that would be impolite and unfriendly.

C. He suggests that you say the following, "Oh...I'm really _____ these days. I can't really tell if I'll have the _____. I'll _____ later, okay?"

D. This way, the other party will likely understand that you are _____.

E. If the other party asks about your availability the next day, you can say, "Tomorrow I

_____."

F. This, Hǎo Píng suggests, is a _____ way of refusing.

Third Viewing: Linguistic Information

4. Please match the English to the Chinese expressions:

nouns

duìfāng 對方／对方   *feeling*

bànfǎ 辦法／办法   *method, way*

gǎnjué 感覺／感觉   *the other party*

adjectives

yǒuhǎo 友好   *polite*

jiǎndān 簡單／简单   *simple*

lǐmào 禮貌／礼貌   *friendly*

verbs

gàosu 告訴／告诉   *refuse*

liǎojiě 了解   *evade, avoid*

jùjué 拒絕／拒绝   *understand*

tuītuō 推托   *decline*

tuīcí 推辭／推辞   *tell*

other

rúguǒ 如果   *if*

xǔduō 許多／许多   *perhaps, maybe*

shuōbudìng 说不定／说不定   *many*

Unit B

5. Hǎo Píng opens with the following presupposition.

Rúguǒ nǐ dào Běijīng lái, e, xǔduō Běijīng fēicháng yǒuhǎo de, nng, lǎoshī ya, tóngxué ya, péngyou, dōu xiǎng qǐng nǐ chī fàn.

如果你到北京來，呃，許多北京非常友好的，嗯，老師呀，
同學呀，朋友，都想請你吃飯。

如果你到北京来，呃，许多北京非常友好的，嗯，老师呀，
同学呀，朋友，都想请你吃饭。

If you come to Beijing, many particularly friendly, er, teachers, or students—friends (in other words)—in Beijing, will want to buy you a meal.

Rewrite his statement as follows:

"If you come to Beijing, many people will invite you to a meal."

---

6. Hǎo Píng elaborates:

Rúguǒ nǐ bù xiǎng qù chī fàn, bù yào jiǎndān shuō: "Wǒ bù qù", "Wǒ bù yào." Zhèi huì gěi duìfāng gǎnjué, ng, bù lǐmào, bù yǒuhǎo.

如果你不想去吃飯，不要簡單說"我不去"、"我不要"。
這會給對方感覺，嗯，不禮貌，不友好。

如果你不想去吃饭，不要简单说"我不去"、"我不要"。
这会给对方感觉，嗯，不礼貌，不友好。

If you don't want to go, don't simply say, "I'm not going." "I don't want to." This will strike the other party as impolite, or unfriendly.

Rewrite his statement as follows:

"Simply saying, 'I don't want to go' is a little impolite."

"If you don't want to go, don't just say, 'I don't want to go.' That's unfriendly."

Lesson 11

7. He elaborates further. (Fill in the blanks, using *pinyin.*)

_____ nǐ xiǎng _____ tā, nǐ kěyǐ hěn _____ de shuō, "Aiya, wǒ zhè jǐ tiān hěn _____. Wǒ hái _____ yǒu méiyǒu shíjiān. Wǒ _____ gěi nǐ dǎ diànhuà ba. Wǒ zài _____ nǐ ba!"

如果你想拒絕他，你可以很禮貌地說"哎呀，我這幾天很忙。
我還說不定有沒有時間。我再給你打電話吧。我再告訴你吧！"

如果你想拒绝他，你可以很礼貌地说"哎呀，我这几天很忙。
我还说不定有没有时间。我再给你打电话吧。我再告诉你吧！"

"If you want to refuse him/her, you can say very politely, "Oh, I'm really busy these days. I don't know if I'll have the time. Why don't I call you later. I'll tell you later, okay?"

8. Finally, he says: "This is a polite way of refusing."

Reorder the terms below to form the Chinese equivalent of this statement.

jùjué de /	lǐmào de /	zhè shì /	bànfǎ /	yī zhǒng
拒絕的 /	禮貌地 /	這是 /	辦法 /	一種 /
拒绝的	礼貌地	这是	办法	一种
☐	☐	☐	☐	☐

Post-Viewing Activities

Speaking

9. You want to do something with someone. Check two of the following options:

_____go to the movies

_____go to lunch

_____go running (pǎobù)

_____go shopping

_____go to dinner

Unit B

10. Walk around the room. Talk to your classmates. Invite them to join you for the activities in which you are interested.

- •If they invite you to do something you do not care for (i.e., to do one of the three activities you did NOT check), find a *polite* way to decline.
- •If you extend them an invitation and they choose to decline, realize that they are declining, back off, and do not take offense.
- •If your invitation is accepted, or you accept someone's invitation (to do one of the activities you DID check), set a date, time, and place to meet.

11. Report back to the class on your plans.

Reading / Writing

12. Read the following message from your Chinese friend.

老朋友：

真对不起！我原先答应你这个周末去参加你的聚会，但我现在不敢肯定我是否一定能去。我原先没料到我这几天这么忙。这样吧，如果我能去的话，我会事先打电话通知你。万一我不能去，也希望你不要介意。

再次抱歉！

你的老朋友

Lesson 11

13. Respond to the following questions.

a. Why do you think your "old friend" is writing you? He or she refers to (select one)

_____ your party this weekend

_____ the study group for the test next week

_____ your movie date this evening

b. Your friend wishes to say that he or she (select one):

_____ definitely cannot come

_____ may or may not not be able to come

_____ definitely will come

c. What's changed since the last time your friend spoke to you? Your friend says he or she has (select one)

_____ become ill

_____ forgotten a previous appointment

_____ become really busy

d. Your friend hopes you will not (select one)

_____ change your mind

_____ take offense

_____ retaliate

14. Fill in the blanks by guessing the missing information (characters, *pinyin*, or English) in the vocabulary list below.

_____ yuánxiān *originally*

答應 / 答应 _____ *agree*

參加 / 参加 cānjiā _____

聚會 / _____ jùhuì *party, get-together*

_____ kěndìng *absolutely, for sure*

是否 _____ *whether or not*

_____ liàodào *foresee, expect*

事先 _____ *in advance, before the event*

_____ tōngzhī *notify, inform*

萬一 / 万一 _____ *just in case*

_____ jièyì *mind, take offense*

再次 zàicì _____

_____ bàoqiàn *apologize, feel sorry*

Unit B

15. Following is the completed vocabulary list to help decode your friend's note. Re-read it, and see how much more of it you can understand.

原先　yuánxiān *originally*

答應 / 答应　dāying *agree*

參加 / 参加　cānjiā *participate in*

聚會 / 聚会　jùhuì *party, get-together*

肯定　kěndìng *absolutely, for sure*

是否　shìfǒu *whether or not*

料到　liàodào *foresee, expect*

事先　shìxiān *in advance, before the event*

通知　tōngzhī *notify, inform*

萬一 / 万一　wànyī *just in case*

介意　jièyì *mind, take offense*

再次　zàicì *once again*

抱歉　bàoqiàn *apologize, feel sorry*

16. Write a brief response to your friend.

我明白你的難處。
我希望你能來,可是萬一你不能來,我不會介意的.

如果你不能來,没关係。我们下个周末还会有聚会。希望你下周末比较有空。请你给我打个电话.

我们这次聚会是为了你办的!要是你不来的话,多么没意思啊?!你一定得来,要不然我们大家都会很失望。请你收到条子来个电话。

Unit B

【北京大學國際交流處處長郝平博士談話】

呃，如果你到北京來，呃，許多北京非常友好的，嗯，老師呀，同學呀，朋友，都想請你吃飯。

那麼，如果你不想去吃飯，不要簡單說："我不去"、"我不要。"這會給對方感覺，嗯，不禮貌，不友好。

如果你想拒絕他，你可以很禮貌地說："哎呀，我這幾天很忙。我還說不定有沒有時間。我再給你打電話吧。我再告訴你吧！"

那麼對方就會了解：噢，他可能推…推托了，推辭了。

或者你說："嗯，我今天有事。"那麼對方還會問你："明天呢？"你就說："我明天（也）有事。"

也是一種禮貌的拒絕的辦法。

【北京大学国际交流处处长郝平博士谈话】

呃，如果你到北京来，呃，许多北京非常友好的，嗯，老师呀，同学呀，朋友，都想请你吃饭。

那么，如果你不想去吃饭，不要简单说："我不去"、"我不要。"这会给对方感觉，嗯，不礼貌，不友好。

如果你想拒绝他，你可以很礼貌地说："哎呀，我这几天很忙。我还说不定有没有时间。我再给你打电话吧。我再告诉你吧！"

那么对方就会了解：噢，他可能推…推托了，推辞了。

或者你说："嗯，我今天有事。"那么对方还会问你："明天呢？"你就说："我明天（也）有事。"

也是一种礼貌的拒绝的办法。

Lesson 11

[*Běijīng Dàxue Guójì Jiāoliúchù chùzhǎng Háo Píng bóshì tánhuà*)

E, rúguǒ nǐ dào Běijīng lái, e, xǔduō Běijīng fēicháng yǒuhǎo de, ng, lǎoshī ya, tóngxué ya, péngyou, dōu xiǎng qǐng nǐ chī fàn.

Nàme, rúguǒ nǐ bù xiǎng qù chī fàn, bù yào jiǎndān shuō "Wǒ bú qù", "Wǒ bù yào". Zhèi huì gěi duìfāng gǎnjué, ng, bù lǐmào, bù yǒuhǎo.

Rúguǒ nǐ xiǎng jùjué tā, nǐ kěyǐ hěn lǐmào de shuō, "Āiya, wǒ zhè jǐ tiān hěn máng. Wǒ hái shuōbùdìng yǒu méiyǒu shíjiān. Wǒ zài gěi nǐ dǎ diànhuà ba. Wǒ zài gàosù nǐ ba!"

Nàme duìfāng jiù huì liǎojiě: O, tā kěnéng tuī ... tuītuō le, tuīcí le.

Huòzhě nǐ shuō "Ng, Wǒ jīntiān yǒu shì." Nàme duìfāng hái huì wèn nǐ, "Míngtiān ne?" Nǐ jiù shuō, "Wǒ míngtiān (yě) yǒu shì."

Yě shì yīzhǒng lǐmào de jùjué de bànfǎ.

[*A chat with Dr. Hao Ping, director of the Office of International Relations of Peking University*]

If you come to Beijing, er ... in Beijing many extremely friendly, er ... teachers, classmates, and friends will all want to invite you out to dinner.

If you don't want to go out with them, don't simply say, "I won't go," "I don't want to go." This will give the other person the feeling that you're not polite, er ... not friendly.
If you want to refuse them, you can politely say, "Oh, for the next couple of days I'm very busy. I can't say when I'll have time. Let me give you a call later. I'll tell you later."

Then the other person will understand: Oh, they are putting ... putting it off, declining.

Or you can say, "Um, today I have something to do." Then the other person may ask you, "How about tomorrow?" Then you can say, "Tomorrow I (also) have something to do."
This is another courteous way of refusing.

Unit B

Unit C: Handling Meals

Lesson 12:

Two Boys Comment on Dinner

We revisit with Xú Zhèngyǔ (screen right) and Lǚ Áng (screen left; pictured here) who tell us what they will eat (or ate) for dinner.

Previewing Activity

1. What do you think the boys might eat (or have eaten)? Circle as appropriate.

| rice | noodles | vegetables | meat | soup |

| fruit | dessert | pizza | hamburgers | spaghetti |

First Viewing: Global Information

2. Which of the items above did the boys mention? Underline as appropriate.

3. How many dishes did Xú (screen right) have?

| | soup plus one dish | | | soup plus two dishes |

| | soup plus three dishes | | | soup plus four dishes |

How many dishes does Lǚ (screen left) predict he is going to have?

| | rice plus one dish | | | rice plus two dishes |

| | rice plus three dishes | | | rice plus four dishes |

Second Viewing: Specific Information

4. Which dishes did Xú have? Which dishes does Lǔ predict he is going to have? Write X (for Xú—screen right) and L (for Lǔ—screen left) in the spaces below.

_____ hāozigǎnr 蒿子桿兒 / 蒿子杆儿 *artemesia greens*

_____ tāng 湯 / 汤 *soup*

_____ páigǔ 排骨 *pork rib sections*

_____ mógu 蘑菇 / 蘑菇 *mushrooms*

_____ mǐfàn 米飯 / 米饭 *rice*

_____ yóucài 油菜 / 油菜 *canola greens, rape greens*

Third Viewing: Linguistic Information

5. The interviewer asks, "What dishes do you think (guess, estimate) you'll probably be eating tonight?" Fill in the blanks for this question, using *pinyin*.

"Nǐ _____ nǐmen jīntiān wǎnshang _____ huì chī shénme cài ne?"
"你估計你們今天晚上大概會吃甚麼菜呢？" ／
"你估计你们今天晚上大概会吃什么菜呢？"

6. Xú's answer is: "This changes constantly. I don't know." Fill in the blank using *pinyin*.

"Zhège biànhuà _____, bù zhīdào."
"這個變化無常，不知道。" ／ "这个变化无常，不知道。"

7. Xú says that he had "Two dishes and a soup, (which is) quite the standard."
Fill in the blank using *pinyin*.

"Liǎngge cài yī ge tāng, _____ biāozhǔn."
"兩個菜一個湯，相當標準。" ／ "两个菜一个汤，相当标准。"

8. Lǔ predicts that his father will make rice and three dishes tonight.

What is the *pinyin* for "to predict"? _____ 預料 ／ 预料

Unit C

Post-Viewing Activities

Speaking

9. Make a list of the following items (write in *pinyin* and/or characters):

your three favorite Chinese dishes   *your three favorite non-Chinese dishes*

_____   _____

_____   _____

_____   _____

10. Work with your classmates and your teacher to determine the most popular dishes among the people in your class. Write in *pinyin* and/or characters.

Chinese dishes   *non-Chinese dishes*

_____   _____

_____   _____

_____   _____

_____   _____

_____   _____

_____   _____

_____   _____

Lesson 12

Sample dishes named by students

Chinese dishes

tiánsuānròu, gūlǎoròu 甜酸肉，咕噜肉 *sweet-sour pork*

jiǎozi 餃子 / 饺子 *dumplings; gyoza*

guōtiē 鍋貼 / 锅贴 *pan-fried dumplings; pot stickers*

zhájiàngmiàn 炸醬麵 / 炸酱面 *noodles in stir-fried bean sauce*

hóngshāo páigǔ 紅燒排骨 / 红烧排骨 *red-cooked rib segments*

gānchǎo niúhé 乾炒牛河 / 干炒牛河 *stir-fried beef with rice noodles*

chǎofàn 炒飯 / 炒饭 *fried rice*

mápó dòufu 麻婆豆腐 *stir-fried tofu in hot sauce; Grandma's tofu*

yúxiāng ròusī 魚香肉絲 / 鱼香肉丝 *stir-fried pork in garlic sauce*

yúxiāng qiézi 魚香茄子 / 鱼香茄子 *stir-fried eggplant in garlic sauce*

hóngshāoròu 紅燒肉 / 红烧肉 *red-cooked pork; stewed pork*

kǎoyā 烤鴨 / 烤鸭 *roast duck*

shuànyángròu 涮羊肉 *lamb hot pot*

húndùntāng 餛飩湯 / 馄饨汤 *dumpling soup; wonton soup*

suānlàtāng 酸辣湯 / 酸辣汤 *hot-sour soup*

non-Chinese dishes

BBQ kǎoniúròu BBQ烤牛肉 *barbequed beef*

hànbǎobāo 漢堡包 / 汉堡包 *hamburger*

huǒjī 火雞 / 火鸡 *turkey*

bǐsàbǐng, Yìdàlì ròubǐng 比薩餅 / 比萨饼；意大利肉餅 / 意大利肉饼 *pizza*

shālā 沙拉 *salad*

huāshēngjiàng jiā guǒjiàng sānmíngzhì 花生醬加果醬三明治 / 花生酱加果酱三
   明治 *peanut butter and jelly sandwich*

Hánguó pàocài 韓國泡菜 / 韩国泡菜 *kimchee; Korean pickled cabbage*

Yìdàlì miàntiáo, Yìdàlì fěn 意大利麵條 / 意大利面条；意大利粉 *spaghetti*

Unit C

11. Write some notes on what would constitute either 1) a typical or 2) an ideal meal for you. Name at least 3–4 items.

12. Speak to at least three of your classmates. Describe your meal to them (using complete and fluent sentences!). Take notes on what they tell you. See if any of them have any overlaps in favorite dishes/foods with you, in the meal they describe to you. Take notes below.

classmate 1	classmate 2	classmate 3

13. Report back to the class on your findings.

Lesson 12

Sample student statements (delivered orally)

Wǒ zuì xǐhuan chī tiánsuān ròu. Zài yào yī wǎn fàn, yīdianr Hánguó pàocài, jiù gòu le. Yīnwèi chá yǒuyīdianr kǔ, suǒyǐ wǒ zhǐ yào hē shuǐ.

Měi tiān chī liǎng ge cài, yī ge tāng, shì xiāngdāng biāozhǔn de. Yī ge ròu cài, yī ge qīngcài, hái yào yī wǎn mǐfàn zuì hǎo. Wǒ tiāntiān dōu yào chī mǐfàn. Ránhòu shénme cài dōu xíng, kěshì wǒ bù xǐhuan chī là de.

*Rúguǒ wǒ chī Zhōngguócài, nàme mǐfàn hěn zhòngyào. Ránhòu, wǒ yào niúròu. Rúguǒ méiyǒu niúròu, wǒ bù gòu chī. Wǒ zuì xǐhuan hóngshāo niúròu, yīnwèi shì xiánxián làlà de. Fàn hòu, shuǐguǒ hěn zhòngyào, yīnwèi chī le niúròu yǐhòu wǒ xǐhuān chī tián de dōngxi.
Rúguǒ bù chī Zhōngguócài, nàme wǒ zuì xǐhuan chī sān ge hànbǎobāo, yī dà bēi Kěkǒu kělè.*

Unit C

Reading / Writing

14. Following is a message from Xiǎo Wáng to Xiǎo Lǐ. Highlight what you can understand of it.

小李：

　　你好！明天是小张的生日，我准备在宿舍的厨房为他搞一个生日聚会，欢迎你参加。聚会大约明晚七点开始，九点结束，不会占用大家太多时间，因为我知道大家最近都在忙著期中考试。我已经定了生日蛋糕，我们每个人再做一道自己最拿手的菜，就够了。

　　小黄要做宫爆鸡丁，小陈要做鱼香肉丝，小曹要做糖醋排骨，老何要做酸辣汤。我呢，会做的菜太多了，还没决定做哪种，你能给我点建议吗？我会做油焖大虾、清蒸桂鱼、红烧肉和菠菜豆腐。

　　请留张条子告诉我，你明天来不来，希望我做哪道菜，还有你准备做什么菜，好吗？注意保密，我想给他一个惊喜！

小王

即日　下午三点

15. Based on what you have highlighted, answer the following questions.

Xiǎo Wáng is trying to organize a _____.

It is set for the following day and times: _____.

Xiǎo Wáng wants Xiǎo Lǐ to do four things:

1. come to the event,

2. bring a _____,

3. give Xiǎo Wáng some advice about _____,

4. and respond to the note.

Lesson 12

16. Match the following English and Chinese terms.

_____ 準備 / 准备	_____ 結束 / 结束	_____ 建議 / 建议
_____ 宿舍	_____ 占用	_____ 油燜大蝦 / 油焖大虾
_____ 廚房 / 厨房	_____ 期中考試 / 期中考试	_____ 清蒸桂魚 / 清蒸桂鱼
_____ 爲他 / 为他	_____ 蛋糕	_____ 紅燒肉 / 红烧肉
_____ 搞	_____ 拿手的菜	_____ 菠菜豆腐 / 菠菜豆腐
_____ 聚會 / 聚会	_____ 宮爆雞丁 / 宫爆鸡丁	_____ 留張條子 / 留张条子
_____ 歡迎 / 欢迎	_____ 魚香肉絲 / 鱼香肉丝	_____ 注意
_____ 參加 / 参加	_____ 糖醋排骨	_____ 保密
_____ 大約 / 大约	_____ 酸辣湯 / 酸辣汤	_____ 驚喜 / 惊喜
_____ 開始 / 开始	_____ 決定 / 决定	_____ 即日

a. yóumèn dàxiā _prawns braised in oil_
b. jùhuì _get-together, gathering_
c. huānyíng _welcome_
d. qīngzhēng guìyú _steamed mandarin fish_
e. bǎomì _keep secret_
f. jīngxǐ _(happy) surprise_
g. jírì _today, this day_
h. hóngshāoyú _red-cooked fish_
i. bōcài dòufu _spinach with tofu_
j. cānjiā _participate_
k. dàyuē _approximately, about_
l. kāishǐ _begin_
m. jiéshù _end_
n. zhànyòng _take up, occupy_
o. qīzhōng kǎoshì _midterm test_
p. dàngāo _cake_

q. zhǔnbèi _prepare_
r. sùshè _dormitory_
s. chúfáng _kitchen_
t. wèi tā _for him, on his behalf_
u. gǎo _make, arrange_
v. náshǒu de cài _dish one is best at making_
w. gōngbào jīdīng _chicken cubes flash-fried in the palace style_
x. yúxiāng ròusī _pork slivers with garlic sauce_
y. tángcù páigǔ _sweet-sour ribs_
z. suānlàtāng _hot-sour soup_
aa. juédìng _decide_
ab. jiànyì _suggest, recommend_
ac. liú zhāng tiáozi _leave a note_
ad. zhùyì _notice, pay attention to_

17. Now re-read the note, and, as best you can, write a response to it.

小王：

明天的聚會我怎麼能不來呢？因為你跟小張是我最好的朋友。

你做的菜，我沒有一個不喜歡。你做哪個都好，一定很好吃。我們一定會很喜歡吃的。請你多做幾個吧！

我呢，我不會做菜。這個你知道了！我會帶一個大比薩餅來給大家吃。

好。明天見！

C orey

小王：

明天我會去。謝謝！我也不會告訴小張明天有聚會。

你寫的菜我沒吃過。不能給你建議。對不起。

我買巧克力冰淇淋帶來，好嗎？

老方

小王：

我一定來！因為我吃素，希望你做一個素菜，所以我建議你做菠菜豆腐。可以嗎？

我做一個蠔油生菜。

安安

Lesson 12

問：你估計你們今天晚上大概會吃甚麼菜呢？

徐：這個變化無常，不知道。

問：昨天晚上吃的甚麼呢？

徐：昨天晚上吃的是油菜和排骨，就沒了。兩菜一湯，相當標準。

呂：我預料今天我爸會給我做米飯，然後，還有，還有蒿子桿兒（笑），還有蘑菇，還有排骨，沒了。

问：你估计你们今天晚上大概会吃什么菜呢？

徐：这个变化无常，不知道。

问：昨天晚上吃的什么呢？

徐：昨天晚上吃的是油菜和排骨，就没了。两菜一汤，相当标准。

吕：我预料今天我爸会给我做米饭，然后，还有，还有蒿子杆儿（笑），还有蘑菇，还有排骨，没了。

Wèn: Nǐ gūjì nǐmen jīntiān wǎnshang dàgài huì chī shénme cài ne?

Xú: Zhège biànhuà-wúcháng, bù zhīdào.

Wèn: Zuótiān wǎnshang chī de shénme ne?

Xú: Zuótiān wǎnshang chī de shì yóucài hé páigǔ, jiù méi le. Liǎng cài yī tāng, xiāngdāng biāozhūn.

Lǚ: Wǒ yùliào jīntiān wǒ bà huì gěi wǒ zuò mǐfàn, ránhòu, háiyǒu, háiyǒu hāozigǎnr (xiào), háiyǒu mógu, háiyǒu páigǔ, méi le.

Interviewer: What dishes do you think you'll probably be eating tonight?

Xú: That changes constantly. I don't know.

Interviewer: What did you eat last night, then?

Xú: Last night we ate canola greens and ribs, and that was it. Two dishes and a soup; pretty standard.

Lǚ: I predict my dad will cook rice for me, and then, also, also artemesia greens *(laughs)*, and also mushrooms, and also ribs, that's it.

Unit C

202

Unit C: Handling Meals

Lesson 13:

Ordering in a
Chinese Restaurant (1)

Péng Qióng takes Robyn Yee, Todd Pavel, and James Yao to lunch at a local restaurant.

Previewing Activities

1. Do you think Péng Qióng will order for everyone, or will each person at lunch order a dish? Check one:

☐ Péng Qióng orders   ☐ each person orders

2. How <u>many</u> of each of the following do you think they'll order? Write a number in the box:

☐ vegetable dishes   ☐ meat dishes   ☐ servings of rice

3. Which of the following do you think they'll order as well? Check all that apply:

☐ soup   ☐ dessert   ☐ drinks

First Viewing: Global Information

4. Confirm the predictions you made above.

Did Péng Qióng order for everyone, or did each person at lunch order a dish? Check one:

☐ Péng Qióng ordered   ☐ each person ordered

5. How <u>many</u> of each of the following did they order? Write a number in the box:

☐ vegetable dishes   ☐ meat dishes   ☐ servings of rice

6. Which of the following did they order as well? Check all that apply:

☐ soup   ☐ dessert   ☐ drinks

Second Viewing: Specific Information

7. Who ordered each of the following dishes?

	Péng	Robyn	Todd	James	everyone	no one
appetizers						
spicy tofu						
hot-sour stir-fried potato slivers						
mushrooms and canola greens						
stir-fried bean sprouts						
snow peas with garlic						
wood ears and bamboo shoots						
hot-sour soup						
garlic pork slivers						
fish with pickled Ch. cabbage						
fatty pork with preserved veg.						
drinks						

Third Viewing: Linguistic Information

8. How does Péng Qióng address the waitress? Write in *pinyin:*_____

Unit C

9. The waitress responds by saying, "Uh-huh. How do you do! What dishes do you think you would like?" Fill in the blanks:

"Ài! Nín haǒ _____! Kànkan_____ shénme cài?"

"哎！您好幾位！看看需要甚麼菜？" ／ "哎！您好几位！看看需要什么菜？"

10. Péng Qióng says, "Let's take a look at this menu." How does she say this in Chinese? Write *pinyin* and/or characters.

_____

11. The waitress tells them they do not need to order appetizers (since these come as a set). She suggests that they just order the hot (main) dishes. Write the Chinese for the following terms in this exchange:

to order _____   hot dishes _____

appetizers (cold dishes) _____

12. How does Péng Qióng ask the waitress to repeat what she said?

"Qǐng nǐ _____, hǎo ma?"

"請你再說一遍，好嗎？" ／ "请你再说一遍，好吗？"

13. After the waitress repeats what she said, Péng Qióng says, "Oh, let's do this, then. What kind of flavors do you like in your dishes?" Fill in the blanks:

"O, _____. Nǐmen xǐhuan chī shénme _____ de cài ne?

"哦，這樣。你們喜歡吃甚麼口味的菜呢？" ／

"哦，这样。你们喜欢吃什么口味的菜呢？"

14. Which of the following flavors does Todd mention next? Check as appropriate.

甜 tián *sweet*	
酸 suān *sour*	
苦 kǔ *bitter*	
辣 là *spicy*	
鹹 / 咸 xián *salty*	

Lesson 13

15. Péng Qióng says that "Mápó dòufu" (variously translated in the US as "Grandma's tofu," "Spicy tofu," "Mapo bean curd," "The Pockmarked Old Woman's Bean curd"; tradition holds that the creator of the dish was a woman who had once suffered from smallpox) is a very good dish. What measure word does she use for the noun "dish"? _____

16. Next, Péng Qióng asks James to select a dish. What is the term for "to select"?

_____ (選擇 / 选择)

17. Robyn asks for a vegetable dish. The waitress says they have many, such as ... (she names several dishes). What word does she use to indicate "such as"?

_____ (像)

18. Rearrange the following phrases to construct a sentence meaning, "We have lots of vegetable dishes, such as stir-fried bean sprouts (清炒豆苗 / 清炒豆苗) and canola greens with mushrooms (香菇油菜)."

香菇油菜 / 香菇油菜   很多青菜 / 很多青菜   像

_____   _____   _____

清炒豆苗 / 清炒豆苗   我們有 / 我们有   還有 / 还有

_____   _____   _____

19. Robyn chooses "the third (dish)." Péng Qióng asks the waitress, "The third one you mentioned just now was ..." What is the term for "just now"? _____

20. Eventually, Péng Qióng says, "Well then, let's have a hot-sour soup." Fill in the blank.

"Nà jiù _____ ge suānlà tāng."

21. In trying to decide on which dish she wants to order, Péng Qióng uses a synonym for 青菜 / 青菜. What is it? Write the *pinyin:* _____ (蔬菜 / 蔬菜).

Unit C

22. Again the waitress asks what flavor/style of cooking Péng Qióng prefers. What does she say? Fill in the blank: "Nǐ xǐhuan chī shénme _____ de?" Then rearrange the following phrases to construct the sentence:

甚麼 / 什么   吃   喜歡 / 喜欢   的   你   口味

_____   _____   _____   _____   _____   _____

23. Péng Qióng decides to order a meat dish. Fill in the vocabulary chart below with the missing items, based on what she says and what you know.

English	*pinyin*	漢字 / 汉字
meat dish		
vegetable dish		蔬菜

24. Péng Qióng searches her memory for the name of a famous Beijing dish. What term does she use to denote "famous"? Write in *pinyin* _____ [著名 / 著名]

The waitress' response is, "It's garlic pork, I suppose?" Fill in the blank using *pinyin*.

"Yúxiāng ròusī _____?"

Note: 魚香 / 鱼香 literally means "fish fragranced = fish flavored"; in actuality any dish cooked in "fish flavored" style is liberally seasoned with garlic. 肉絲 / 肉丝 literally means "meat threads." However, *ròu* by itself refers to pork; other meats are marked by the name of the animal as well, eg: 牛肉 *niúròu* beef, and 雞肉 / 鸡肉 *jīròu* chicken. *Sī* (threads) refers to meat cut into thin slivers. Thus, *ròusī* are "pork slivers."

25. Péng Qióng asks, "What is (the dish) called that has that sour Chinese cabbage on the bottom?" Fill in the blanks.

"Yǒu nèige suāncài zài xiàmian _____ nèige _____ shénme?"

Rearrange the words and phrases below to form this sentence.

那個   那個   甚麼 / 什么   酸菜 / 酸菜   下面   的   叫   在   有

_____   _____   _____   _____   _____   _____

26. The waitress guesses again.

Fill in the blank, using <u>English</u>: "Pickled cabbage _____?"

What is the name of this dish in Chinese? Write it in *pinyin* _____

27. What is the name of the dish Péng Qióng actually orders? Fill in the blanks, using *pinyin*.

      Méi_____ kòu_____ [梅菜扣肉]

Literally, 梅菜 *méicài* means "plum vegetables," or by extension "Chinese cabbage preserved with salt and spices in the style of salted plums." 扣 *kòu* is a verb meaning "to turn upside down, to upend," which refers to the style of cooking: thick slices of seasoned fatty pork [肉] are placed on the bottom of a pot and covered with *méicài* to cook. To serve, the pot is upended onto a serving plate, so that the pork appears on the top.

In describing this dish, Péng Qióng says:

你可以嚐一嚐。它雖然有很多的肥肉和瘦肉在一起，
但是你吃的時候很香，一點都不覺得油膩。／
你可以尝一尝。它虽然有很多的肥肉和瘦肉在一起，
但是你吃的时候很香，一点都不觉得油腻。

28. First, fill in the blanks in the *pinyin*:

Nǐ kěyǐ cháng yī cháng. Tā _____ yǒu hěn duō de _____ hé shòuròu zài _____, dànshi nǐ chī de shíhou hěn _____, yī diǎnr dōu bù yóunì.

29. Now, fill in the blanks in the English:

You can have a _____. Although there is a lot of fat together with the _____ meat, still, when you eat it (it's) really _____. You won't find it at all greasy.

30. The waitress ends the exchange by saying, "Just a moment, then ..." which is a very common way to end the conversation when a request for service has been made. Literally, the phrase means, "Slightly wait one while, oh." Fill in the blanks in the *pinyin*:

      "Shāo _____ yì _____, a."

      稍等一會，啊／稍等一会，啊。

31. Reorder the words below to obtain another way to say the same thing:

      下   等   稍   一

      _____   _____   _____   _____

Unit C

Speaking

Food stalls

32. Break into groups of 3–4 persons each. Half the groups are "A" and the other half are "B."

√ The "A"s are food concession operators: In your small group, decide on ten dishes you will offer that are most likely to "sell." List them below in the space marked #1. Work with your teammates and learn how to say at least one descriptive sentence about each dish.

√ The "B"s are customers. Get together and decide on what an ideal meal for you would consist of: what starch, how many dishes, what kind of dishes (vegetable? meat? what style of cooking? spicy? salty? sweet?). List these characteristics below in the space marked #1. Also list 4–5 dishes as examples of what you might like to have.

√ Check to record which group you in.   ☐ I am "A"; I sell food.

                                                             ☐ I am "B"; I am buying food.

√ Next, regroup so that at least one "A" works with at least one "B." If you are a customer, ask what the concessionaire has to offer, and negotiate an acceptable meal. Write the specifics of that meal in the space marked #2. If you are a concessionaire, find out what your customer would like, and do your best to meet their needs. In the space marked #2, write the specifics of what the customer will be buying from you.

√ Report the result of your transaction to the class.

#1	#2

Lesson 13

Useful vocabulary suggested by students

Condiments, ingredients

胡椒 hújiāo *black pepper*

辣椒 làjiāo *hot red pepper*

醋 cù *vinegar*

醬油 / 酱油 jiàngyóu *soy sauce*

糖 táng *sugar*

鹽 / 盐 yán *salt*

蒜 / 蒜 suàn *garlic*

蔥頭 / 葱头，洋蔥 / 洋葱 cōngtóu, yángcōng *onion*

姜 jiāng *ginger*

海鮮 / 海鲜 hǎixiān *seafood*

More names of favorite dishes

宮爆雞丁 / 宫爆鸡丁 gōngbào jīdīng
stir-fried chicken with hot pepper

糖醋排骨 tángcù páigǔ *sweet-sour spareribs*

油燜大蝦 / 油焖大虾 yóumèn dàxiā *oil-braised prawns*

清蒸桂魚 / 清蒸桂鱼 qīngzhēng guìyú *steamed salmon*

乾扁四季豆 / 干扁四季豆 gānbiān sìjìdòu *stir-fried string beans*

Unit C

33. Imagine that you are Tom Chang, studying at a PRC university. Your roommate has left you the following note and menu. Skim through both, and highlight what you can understand.

张汤姆：

　　你好！欢迎你们美国同学们来到中国学习、访问。我准备明晚七点在京都酒店请你们吃顿便饭，为你们接风洗尘。那家酒店的菜是纯正的北京风味，我想你们既然是来了解中国文化的，那么就从了解中国的饮食文化开始吧！因此，我附上了一份酒店的菜单，请你们自己先试著点菜。如果你们想全面地了解中国人的饮食习惯，我建议你们最好凉菜、热菜、汤、粥、主食和饮料每样都点一些，尝一尝。

　　不过，了解是一回事，能否接受是另一回事，不知你们的口味如何，在饮食上有无特别的禁忌。珍妮点了酸辣黄瓜，比尔点了麻辣鸡丝，莫妮卡点了酸辣汤，看来他们都爱吃辣的。你也能吃辣的吗？

　　请留张便条告诉我，你想点哪些菜，喜欢什么口味的菜，饮食上有没有什么禁忌。如果你对菜单有什么不懂的地方，也请告诉我。我很喜欢跟别人讨论任何关于吃的问题。

王小明

即日　下午三点半

菜单

凉菜

一。皮蛋豆腐....¥15

二。酸辣黄瓜....¥15

三。泡菜.......¥12

四。炸花生米....¥10

五。卤凤爪.....¥11

热菜

一。麻辣鸡丝....¥25

二。北京烤鸭....¥45

三。红烧鲤鱼....¥50

四。滑溜里脊....¥45

五。铁板牛柳....¥45

六。梅菜扣肉....¥45

七。孜然羊肉....¥60

八。回锅肉.....¥25

九。香芋牛腩煲..¥45

十。油焖大虾....¥50

十一。冬笋蘑菇..¥30

十二。清炒蒜苗..¥35

十三。鱼香茄子..¥30

十四。蚝油生菜..¥25

十五。油炸臭豆腐¥25

汤

一。西湖牛肉羹....¥15

二。酸辣汤.......¥13

三。西红柿鸡蛋汤..¥11

四。紫菜肉丝汤....¥15

五。菠菜豆腐汤....¥13

粥

一。皮蛋瘦肉粥....¥3

二。八宝粥.......¥5

三。紫米粥.......¥3

四。绿豆粥.......¥4

五。鱼片粥.......¥3

主食

一。饺子（半斤）..¥20

二。米饭.........¥3

三。馅饼.........¥8

四。面条.........¥5

五。馒头.........¥2

饮料

一。青岛啤酒......¥8

二。八宝茶.......¥6

三。矿泉水.......¥6

四。果汁.........¥6

Unit C

34. Consider the note first, and fill in the blanks below.

Wáng Xiǎomíng is inviting you to dinner. When? _____

Where?_____

He asks you to write him a note back. What does he want you to tell him?

1. _____

2. _____

3. _____

35. Now consider the menu. List five items you would consider ordering. Next to each, write in English what you think each of these items are. Share your list with your classmates.

1. _____

2. _____

3. _____

4. _____

5. _____

36. Match the following Chinese terms with their glosses.

_____訪問 / 访问   a. liáojiě *understand*

_____準備 / 准备   b. wénhuà *culture*

_____京都   c. yǐnshí *food and drink*

_____頓   d. kāishǐ *begin*

_____便飯 / 便饭   e. jīngdū *capital city*

_____接風洗塵 / 接风洗尘   f. dùn *(measure word for a meal)*

_____純正 / 纯正   g. biànfàn *a simple meal*

_____風味 / 风味   h. jiēfēng-xǐchén *welcome to town*

_____既然   i. fǎngwèn *visit*

_____了解   j. zhǔnbèi *prepare to*

_____文化   k. chúnzhèng *pure, unadulterated*

_____飲食 / 饮食   l. fēngwèi *taste and style of food*

_____開始 / 开始   m. jìrán *since*

_____因此   n. yīncǐ *because of this*

Lesson 13

_____附上

_____試著 / 试著

_____點菜 / 点菜

_____如果

_____全面地

_____飲食習慣 / 饮食习惯

_____建議 / 建议

_____涼菜 / 凉菜

_____熱菜 / 热菜

_____粥

_____主食

_____嘗一嘗 / 尝一尝

_____一回事

_____能否

_____接受

_____另一回事

_____如何

_____有無 / 有无

_____特別

_____禁忌

_____珍妮

_____酸辣黃瓜

_____比爾 / 比尔

_____麻辣雞絲 / 麻辣鸡丝

_____莫妮卡 / 莫妮卡

_____便條 / 便条

_____討論 / 讨论

_____任何

_____關于 / 关于

_____敬上

_____即日

o. jiànyì *suggest*

p. liángcài *appetizer (cold plate)*

q. rècài *main courses (hot food)*

r. zhōu *congee, rice gruel*

s. fùshàng *attach, append*

t. shìzhe *try to*

u. diǎncài *order dishes*

v. rúguǒ *if*

w. quánmiàn de *complete, comprehensive*

x. zhǔshí *staple (starch)*

y. cháng yī cháng *have a taste*

z. yī huí shì *one matter*

aa. yǒuwú *have or not*

ab. tèbié *special*

ac. jìnjì *taboo, abstinence*

ad. Zhēnní *Jenny*

ae. suānlà huángguā *pickled cucumbers*

af. Bǐ'ěr *Bill*

ag. néngfǒu *able to or not*

ah. jiēshòu *tolerate, accept*

ai. lìng yī huí shì *a different matter*

aj. rúhé *how*

ak. málà jīsī *peppery chicken slivers*

al. Mòníkǎ *Monica*

am. biàntiáo *a note*

an. tǎolùn *discuss*

ao. jìngshàng *respectfully present*

ap. jírì *this day, today*

aq. rènhé *any*

ar. guānyú *concerning*

as. yǐnshí xíguàn *habits in food and drink*

Unit C

37. Re-read the note with the help of the vocabulary list. Highlight everything you can understand this time.

38. Following are the items appearing on the menu. Fill in the blanks.

皮蛋豆腐　pídàn dòufu ＿＿＿＿＿＿＿ *with preserved eggs*

酸辣黄瓜　suānlà huángguā　*pickled (hot & ＿＿＿＿＿＿＿) cucumbers*

泡菜／泡菜　pàocài　*pickled vegetables*

炸花生米　zhá huāshēngmǐ ＿＿＿＿＿＿＿ *peanuts*

滷鳳爪／卤凤爪　lǔ fèngzhǎo　*stewed chicken feet*

麻辣雞絲／麻辣鸡丝　málà jīsī ＿＿＿＿＿＿＿＿＿＿

北京烤鴨／北京烤鸭　Běijīng kǎoyā ＿＿＿＿＿＿＿＿＿＿

紅燒鯉魚／红烧鲤鱼　hóngshāo lǐyú　*red-cooked carp*

滑溜里脊　huáliū lǐjī　*flash-fried pork tenderloin*

鐵板牛柳／铁板牛柳　tiěbǎn niúliǔ　*beef on a sizzling platter*

梅菜扣肉／梅菜扣肉　méicài kòuròu ＿＿＿＿＿＿＿＿＿＿

孜然羊肉　zīrán yángròu　*cumin-flavored lamb*

回鍋肉／回锅肉　huíguōròu　*twice-cooked pork*

香芋牛腩煲　xiāngyù niúnán bǎo　*beef sirloin and taro stew*

油燜大蝦／油焖大虾　yóumèn dàxiā ＿＿＿＿＿＿＿＿＿＿

冬筍蘑菇／冬笋蘑菇　dōngsǔn mógu　*mushrooms with bamboo shoots*

清炒蒜苗／清炒蒜苗　qīngchǎo suànmiáo　*stir-fried garlic shoots*

魚香茄子／鱼香茄子　yúxiāng qiézi　*eggplant in ＿＿＿＿＿＿＿ sauce*

蠔油生菜／蚝油生菜　háoyóu shēngcài　*lettuce with oyster sauce*

油炸臭豆腐　yóuzhá chòudòufu　*deep-fried stinky (fermented) tofu*

西湖牛肉羹　Xīhú niúròugēng　*West Lake beef soup*

酸辣湯／酸辣汤　suānlàtāng ＿＿＿＿＿＿＿＿＿＿

西紅柿雞蛋湯／西红柿鸡蛋汤　xīhóngshì jīdàn tāng　*egg & tomato ＿＿＿＿*

紫菜肉絲湯／紫菜肉丝汤　zǐcài ròusī tāng　*seaweed & ＿＿＿＿＿＿＿*

菠菜豆腐湯／菠菜豆腐汤　bōcài dòufu tāng ＿＿＿＿＿＿＿＿＿＿

皮蛋瘦肉粥　pídàn shòuròu zhōu　*rice gruel with lean pork & ＿＿＿＿＿*

八寶粥／八宝粥　bābǎozhōu　*rice gruel with eight (sweet) ingredients*

紫米粥　zǐmǐzhōu　*purple rice gruel*

綠豆粥／绿豆粥　lùdòuzhōu　*green bean gruel*

魚片粥／鱼片粥　yúpiànzhōu　*rice gruel with slices of ＿＿＿＿＿*

餃子（半斤）／饺子（半斤）jiǎozi (bàn jīn)　*dumplings (gyoza; 250 grams)*

餡餅／馅饼　xiànrbǐng　*hotcakes filled with meat & vegetables*

麵條／面条　miàntiáo ＿＿＿＿＿＿＿＿＿＿

饅頭／馒头　mántou　*steamed buns*

青島啤酒／青岛啤酒　Qīngdǎo píjiǔ　*Tsingtao ＿＿＿＿＿＿＿*

八寶茶／八宝茶　bābǎochá　*tea with ＿＿＿＿＿＿＿＿＿＿*

礦泉水／矿泉水　kuàngquánshuǐ　*mineral water*

Lesson 13

39. List 10 items you might like to order from this menu.

_____

_____

_____

_____

_____

_____

_____

_____

_____

_____

40. Write a response to Wáng Xiǎomíng.

王小明：

你給我的菜單上的菜，我每樣都能吃，沒有甚麼禁忌，也很愛吃辣的。謝謝你請我們吃飯。你真是個有心人。明晚見。

馬克上

王小明：

麻辣鸡丝特别辣吗？要是有一点辣可是不太辣，我想尝一尝。还有，我很喜欢韩国泡菜，所以大概会喜欢酸辣黄瓜。我也想尝一尝回锅肉，可以吗？改天我请你去吃汉堡包！

李青

小王：我想點滷鳳爪、皮蛋豆腐、鐵板牛柳、北京烤鴨、菠菜豆腐湯、還有米飯。飲料明天再點。我飲食沒有甚麼禁忌，可是我很怕吃辣的。我比較喜歡吃鹹的。好，明天見吧。謝謝你請我們吃飯。

小劉

小明：你附上的菜单上的菜都很好。我没有不想尝的。你来点吧。然后我来猜每道是什么菜。好吗？

Jeannie

彭瓊： 小姐！

服務員： 哎！您好幾位！看看需要
甚麼菜？

彭瓊： 我們，看，看一下這個菜
單。

服務員： 就不用點涼菜了。涼菜我
們有，你就點熱菜吧，好嗎？

彭瓊： 哦，請你再說一遍，好嗎？

服務員： 哦，你點一下熱菜，看需
要甚麼熱菜。

彭瓊： 哦，這樣，你們喜歡吃甚麼
口味的菜呢？

彭德： 我喜歡吃辣的。

彭瓊： 噢，辣的，你覺得麻婆豆腐
怎麼樣？那個是很好的一道菜。

彭德： 啊，很好，很好。

彭瓊： 嗯，很好。

服務員： 要一個麻婆豆腐是嗎？

彭瓊： 嗯，一個麻婆豆腐。

服務員： 哎。

彭瓊： 哦，你可以來選擇一個菜嗎？

姚守正：我要吃，哦，酸辣土豆絲。

彭瓊： 酸辣土豆絲。（對余修明）
嗯，你想吃甚麼菜？

余修明：我喜歡吃青菜。

彭瓊： 吃青菜。嗯，好。

彭琼： 小姐！

服务员： 哎！您好几位！看看需要
什么菜？

彭琼： 我们，看，看一下这个菜
单。

服务员： 就不用点凉菜了。凉菜我
们有，你就点热菜吧，好吗？

彭琼： 哦，请你再说一遍，好吗？

服务员： 哦，你点一下热菜，看需
要什么热菜。

彭琼： 哦，这样，你们喜欢吃什么
口味的菜呢？

彭德： 我喜欢吃辣的。

彭琼： 噢，辣的，你觉得麻婆豆腐
怎么样？那个是很好的一道菜。

彭德： 啊，很好，很好。

彭琼： 嗯，很好。

服务员： 要一个麻婆豆腐是吗？

彭琼： 嗯，一个麻婆豆腐。

服务员： 哎。

彭琼： 哦，你可以来选择一个菜吗？

姚守正：我要吃，哦，酸辣土豆丝。

彭琼： 酸辣土豆丝。（对余修明）
嗯，你想吃什么菜？

余修明：我喜欢吃青菜。

彭琼： 吃青菜。嗯，好。

Unit C

Péng Qióng: Xiǎojiě!

Fúwùyuán: Ai! Nín hǎo jǐ wèi!
Kànkan xūyào shénme cài?

Péng Qióng: Wǒmen, kàn, kàn yīxia
zhège càidān.

Fúwùyuán: Jiù bùyòng diǎn liángcài le.
Liángcài wǒmen yǒu, nǐ jiù
diǎn rècài ba, hǎo me?

Péng Qióng: O, qǐng nǐ zài shuō
yībiàn hǎo ma?

Fúwùyuán: O, nǐ diǎn yīxià rècài,
kàn xūyào shénme rècài.

Péng Qióng: O, zhèyàng, nǐmen xǐhuan
chī shénme kǒuwèi de cài ne?

Péng Dé: Wǒ xǐhuan chī là de.

Péng Qióng: O, là de, nǐ juéde mápó
dòufu zěnmeyàng? Nàge shì hěn
hǎo de yī dào cài.

Péng Dé: A, hěn hǎo, hěn hǎo.

Péng Qióng: Nng, hěn hǎo.

Fúwùyuán: Yào yī ge mápó dòufu shì
ma?

Péng Qióng: Ng, yī ge mápó dòufu.

Fúwùyuán: Ai.

Péng Qióng: O, nǐ kěyǐ lái xuǎnzé yī
ge cài ma?

Yáo Shǒuzhèng: Wǒ yào chī, o, suānlà
tǔdòusī.

Péng Qióng: Suānlà tǔdòusī.
(Duì Yú Xiūmíng) Ng, nǐ xiǎng chī
shénme cài?

Yú Xiūmíng: Wǒ xǐhuan chī qīngcài.

Péng Qióng: Chī qīngcài. Ng, hǎo.

Peng Qiong: Miss!

Waitress: Yes. Hello, everyone!
What dishes do you think you'll
be wanting?

Peng Qiong: Let's, let's take a look at this
menu.

Waitress: You don't need to order
appetizers. We have those, just order
the main (hot) dishes, okay?

Peng Qiong: Oh, could you say that
again, please?

Waitress: Oh, just order the hot
dishes, see what hot dishes you'd like.

Peng Qiong: Oh, I see. So what are your
tastes in food?

Todd: I like spicy food.

Peng Qiong: Oh, spicy food. What do you
think of hot & spicy bean curd? That
is a very good dish.

Todd: Ah, very good, very good.

Peng Qiong: Uh-huh, great.

Waitress: So you'd like a hot &
spicy bean curd?

Peng Qiong: Uh-huh, a hot & spicy
bean curd.

Waitress: Okay.

Peng Qiong: Oh, can you pick a dish?

James: I'd like to have, er, hot & sour
potato slivers.

Peng Qiong: Hot & sour potato slivers.
(To Robyn) Mmm, what would you
like to eat?

Robyn: I like vegetables.

Peng Qiong: Vegetables. Mmm, fine.

Lesson 13

讓我來看一看哪有青菜。
請問小姐， 有青菜嗎？

服務員：有哇，你象香菇油菜，清
　　　　炒豆苗，蒜茸荷蘭豆，喜歡吃
　　　　嗎？蒜茸荷蘭豆，象冬筍木耳
　　　　…

彭瓊：這有很多的青菜，你 ... 比
　　　較喜歡吃哪，哪一種呢？

余修明：嗯，第三個。

彭瓊：好，你剛纔説的第三個是…

服務員：蒜茸，嗯，蒜茸荷蘭豆。

彭瓊：蒜茸荷蘭豆吧。我們是不
　　　是應該點一個湯？你們喜歡甚
　　　麼樣的湯？

姚守正：我喜歡酸辣湯。

彭瓊：酸辣湯？

彭德：我也喜歡。那，你呢？

彭瓊：酸辣湯你也喜歡嗎？

余修明（同時）：我也喜歡。

彭瓊：請問，有酸辣湯嗎？

服務員：有。

彭瓊：那就來個酸辣湯。還有我
　　　想應該是四碗米飯，對嗎？

彭德：對。你還沒決定，對不對？

彭瓊：What?

彭德：你吃甚麼？

让我来看一看哪有青菜。
请问小姐， 有青菜吗？

服务员：有哇，你象香菇油菜，清
　　　　炒豆苗，蒜茸荷兰豆，喜欢吃
　　　　吗？蒜茸荷兰豆，象冬笋木耳
　　　　…

彭琼： 这有很多的青菜，你 ... 比
　　　较喜欢吃哪，哪一种呢？

余修明：嗯，第三个。

彭琼：好，你刚才说的第三个是…

服务员：蒜茸，嗯，蒜茸荷兰豆。

彭琼：蒜茸荷兰豆吧。我们是不
　　　是应该点一个汤？你们喜欢什
　　　么样的汤？

姚守正：我喜欢酸辣汤。

彭琼：酸辣汤？

彭德：我也喜欢。那，你呢？

彭琼：酸辣汤你也喜欢吗？

余修明（同时）：我也喜欢。

彭琼：请问，有酸辣汤吗？

服务员：有。

彭琼：那就来个酸辣汤。还有我
　　　想应该是四碗米饭，对吗？

彭德：对。你还没决定，对不对？

彭琼：What?

彭德：你吃什么？

Unit C

Ràng wǒ lái kàn yi kàn nǎr yǒu qīngcài. Qǐngwèn xiǎojiě, yǒu qīngcài ma?

Fúwùyuán: Yǒu wa, nǐ xiàng xiānggū yóucài, qīngchǎo dòumiáo, suànróng hélándòu, xǐhuan chī ma? Suànróng hélándòu, xiàng dōngsǔn mùěr ...

Péng Qióng: Zhè yǒu hěn duō de qīngcài, nǐ...bǐjiào xǐhuan chī nǎ, nǎ yī zhǒng ne?

Yú Xiūmíng: Ng, dì-sān ge.

Péng Qióng: Hǎo, nǐ gāngcái shuō de dì-sān ge shì ...

Fúwùyuán: Suànróng, ng, suànróng hélándòu.

Péng Qióng: Suànróng hélándòu ba. Wǒmen shì bu shì yīnggāi diǎn yī ge tāng? Nǐmen xǐhuan shénmeyàng de tāng?

Yáo Shǒuzhèng: Wǒ xǐhuan suānlà tāng.

Péng Qióng: Suānlà tāng?

Péng Dé: Wǒ yě xǐhuan. Nà, nǐ ne?

Péng Qióng: Suānlà tāng nǐ yě xǐhuan ma?

Yú Xiūmíng (tóngshí): Wǒ yě xǐhuan.

Péng Qióng: Qǐngwèn, yǒu suānlà tāng ma?

Fúwùyuán: Yǒu.

Péng Qióng: Nà jiù lái ge suānlàtāng. Háiyǒu wǒ xiǎng yīnggāi shì sì wǎn mǐfàn, duì ma?

Péng Dé: Duì. Nǐ hái méi juédìng, duì bu duì?

Péng Qióng: What?

Péng Dé: Nǐ chī shénme?

Let me see where the vegetables are. Miss, may I ask, do you have vegetables?

Waitress: Of course, like rape greens with mushrooms, stir-fried bean sprouts, snow peas with garlic, do you like those? Snow peas with garlic, or bamboo shoots with fungus ...

Peng Qiong: They have a lot of vegetable dishes. Which, which dish would you prefer to eat?

Robyn: Mmm, the third one.

Peng Qiong: Okay, the third one you said just now was ...

Waitress: Garlic, mmm, snowpeas with garlic.

Peng Qiong: Snowpeas with garlic, then. We ought to order a soup, no? What kind of soup do you like?

James: I like hot-sour soup.

Peng Qiong: Hot-sour soup?

Todd: I like that too. And, how about you?

Peng Qiong: Do you like hot-sour soup too?

Robyn (concurrently): I like it too.

Peng Qiong: Do you have hot-sour soup, may we ask?

Waitress: Yes we do.

Peng Qiong: Then let's have a hot-sour soup. And then I think it's four bowls of rice, right?

Todd: Right. You haven't decided yet, right?

Peng Qiong: What?

Todd: What are you having?

Lesson 13

221

彭瓊：啊，對，對，對，我忘了。
　　　哦，我想我應該點個肉菜，因
　　　為你們大家點的都是蔬菜。小
　　　姐，請問您這兒有 ...
服務員：您喜歡吃甚麼口味的？
　　　　小姐？
彭瓊：我想北京有一個最著名的一
　　　個菜，應該是叫 ...
服務員：魚香肉絲吧？
彭瓊：不是，不是。酸，有那個酸
　　　菜在下面的那叫甚麼？
服務員：酸菜魚？
彭瓊：不是，是肉，叫 ... 上面是
　　　肉，肥肉，和，瘦肉有一點的。
服務員：哦，梅菜扣肉。
彭瓊：梅菜扣肉。對，對，對。有
　　　嗎？
服務員：就點梅菜扣肉是吧？
彭瓊：對，對，對。嗯，那個很好
　　　吃的，很著名的。在北京，很
　　　多人，外國來中國的時候都吃
　　　這個梅菜扣肉。你可以嚐一嚐，
　　　它雖然有很多的肥肉和瘦肉在
　　　一起，但是，嗯，你吃的時候
　　　很香，一點都不覺得油膩。

彭琼：啊，对，对，对，我忘了。
　　　哦，我想我应该点个肉菜，
　　　因为你们大家点的都是蔬
　　　菜。小姐，请问您这儿有 ...
服务员：您喜欢吃什么口味的？
　　　　小姐？
彭琼：我想北京有一个最著名的一
　　　个菜，应该是叫 ...
服务员：鱼香肉丝吧？
彭琼：不是，不是。酸，有那个酸
　　　菜在下面的那叫什么？
服务员：酸菜鱼？
彭琼：不是，是肉，叫 ... 上面是
　　　肉，肥肉，和，瘦肉有一点的。
服务员：哦，梅菜扣肉。
彭琼：梅菜扣肉。对，对，对。有
　　　吗？
服务员：就点梅菜扣肉是吧？
彭琼：对，对，对。嗯，那个很好
　　　吃的，很著名的。在北京，很
　　　多人，外国来中国的时候都吃
　　　这个梅菜扣肉。你可以一尝，
　　　它虽然有很多的肥肉和瘦肉在
　　　一起，但是，嗯，你吃的时候
　　　很香，一点都不觉得油腻。

Unit C

Péng Qióng: A, duì, duì, duì, wǒ wàng le.
O, wǒ xiǎng wǒ yīnggāi diǎn ge
ròucài, yīnwei nǐmen dàjiā diǎn de
dōu shì shūcài. Xiǎojie, qǐngwèn nín
zhèr yǒu ...

Fúwùyuán: Nín xǐhuān chī shénme
kǒuwèi de? Xiǎojie?

Péng Qióng: Wǒ xiǎng Běijīng yǒu yī ge
zuì zhùmíng de yī ge cài, yīnggāi
shì jiào ...

Fúwùyuán: Yúxiāng ròusī ba?

Péng Qióng: Bù shì, bù shì. Suān, yǒu
nàge suāncài zài xiàmian de nà jiào
shénme?

Fúwùyuán: Suāncài yú?

Péng Qióng: Bù shì, shì ròu, jiào...
shàngmian shì ròu, féiròu, hé,
shòuròu yǒu yīdiǎnr de.

Fúwùyuán: O, méicài kòuròu.

Péng Qióng: Duì, duì, duì. Méicài kòuròu.
Yǒu ma?

Fúwùyuán: Jiù diǎn méicài kòuròu shì ba?

Péng Qióng: Duì, duì, duì. N, nàge hěn
hǎochī de, hěn zhùmíng de. Zài
Běijīng, hěn duō rén, wàiguó lái
Zhōngguó de shíhou dōu chī zhège
méicài kòuròu. Nǐ kěyǐ cháng yī
cháng, tā suīrán yǒu hěn duō de
féiròu hé shòuròu zài yīqǐ, dànshì, n,
nǐ chī de shíhou hěn xiāng, yīdiǎnr
bù juéde yóunì.

Peng Qiong: Oh, right, right, right, I forgot.
Er, I think I'd better order a meat dish,
because what you have all ordered are
vegetable dishes. Miss, may I ask, do
you have ...

Waitress: What flavors do you like? Miss?

Peng Qiong: I think there's a famous
dish in Beijing, it's called ...

Waitress: Garlic pork?

Peng Qiong: No, no. Sour, what is the
dish that has sour cabbage on the
bottom called?

Waitress: Sour cabbage fish?

Peng Qiong: No, it's pork, it's called ...
on top there's pork, it's fatty pork
together with some lean pork.

Waitress: Oh, marbled pork with
pickled vegetables.

Peng Qiong: That's right, that's right.
Marbled pork with pickled vegetables.
Do you have it?

Waitress: Then you want a marbled
pork with pickled vegetables, right?

Peng Qiong: Right, right, right. Mmm,
that's very delicious, and very famous.
In Beijing, many people, when they
come from overseas to China, they'll
try this marbled pork with pickled
vegetables. You can try it, although
there's a lot of fatty meat together
with the lean meat, however, mmm,
when you taste it you'll find it
fragrant, you won't find it greasy at all.

Lesson 13

彭德：好。

彭瓊：嗯，可以試一下。

　　　還有四碗米飯，好嗎？

服務員：哎，請問還需要甚麼

　　　　飲料嗎？

彭瓊：我們已經點了湯，不要飲

　　　料了。

服務員：哎，好了。

彭瓊：好，謝謝。

服務員：稍等一會啊。

Péng Dé: Hǎo.

Péng Qióng: Nng, kěyǐ shìyixia.

　　　　　Háiyǒu sì wǎn mǐfàn, hǎo ma?

Fúwùyuán: Ai, qǐngwèn hái xūyào shénme

　　　　　yǐnliào ma?

Péng Qióng: Wǒmen yǐjīng diǎnle

　　　　　tāng, bù yào yǐnliào le.

Fúwùyuán: Ai, hǎo le.

Péng Qióng: Hǎo, xièxie.

Fúwùyuán: Shāo děng yīhuìr a.

彭德：好。

彭琼：嗯，可以试一下。

　　　还有四碗米饭，好吗？

服务员：哎，请问还需要什么

　　　　饮料吗？

彭琼：我们已经点了汤，不要饮

　　　料了。

服务员：哎，好了。

彭琼：好，谢谢。

服务员：稍等一会啊。

Todd: Okay.

Peng Qiong: Mmm. You can try it.

　　　　　And then we'll have four bowls of
　　　　　rice, okay?

Waitress: Uh-huh, may I ask, would
　　　　　you like something to drink?

Peng Qiong: We've ordered a soup, we
　　　　　don't need any drinks, then.

Waitress: Uh-huh, all right then.

Peng Qiong: Good. Thank you.

Waitress: It'll just be a while.

Unit C

Lesson 14:

Ordering in a Chinese Restaurant (2)

Péng Qióng and her girlfriend bike to a nearby restaurant to have lunch together.

Previewing Activity

1. What kind of food do you think they will have? Check one:

☐ Chinese (Zhōngcān) ☐ other Asian (qítā Yàzhōu) ☐ Western (Xīcān) ☐ other (qítā)

First Viewing: Global Information

2. Confirm the prediction you made above. What kind of food are they having?

_____

3. Who decided which restaurant to go to?

☐ Péng Qióng (彭瓊 / 彭琼) ☐ her friend (她朋友) ☐ both together (兩個人一起 / 两个人一起)

4. How many dishes did they order?

☐ one dish (一道) ☐ two dishes (兩道 / 两道) ☐ three dishes (三道) ☐ four dishes (四道)

5. When the waitress came back, what happened?

☐ one dish was canceled (jiǎnshǎo le yī dào cài)

☐ one dish was changed (huàn le yī dào cài)

☐ an additional dish was ordered (jiā le yī dào cài)

Second Viewing: Specific Information

6. Which of the two following chain restaurant was mentioned first? Check, then write the *pinyin* below:

☐ Teddy Bear's (A & W's).   ☐ McDonald's.

_____   _____

（愛德熊 / 爱德熊）   （麥當勞 / 麦当劳）

7. What is the name of the restaurant at which they end up eating? Fill in the blanks in *pinyin*.

_____ jü _____ _____ yä diàn

Rearrange the characters (by writing numbers in the blanks) to form the name of the restaurant:

店	聚	鴨 / 鸭	全	烤	德

8. Fill in the blanks using *pinyin* for the names of the dishes the friends <u>first</u> order:

_____ yā | |

_____ gū _____ xīn | |

jú _____ lǐjī | *pork* |

What is the main ingredient in each of these three dishes? Fill in the boxes above, right.

9. What drinks do they order? Match the item with the person:

(yēzi zhī 椰子汁 *coconut juice*)

(guǒchá 果茶 / 果茶 *hawthorne berry nectar*)

(kuàngquánshuǐ 礦泉水 / 矿泉水 *mineral water*)

(彭瓊 / 彭琼)

(朋友)

Unit C

10. When the waitress returns, she says that one dish is (check one):

[ ] not on the menu (*càidān shang méiyǒu*)   [ ] sold out (*màiwán le*)

11. Péng Qióng and her friend replace it with the following (fill in the blanks using *pinyin*):

_____ cù _____ jī (pork tenderloin fillet)

12. Check the flavors mentioned in this exchange:

甜 tián *sweet*	
酸 suān *sour*	
苦 kǔ *bitter*	
辣 là *spicy*	
鹹 / 咸 xián *salty*	

13. Waiting for the food to arrive, the friends chat about (check one):

[ ] friends (*péngyou*)   [ ] school work (*gōngkè*)   [ ] parents (*fùmǔ*)

14. When the first dish, *choysum* (greens) with Chinese mushrooms, is served, Péng Qióng says, "Let's eat" (Zánmen chī ba). Her friend asks, "Shall we eat for real?" (Or shall we *pretend* to eat, for the camera?) In Chinese, she asks (fill in the blanks using *pinyin* [and characters if you can]):

Zánmen _____ chī ma? 咱們_____ 吃嗎 / 咱们_____吃吗?

Péng Qióng replies, "Tàng! Xiǎoxīn! 燙 / 烫！小心！" which means (fill in the blank in English):   "It's _____! Be careful!"

15. Finally, when her friend asks if she can make this dish, Péng Qióng replies that she (circle one):

    can (*huì*)   cannot (*bù huì*)

Further, Péng Qióng says that the dish is, "for sure, perhaps not too _____."
(Fill in the blank in English.)

Lesson 14

Third Viewing: Linguistic Information

16. Match the Chinese with the English:

_____ "我已經餓了！ / 我已经饿了！"
     wǒ yǐjīng è le   "I'm almost dead of hunger!"

_____ "我早就餓了！ / 我早就饿了！"
     wǒ zǎo jiù è le   "I'm already hungry!"

_____ "我都快餓死了！ / 我都快饿死了！"
     wǒ dōu kuài èsi le   "I've been hungry for a long time now!"

17. Who says each of the utterances above?
Write 1 for Péng Qióng and 2 for her friend in the spaces above left.

18. What do you think the function of the 了 at the end of each sentence is? Check one:

[   ] indicates completed action

[   ] indicates a change of status

19. Using the terms 累 lèi *to be tired* and 睡覺 / 睡觉 shuìjiào *to sleep*, translate the sentences below following the model provided by Péng Qióng and her friend:

I'm already tired! _____

I've been wanting for a while now to go to sleep! _____

I'm so tired I'm almost dead! _____

20. How about using 煩 / 烦 fán *to be bored, to be sick of something* and 出去 chūqù *to go out*?

I'm already sick of this! _____

I've been wanting to go out for ages! _____

I'm dying of boredom! _____

Unit C

Note: "Oh, I'm dying of hunger" is loosely "我餓死了啊！/ 我饿死了啊！" where the 啊 at the end of the sentence is roughly equivalent to "oh." In colloquial speech, 了 le + 啊 a = 啦 la; thus, "我餓死啦！/ 我饿死啦！"

21. Péng Qióng says the following (fill in the blanks in the English):

不是吃烤鴨嗎？烤鴨也不錯。其實，我挺想吃那個愛德熊的 /
不是吃烤鸭吗？烤鸭也不错。其实，我挺想吃那个爱德熊的。

Bù shì chī kǎoyā ma? Kǎoyā yě bù cuò. Qíshí, wǒ tǐng xiǎng chī nèige Àidéxióng de.

Weren't we going to eat _____? Roast duck's not bad either. Actually, I'd rather

like to _____ at that _____.

22. Just for practice, write the following, using 去看電影 /去看电影 qù kàn diànyǐng and 呆在家裡 /呆在家里 dāi zài jiāli.

• Weren't we going to the movies?

_____

• Actually, I'd rather like to stay at home tonight.

_____

23. Péng Qióng asks two questions of her friend:

你去過愛德熊嗎／你去过爱德熊吗？ and
你以前來過這兒嗎／你以前来过这儿吗？

What is the function of 過 ? Check one of the following.

☐ It marks past experience.

☐ It marks completed action.

24. Ask the following questions in Chinese:

Have you ever had hot-sour soup? _____

Have you ever made roast duck? _____

Now answer these questions, based on your own situation.

(hot-sour soup):_____

(roast duck): _____

Lesson 14

25. Péng Qióng says of eating duck:

（我）好久沒吃了。 *I haven't had any for a long time now.*

Her friend replies (fill in the blank in the English):

我也好久沒吃了。我記得上次吃是一年前 /

我也好久没吃了。我记得上次吃是一年前。

I haven't had any for a long time now either.

I remember the last time I ate it was _____.

26. Now you say:

I haven't seen a movie in a long time now. The last time I saw one was a month ago.

_____]

27. Opposites: Match the English to the Chinese.

記得 / 记得 jìde **d**	<===>	忘了 wàng le **b**	a. *don't necessarily have to eat duck*
			√ b. *to forget*
肯定得吃鴨子 / 肯定得吃鸭子 kěndìng děi chī yāzi	<===>	不一定要吃鴨子 / 不一定要吃鸭子 bùyīdìng yào chī yāzi	c. *pretty relaxed*
			√ d. *to remember*
差不多了 chà bù duō le	<===>	還不夠 / 还不够 hái bù gòu	e. *not quite enough yet*
			f. *definitely have to eat duck*
挺緊張 / 挺紧张 tǐng jǐnzhāng	<===>	挺輕鬆 / 挺轻松 tǐng qīngsōng	g. *pretty tense, nervous*
			h. *that's about it (enough)*

Unit C

28. Think of three synonyms for "成嗎 / 成吗 chéng ma?"

可以嗎 / 可以吗		

29. The waitress says, on separate occasions:

☐ ☐ 請您稍等 / 请您稍等 Qǐn nín shāo děng.

☐ ☐ 對不起，打擾一下 / 对不起，打扰一下 Duìbuqǐ, dǎrǎo yīxia.

Match each of the following English expressions to the two Chinese expressions by writing a letter in the boxes above left.

    a. Sorry for the intrusion.

    b. This will take just a little while.

    c. If I could interrupt a moment ...

    d. Could you wait a while please, then ...

Post-Viewing Activities

Speaking

30. Try your luck.

Form pairs. Take out one coin between each pair. Each person should have paper and pen.
  A = the customer; B = the waitperson.

A begins by requesting a dish (choose any).
B flips the coin. Heads = the dish is available; tails = the dish is unavailable.

If heads, B repeats the order and notes it down. (A notes the order as well.) If tails, B explains why the dish is not available, and suggests something similar to replace it. If A accepts the suggestion, B (and A) note the order. Continue until A and B have agreed on four dishes that are "available."

Report your order to the class.

Lesson 14

31. Guided dialogue.

Break into pairs, and role-play the following exchange. (Pick one role, and cover up your classmate's instructions.)

甲 :	Say you've gotten very hungry.	乙 :	Ask where your partner would like to eat.
甲 :	Ask what your partner feels like eating.	乙 :	Say that anything would be fine.
甲 :	Suggest a fast food restaurant.	乙 :	Say that you'd actually like to have some roast duck.
甲 :	Say that roast duck would be fine by you too.	乙 :	Suggest a restaurant where you can have some roast duck.
甲 :	Ask if your partner has ever eaten there before.	乙 :	Say you often eat there. Ask if your partner has eaten there before.
甲 :	Say the last time you ate there was a year ago.	乙 :	Say something complimentary about the restaurant.
甲 :	Ask if your partner remembers what his or her favorite dishes at that restaurant are.	乙 :	Say "of course"; name 4–5 dishes, including roast duck.
甲 :	Say you'll definitely have to try those dishes.	乙 :	Say there's only two of you, so you don't have to order ALL of them.
甲 :	Say but you'll definitely try some.	乙 :	Agree.
甲 :	Suggest that you be on your way, then.	乙 :	Offer to pay for the meal.
甲 :	Say, "No, no, no, no ..."	乙 :	Insist.
甲 :	Suggest that you'll decide later. (Yǐhòu zài shuō ba.)	乙 :	Insist.

Unit C

Reading / Writing

32. Someone has left you the following recipe, written in both traditional and simplified Chinese. Scan through it and highlight what you can understand of it.

麻婆豆腐

- 豆腐（硬）一盒
- 蔥末一大匙／葱末一大匙
- 蒜末一小匙／蒜末一小匙
- 薑末一小匙／姜末一小匙
- 絞肉四兩／绞肉四两
- 辣豆瓣醬一大匙／辣豆瓣酱一大匙
- 料酒一大匙

- 醬油一大匙／酱油一大匙
- 水一杯
- 油三大匙
- 太白粉一小匙、水一大匙，攪在一起／太白粉一小匙、水一大匙，搅在一起
- 鹽、花椒粉各少許／盐、花椒粉各少许

1. 把豆腐切成半寸方塊。
2. 燒熱油三大匙。炒香蔥、蒜、薑末。
3. 放進絞肉及辣豆瓣醬拌炒幾秒。
4. 加料酒、醬油、水及豆腐。等燒開後改小火煮約三分鐘。
5. 放進水加太白粉，構成薄汁。灑下鹽、花椒粉。

1. 把豆腐切成半寸方块。
2. 烧热油三大匙。炒香葱、蒜、姜末。
3. 放进绞肉及辣豆瓣酱拌炒几秒。
4. 加料酒、酱油、水及豆腐。等烧开后改小火煮约三分钟。
5. 放进水加太白粉，构成薄汁。洒下盐、花椒粉。

Lesson 14

233

33. Fill in the blanks in the following English version of the recipe, based on the Chinese.

Mapo Bean Curd

(literally: the tofu dish invented by the old woman with the pockmarked face)

•Tofu (firm) 1 box
•chopped green onion 1 tablespoon
•chopped garlic 1 teaspoon
•chopped ginger 1 _____
•ground pork 4 ounces
•hot bean paste 1 _____
•cooking wine 1 _____
•_____ 1 tablespoon
•_____ 1 _____
•oil 3 _____
•cornstarch 1 _____, _____ 1 tablespoon, mixed together
•pinch each of salt and pepper

1. Cut the _____ into 1/2 inch squares.
2. Heat the _____. Stir-fry the _____, _____, and _____ till fragrant.
3. Add the _____ and the _____, stir-fry a few seconds.
4. Add the _____, _____, _____ and _____. Bring to a boil, then cook over low heat for _____.
5. Add the cornstarch mixture to thicken. Sprinkle on the _____ and _____, and the dish is done.

34. Match the items below.

____ ____ 麻	1. yìng	a. old woman
____ ____ 婆	2. mò	b. green onion
____ ____ 硬	3. pó	c. garlic
____ ____ 盒	4. chí	d. box
____ ____ 蔥／葱	5. suàn	e. pockmarked
____ ____ 末	6. jiāng	f. powder, ground substance
____ ____ 匙	7. cōng	g. spoon
____ ____ 蒜／蒜	8. jiǎoròu	h. firm, hard
____ ____ 薑／姜	9. má	i. ginger
____ ____ 絞肉／绞肉	10. hé	j. ground pork

Unit C

_____ _____ 辣豆瓣醬 / 辣豆瓣酱   11. huājiāofěn   _k. salt_

_____ _____ 料酒   12. shǎoxǔ   _l. constitute, form_

_____ _____ 醬油 / 酱油   13. qiē   _m. boil_

_____ _____ 太白粉   14. bàn   _n. ground pepper_

_____ _____ 攪在一起 / 搅在一起   15. là dòubànrjiàng   _o. spicy bean paste_

_____ _____ 鹽 / 盐   16. báo zhī   _p. stirred together_

_____ _____ 花椒粉   17. liàojiǔ   _q. cornstarch_

_____ _____ 少許 / 少许   18. jiàngyóu   _r. cook, heat_

_____ _____ 切   19. shāo   _s. bring to a boil_

_____ _____ 燒 / 烧   20. gǎi   _t. change_

_____ _____ 拌   21. tàibáifěn   _u. approximately_

_____ _____ 秒   22. jiǎo zài yìqǐ   _v. cooking wine_

_____ _____ 燒開 / 烧开   23. yán   _w. soy sauce_

_____ _____ 改   24. zhǔ   _x. thin sauce_

_____ _____ 煮   25. yuē   _y. stir, mix_

_____ _____ 約 / 约   26. miǎo   _z. second (of time)_

_____ _____ 勾成   27. shāokāi   _aa. sprinkle_

_____ _____ 薄汁   28. gōuchéng   _ab. small amount_

_____ _____ 灑 / 洒   29. sǎ   _ac. cut_

34. Try to write a brief recipe of your own for a simple dish (a salad? a sandwich?). After editing, share it with a classmate, and see if s/he can identify the dish.

[blank box]

Lesson 14

Sample student responses (edited)

拿兩片麵包。一片的一面塗花生醬。另一片的一面塗果醬。把塗過醬的兩面放在一起，就可以吃了。這個食品又好吃又健康。做起來又省事又便宜。

把一根香蕉剝了皮以后切成片。拿五个草莓，每个切成两半。把三个猕猴桃削了皮，然后也切成片。把所有的水果放在一起。然后把一杯酸奶和两汤匙的橙皮果酱搅拌在一起，倒到水果上面，拌一拌，就好了。够四五个人吃。

把一杯水煮開了。把半杯乾麥片倒進去，加一點葡萄乾。煮五分鐘，就熟了。吃的時候可以加牛奶和糖。

拿一塊牛排。每面煎一分鐘。兩面煎好了就可以吃了。也可以加一點A-1醬。好吃極了！

Unit C

236

彭瓊：咱們去吃飯吧。	彭琼：咱们去吃饭吧。
朋友：好吧。	朋友：好吧。
彭瓊：去…	彭琼：去…
朋友：我已經餓啦！	朋友：我已经饿啦！
彭瓊：我早就餓啦！我早就想吃飯了！	彭琼：我早就饿啦！我早就想吃饭了！
朋友：你想吃甚麼？	朋友：你想吃什么？
彭瓊：不是吃烤鴨嗎？烤鴨也不錯。其實我挺想吃那個愛德熊的。	彭琼：不是吃烤鸭吗？烤鸭也不错。其实我挺想吃那个爱德熊的。
朋友：愛德熊啊？	朋友：爱德熊啊？
彭瓊：嗯。	彭琼：嗯。
朋友：今天吃烤鴨吧。明天吃愛德熊。	朋友：今天吃烤鸭吧。明天吃爱德熊。
彭瓊：嗯，好。	彭琼：嗯，好。
朋友：後天吃麥當勞。	朋友：后天吃麦当劳。
彭瓊：對，對。	彭琼：对，对。
彭瓊：你去過愛德熊嗎？	彭琼：你去过爱德熊吗？
朋友：去過。	朋友：去过。
朋友：到啦！	朋友：到啦！
彭瓊：你以前來過這兒嗎？	彭琼：你以前来过这儿吗？
朋友：以前…我這是第一次來。	朋友：以前…我这是第一次来。
彭瓊：哎呀，我都快餓死了。	彭琼：哎呀，我都快饿死了。
彭瓊：謝謝。	彭琼：谢谢。
朋友：我餓了。	朋友：我饿了。
彭瓊：哎呀，我都快餓死了。	彭琼：哎呀，我都快饿死了。
朋友：你想吃甚麼？	朋友：你想吃什么？
彭瓊：我挺想吃烤鴨的。好久沒吃了。	彭琼：我挺想吃烤鸭的。好久没吃了。

Lesson 14

Péng Qióng: Zǎnmen qù chīfàn ba.

Péngyou: Hǎo ba.

Péng Qióng: Qù ...

Péngyou: Wǒ yǐjīng è la!

Péng Qióng: Wǒ zǎojiù è la! Wǒ zǎojiù
xiǎng chīfàn le!

Péngyou: Nǐ xiǎng chī shénme?

Péng Qióng: Bù shì chī kǎoyā me? Kǎoyā yě
bù cuò. Qíshí wǒ tǐng xiǎng chī nàge
Àidéxióng de.

Péngyou: Àidéxióng a?

Péng Qióng: Ng.

Péngyou: Jīntiān chī kǎoyā ba. Míngtiān chī
Àidéxióng.

Péng Qióng: Ng, hǎo.

Péngyou: Hòutiān chī Màidāngláo.

Péng Qióng: Duì, duì.

Péng Qióng: Nǐ qùguo Àidéxióng ma?

Péngyou: Qùguo.

Péngyou: Dào la!

Péng Qióng: Nǐ yǐqián láiguo zhèr ma?

Péngyou: Yǐqián ... wǒ zhè shì dì-yī cì lái.

Péng Qióng: Aiya, wǒ dōu kuài èsi le.

Péng Qióng: Xièxie.

Péngyou: Wǒ è le.

Péng Qióng: Aiya, wǒ dōu kuài èsi le.

Péngyou: Nǐ xiǎng chī shénme?

Péng Qióng: Wǒ tǐng xiǎng chī kǎoyā de.
Hǎojiǔ méi chī le.

Peng Qiong: Let's go eat.

Friend: Okay.

Peng: Let's go ...

Friend: I'm hungry already!

Peng: I was hungry long ago! I've
been wanting to eat for a long time
now!

Friend: What do you feel like eating?

Peng: Weren't we talking about
having Peking duck? Duck is pretty
good. Actually, I feel like eating at
A &W's.

Friend: A & W's?

Peng: Uh-huh.

Friend: Let's have Peking duck today. We'll
have A & W's tomorrow.

Peng: Uh-huh, okay.

Friend: The day after we'll have McDonald's.

Peng: Right, right.

Peng: Have you been to A & W's?

Friend: I have.

Friend: We're there!

Peng: Have you been here before?

Friend: Before ... this is my first time here.

Peng: Wow, I'm starving!

Peng: Thank you.

Friend: I'm hungry.

Peng: I'm staaarv-ing.

Friend: What do you feel like eating?

Peng: I'd rather like to have Peking duck. I
haven't had it in a long time.

Unit C

朋友：是，我也好久沒吃了。我記得上次吃是一年前。

彭瓊：我大概...嗯...也有很長時間了，但是如果有機會的話，我還是很想吃的。

朋友：今天就有機會啦！

彭瓊：嗯。

朋友：咱們吃甚麼呢？

彭瓊：咱們吃...我想吃鴨子。

朋友：肯定得吃鴨子，全聚德烤鴨店嘛！

服務員：您好，是兩位啊。

彭瓊：啊，您好。

服務員：這是我們的菜單，您看一下需要幾個甚麼菜，我幫您點。

彭瓊：好的。請問一下您這兒的主要的特色菜是甚麼？主要是鴨子，是麼？

服務員：對，我們是全聚德烤鴨店。

彭瓊：哦，哦，那吃甚麼呢，咱們？

朋友：那當然要點鴨子啦！

彭瓊：半只鴨。

服務員：可以。兩位。

彭瓊：怎麼樣？

朋友：好的。青菜...看一下。

服務員：...我們有那個全是素菜的一個菜。

朋友：點一個香菇菜心吧？

朋友：是，我也好久没吃了。我记得上次吃是一年前。

彭琼：我大概...嗯...也有很长时间了，但是如果有机会的话，我还是很想吃的。

朋友：今天就有机会啦！

彭琼：嗯。

朋友：咱们吃什么呢？

彭琼：咱们吃...我想吃鸭子。

朋友：肯定得吃鸭子，全聚德烤鸭店嘛！

服务员：您好，是两位啊。

彭琼：啊，您好。

服务员：这是我们的菜单，您看一下需要几个什么菜，我帮您点。

彭琼：好的。请问一下您这儿的主要的特色菜是什么？主要是鸭子，是么？

服务员：对，我们是全聚德烤鸭店。

彭琼：哦，哦，那吃什么呢，咱们？

朋友：那当然要点鸭子啦！

彭琼：半只鸭。

服务员：可以。两位。

彭琼：怎么样？

朋友：好的。青菜...看一下。

服务员：...我们有那个全是素菜的一个菜。

朋友：点一个香菇菜心吧？

Lesson 14

Péngyou: Shì, wǒ yě hǎojiǔ méi chī le. Wǒ jìde shàngcì shì yī nián qián.

Péng Qióng: Wǒ dàgài ...ng ... yě yǒu hěn cháng shíjiān le, dànshì rúguǒ yǒu jīhuì de huà, wǒ háishi hěn xiǎng chī de.

Péngyou: Jīntiān jiù yǒu jīhuì la!

Péng Qióng: Ng.

Péngyou: Zánmen chī shénme ne?

Péng Qióng: Zánmen chī ... wǒ xiǎng chī yāzi.

Péngyou: Kěndìng děi chī yāzi, Quánjùdé Kǎoyādiàn ma!

Fúwùyuán: Nín hǎo, shì liǎng wèi a.

Péng Qióng: A, nín hǎo.

Fúwùyuán: Zhè shì wǒmen de càidān, nín kàn yīxià xūyào jǐ ge shénme cài, wǒ bāng nín diǎn.

Péng Qióng: Hǎo de. Qǐngwèn yīxià nín zhèr de zhǔyào de tèsècài shì shénme? Zhǔyào shì yāzi, shì me?

Fúwùyuán: Duì, wǒmen shì Quánjùdé Kǎoyādiàn.

Péng Qióng: O, o, nà chī shénme ne, zánmen?

Péngyou: Nà dāngrán yào diǎn yāzi la!

Péng Qióng: Bàn zhī yā.

Fúwùyuán: Kěyǐ. Liǎng wèi.

Péng Qióng: Zěnmeyàng?

Péngyou: Hǎo de. Qīngcài ... kàn yīxià.

Fúwùyuán: ...Wǒmen yǒu nàge quán shì sùcài de yī ge cài.

Péngyou: Diǎn yī ge xiānggū càixīn ba?

Friend: Me too, I haven't had it in a long time either. I remember the last time was a year ago.

Peng: I probably ... mmm ... it's been a long time too, but when I have a chance I still really like to eat it.

Friend: We'll have a chance today!

Peng: Uh-huh.

Friend: What shall we have?

Peng: Let's have... I feel like having duck.

Friend: Of course we'll have duck. This is the Quanjude Duck Restaurant, after all!

Waitress: Hello, for two?

Peng: Uh-huh, hello.

Waitress: This is our menu, take a look and see which dishes you would like, and I'll order them for you.

Peng: Fine. May I just ask, what are your main specialties here? It's primarily duck, right?

Waitress: Right, we are the Quanjude Duck Restaurant.

Peng: Oh, oh, then what shall we eat, the two of us?

Friend: Of course we'll have to order duck!

Peng: A half duck.

Waitress: That's fine. For two.

Peng: How about it?

Friend: Okay. Vegetables ... let's see.

Waitress: ... We have a dish that's all vegetarian.

Friend: Shall we order a *choysum* with shiitake mushrooms?

Unit C

服務員：行。

朋友：還有甚麼？你再點一個。

彭瓊：還有一個 ... 再點一個 ... 點一
　　　個甚麼呢？ ... 菊花里脊？

朋友：行，菊花里脊。

服務員：菊花里脊？

彭瓊：有菊花里脊這個菜嗎？

服務員：有。

彭瓊：好，菊花里脊吧。

朋友：差不多了吧？那 ... 來點兒飲
　　　料？

服務員：飲料喝點甚麼？

彭瓊：我想喝果茶。

服務員：果茶。

朋友：那我來一瓶礦泉水吧。

服務員：一個果茶一個礦泉水。

朋友：對。好的。

服務員：請您稍等。別的還 ... 不需要
　　　了吧？

朋友、彭瓊：不需要了。

彭瓊：好，謝謝。

服務員：對不起，打擾一下。剛纔您
　　　點的那個菊花里脊我們今天賣完
　　　了。您再吃，換一個菜，成麼？

朋友：哦，那你們還有甚麼里脊呀？

侍者：行。

朋友：还有什么？你再点一个。

彭琼：还有一个 ... 再点一个 ... 点一
　　　个　　什么呢？ ... 菊花里脊？

朋友：行，菊花里脊。

服务员：菊花里脊？

彭琼：有菊花里脊这个菜吗？

服务员：有。

彭琼：好，菊花里脊吧。

朋友：差不多了吧？那 ... 来点儿饮
　　　料？

服务员：饮料喝点什么？

彭琼：我想喝果茶。

服务员：果茶。

朋友：那我来一瓶矿泉水吧。

服务员：一个果茶一个矿泉水。

朋友：对。好的。

服务员：请您稍等。别的还 ... 不需要
　　　了吧？

朋友、彭琼：不需要了。

彭琼：好，谢谢。

服务员：对不起，打扰一下。刚才您
　　　点的那个菊花里脊我们今天卖完
　　　了。您再吃，换一个菜，成么？

朋友：哦，那你们还有什么里脊呀？

Lesson 14

Fúwùyuán: Xíng.

Péngyou: Háiyǒu shénme? Nǐ zài diǎn yī ge.

Péng Qióng: Háiyǒu yī ge ... zài diǎn yī ge
... diǎn yī ge shénme ne? Júhuā lǐji?

Péngyou: Xíng, júhuā lǐji.

Fúwùyuán: Júhuā lǐji?

Péng Qióng: Yǒu júhuā lǐji zhège cài ma?

Fúwùyuán: Yǒu.

Péng Qióng: Hǎo, júhuā lǐji ba.

Péngyou: Chàbuduō le ba? Nà ... lái diǎnr
yǐnliào?

Fúwùyuán: Yǐnliào hē diǎn shénme?

Péng Qióng: Wǒ xiǎng hē guǒchá.

Fúwùyuán: Guǒchá.

Péngyou: Nà wǒ lái yī píng kuàngquánshuǐ
ba.

Fúwùyuán: Yī ge guǒchá, yī ge
kuàngquánshuǐ.

Péngyou: Duì. Hǎo de.

Fúwùyuán: Qǐng nín shāo děng. Bié de hái
... bù xūyào le ba?

Péngyou, Péng Qióng: Bù xūyào le.

Péng Qióng: Hǎo, xièxie.

Fúwùyuán: Duìbuqǐ, dǎrǎo yīxià. Gāngcái
nín diǎn de nàge Júhuā lǐji wǒmen
jīntiān mài wán le. Nín zài chī, huàn yī
ge cài, chéng me?

Péngyou: O, nà nǐmen háiyǒu shénme lǐji
ya?

Waitress: Okay.

Friend: What else? You order another.

Peng: Then there's the ... we'll order
one more ... what shall we order? The
chrysanthemum tenderloin?

Friend: Fine, the chrysanthemum tenderloin.

Waitress: The chrysanthemum tenderloin?

Peng: Is there a dish called the chrysanthemum tenderloin?

Waitress: There is.

Peng: Okay, the chrysanthemum tenderloin,
then.

Friend: Is that about it, then? Shall we order
some drinks?

Waitress: What would you like to have for
drinks?

Peng: I'll have hawthorn berry nectar.

Waitress: Hawthorn berry nectar.

Friend: Then I'll have a bottle of mineral
water.

Waitress: One hawthorn berry nectar, one
mineral water.

Friend: Right. Fine, then.

Waitress: Please wait a while. Is there
anything ... you don't want anything
else, right?

Friend, Peng: Nothing else.

Peng: Okay, thanks.

Waitress: Sorry, may I interrupt a moment.
The chrysanthemum tenderloin you
ordered just now we are sold out of
today. Will you have, could you
change a dish?

Friend: Oh, what other pork tenderloin dish
do you have, then?

Unit C

242

服務員：那個，糖醋里脊也是酸甜
　　　　口味的。

朋友：糖醋里脊，行嗎？

彭瓊：可以。

服務員：可以啊？

朋友：好吧，那我們點一個 ...

服務員：那來一個 ... 糖醋里脊。

朋友：好的。

服務員：你稍等啊。

朋友：謝謝。

朋友：一個英語考試。

彭瓊：哦，對對對。

朋友：所以我最近在挺緊張的復習
　　　呢！

彭瓊：哎，好的 ... 香菇 ...

服務員：這是香菇菜心。

彭瓊：香菇菜心。

朋友、彭瓊：好，謝謝。

彭瓊：咱們吃吧。

朋友：咱們真吃嗎？

彭瓊：燙！小心！

朋友：是嗎？

朋友：挺好吃的。

彭瓊：嗯，不錯。

朋友：你會做這個菜嗎？

彭瓊：嗯，我不會做。不會做。
　　　不過我想這個肯定 ... 可能不
　　　太難吧。

服务员：那个，糖醋里脊也是酸甜
　　　　口味的。

朋友：糖醋里脊，行吗？

彭琼：可以。

服务员：可以啊？

朋友：好吧，那我们点一个 ...

服务员：那来一个 ... 糖醋里脊。

朋友：好的。

服务员：你稍等啊。

朋友：谢谢。

朋友：一个英语考试。

彭琼：哦，对对对。

朋友：所以我最近在挺紧张的复习
　　　呢！

彭琼：哎，好的 ... 香菇 ...

服务员：这是香菇菜心。

彭琼：香菇菜心。

朋友、彭琼：好，谢谢。

彭琼：咱们吃吧。

朋友：咱们真吃吗？

彭琼：烫！小心！

朋友：是吗？

朋友：挺好吃的。

彭琼：嗯，不错。

朋友：你会做这个菜吗？

彭琼：嗯，我不会做。不会做。
　　　不过我想这个肯定 ... 可能不
　　　太难吧。

Lesson 14

Fúwùyuán: Nàge, Tángcù lǐji yě shì suān tián kǒuwèir de.

Péngyou: Tángcù lǐji, xíng me?

Péng Qióng: Kěyǐ.

Fúwùyuán: Kěyǐ a?

Péngyou: Hǎo ba, nà wǒmen diǎn yī ge ...

Fúwùyuán: Nà lái yī ge ... tángcù lǐji.

Péngyou: Hǎo de.

Fúwùyuán: Nǐ shāo děng a.

Péngyou: Xièxie.

Péngyou: Yī ge Yīngyǔ kǎoshì.

Péng Qióng: O, duì duì duì.

Péngyou: Suǒyǐ wǒ zuìjìn zài tīng jǐnzhāng de fùxí ne!

Péng Qióng: Ai, hǎo de ... xiānggū ...

Fúwùyuán: Zhè shì xiānggū càixīn.

Péng Qióng: Xiānggū Càixīn.

Péngyou, Péng Qióng: Hǎo, xièxie.

Péng Qióng: Zánmen chī ba.

Péngyou: Zánmen zhēn chī me?

Péng Qióng: Tàng! Xiǎoxīn!

Péngyou: Shì ma?

Péngyou: Tǐng hǎo chī de.

Péng Qióng: Ng, bù cuò.

Péngyou: Nǐ huì zuò zhège cài ma?

Péng Qióng: Ng, wǒ bù huì zuò. Bù huì zuò. Bùguò wǒ xiǎng zhège kěndìng ... kěnéng bù tài nán ba.

Waitress: There's ... the sweet-sour tenderloin is also sour with sweet.

Friend: The sweet-sour tenderloin, all right?

Peng: Fine.

Waitress: All right?

Friend: Okay, then, we'll order a ...

Waitress: We'll order a ... sweet-sour tenderloin.

Friend: Okay.

Waitress: Just a while longer, then.

Friend: Thank you.

Friend: An English exam.

Peng: Oh, right, right, right.

Friend: That's why I've been reviewing frantically, recently!

Peng: Oh, okay ... mushrooms ...

Waitress: This is the *choysum* with shiitake mushrooms.

Peng: *Choysum* with shiitake mushrooms.

Friend, Peng: Okay, thanks.

Peng: Let's eat.

Friend: Are we eating for real?

Peng: It's hot! Careful!

Friend: Really?

Friend: It's pretty good.

Peng: Mmm, not bad.

Friend: Can you make this dish?

Peng: Mmm, I don't know how. I don't know how. But I think this is definitely ... probably not too hard.

Unit C

Unit D: Shopping

Lesson 15:
Buying T-Shirts

Péng Qióng and Robyn shop in the sundry goods store on the Peking University campus.

Previewing Activity

1. Check four of the following that you think might be mentioned in this context:

☐ *size* dàxiǎo, mǎ 大小，碼 / 码	☐ *color* yánsè 顏色 / 颜色
☐ *quality* zhìliàng 質量 / 质量	☐ *price* jiàqian 價錢 / 价钱
☐ *style* yàngzi 樣子 / 樣子	☐ *pattern, design* tú'àn 圖案 / 图案

First Viewing: Global Information

2. Confirm the predictions you made by underlining the items above that were actually mentioned in the scene.

3. Which three of the following items does Péng Qióng point out to Robyn?

_____ towels   _____ T-shirts   _____ slippers   _____ material   _____ caps

4. How many T-shirts does Robyn buy? Circle one.

one T-shirt	two T-shirts	three T-shirts
（一件T恤衫）	（兩件T恤衫 / 两件T恤衫）	（三件T恤衫）

245

Second Viewing: Specific Information

5. Number the following colors in the order by which they were mentioned in the conversation.

_____ multicolored   _____ grey   _____ blue

6. Check which of the following Robyn says she prefers:

_____ multicolored (flowery) material   _____ blue material

7. Which of the following sizes does Robyn ask for, for her T-shirt? Check one.

_____ extra-small   _____ small   _____ medium   _____ large   _____ extra-large

8. Fill in the blanks in the chart below, to indicate the exchange of money that took place.

cost of T-shirt 1		cost of T-shirt 2		total cost		Robyn handed over		Robyn's change
¥	+	¥	=	¥	∴	¥	∴	¥

Third Viewing: Linguistic Information

9. Match the English sizes on the left with their Chinese equivalents on the right.

extra-small	中 (zhōng)
small	超小 (chāoxiǎo)
medium	加大 (jiādà)
large	大 (dà)
extra-large	小 (xiǎo)

10. Match the Chinese questions on the left with the English answers on the right.

哪種布料／哪种布料？	Extra-small, please.
甚麼顏色的布料／什么颜色的布料？	Crew-neck, please.
甚麼樣的T恤衫／什么样的T恤衫？	Nothing more, thanks.
甚麼號的T恤衫／什么号的T恤衫？	Polyester, please.
還要甚麼／还要什么？	Blue, please.

Unit D

11. The salesclerk hands Robyn her change and advises, "Nín ná hǎo ±zÆ≥¶n." "Ná" means "to take in the hands, to hold." This admonishment in reference to money means, "Here, be careful with it, keep it safe." Match the commonly used admonishments below with their English counterparts.

收好 (shōu, *receive*)   Look out; look carefully.

坐好   Go carefully. Stay safe.

站好   Listen carefully.

走好   Put it away; keep it safe.

看好   Sit properly (*generally said to children*).

聽好 / 听好   Stand up straight.

Post-Viewing Activities
Speaking

12. What are the last clothing items you bought? Select ANY TWENTY from the list below, and make a note of WHERE you purchased them. Now chat with a classmate. Tell your partner something about your recent purchases, and take some notes about his or hers.

___ *underpants* nèikù, sānjiǎokù 内褲，三角褲 / 内裤，三角裤

___ *undershirt* nèiyī 内衣

___ *bra* xiōngzhào 胸罩

___ *trousers, pants* chángkù 長褲 / 长裤

___ *jeans* niúzǎikù 牛仔褲 / 牛仔裤

___ *T-shirt* T-xùshān T恤衫

___ *skirt* qúnzi 裙子

___ *shirt , blouse* chènshān 襯衫 / 衬衫

___ *sleeveless shirt* wúxiù chènshān 無袖襯衫 / 无袖衬衫

___ *short-sleeved shirt* duǎnxiù chènshān 短袖襯衫 / 短袖衬衫

___ *long-sleeved shirt* chángxiù chènshān 長袖襯衫 / 长袖衬衫

___ *vest* bèixīn 背心

___ *dress* liányīqún 連衣裙 / 连衣裙

___ *cheungsam* qípáo (chángshān 長衫 / 长衫 in Cantonese) 旗袍

___ *evening gown* wǎn lǐfú 晚禮服 / 晚礼服

___ *sports jacket* xīfú shàngyī 西服上衣

___ *business suit* xīzhuāng 西裝 / 西装

___ *tuxedo* lǐfú 禮服 / 礼服

___ *tie* lǐngdài 領帶 / 领带

___ *bow tie* húdié lǐngdài 蝴蝶領帶 / 蝴蝶领带

___ *shorts* duǎnkù 短褲 / 短裤

(Write notes about your purchases in this space)

Lesson 15   247

___ *swim shorts* yóuyǒngkù 游泳褲 / 游泳裤

___ *swimming suit* yóuyǒngyī 游泳衣

___ *nightgown* shuìpáo 睡袍

___ *pajamas* shuìyī 睡衣

___ *tracksuit top* yùndòngshān 運動衫 / 运动衫

___ *tracksuit bottom* yùndòngkù 運動褲 / 运动裤

___ *sweater* máoyī 毛衣

___ *jacket* jiákè 夾克 / 夹克

___ *raincoat* yǔyī 雨衣

___ *winter coat* miándàyī 棉大衣

___ *pantyhose* liánkùwà 連褲襪 / 连裤袜

___ *socks* wàzi 襪子 / 袜子

___ *sports socks* yùndòngwà 運動襪 / 运动袜

___ *dress socks* chángtǒngwà 長筒襪 / 长筒袜

___ *tennis shoes* wǎngqiúxié 網球鞋 / 网球鞋

___ *running shoes* pǎoxié 跑鞋

___ *sneakers* lǚyóuxié 旅遊鞋 / 旅游鞋

___ *hiking boots* páshānxié 爬山鞋

___ *high-heeled shoes* gāogēnrxié 高跟鞋

___ *sandals* liángxié 涼鞋 / 凉鞋

___ *loafers* fāngbiàn píxié 方便皮鞋

___ *slippers* tuōxié 拖鞋

___ *rain boots* yǔxuē 雨靴

___ *umbrella* yǔsǎn 雨傘 / 雨伞

___ *gloves* shǒutào 手套

___ *scarf* wéijīn, lǐngjīn 圍巾，領巾 / 围巾，领巾

___ *baseball cap* bàngqiúmào 棒球帽

___ *hat* màozi 帽子

___ *belt* yāodài, pídài 腰帶，皮帶 / 腰带，皮带

___ *buttons* kòuzi, niǔkòu 扣子，紐扣 / 扣子，纽扣

___ *pockets* kǒudài 口袋

___ *shoelaces* xiédài 鞋帶 / 鞋带

(Write notes about your purchases in this space)

(Notes about your classmate's purchases)

Unit D

Reading/ Writing

13. Pretend you are Xiǎo Míng, and have received the following note from your friend. Highlight what you can read of it, and fill in the blanks in the English summary below.

小明：

　　你好！我今天下午和我男朋友一起去了趟当代商城。那里的女装部正在进行换季大减价，T—恤衫、连衣裙、无袖衬衫、背心、游泳衣、凉鞋、牛仔裤等许多夏装都有五折以上的折扣。这些服装不但款式新潮、做工精良，而且大多是名牌，衣料也都不错，穿起来很舒适。

　　我逛了个下午，一口气买了八件衣服，还觉得不过瘾，你要是感兴趣，赶快跟我联系，我们明天可以一块儿打的去。替我向你男朋友小东问好！

小云
即日下午6：20分

Xiǎo Yún is writing you because she went to a big _____

at _____ (_____% off), and

would like you to _____ tomorrow.

14. *Name five items that Xiǎo Yún saw on sale.*

1	2	3	4	5

15. Xiǎo Yún describes some specifics of the things on sale. Match the English with the Chinese below.

the material is not bad

the styles are fashionable

they are mostly brand names

they are over 50% off

they are comfortable to wear

the workmanship is good

五折以上的折扣
wǔ zhé yǐshàng de zhékòu

款式新潮
kuǎnshì xīncháo

做工精良
zuògōng jīngliáng

大多是名牌
dàduō shì míngpái

衣料不錯 / 衣料不错
yīliào bù cuò

穿起來很舒適 / 穿起来很舒适
chuānqilai hěn shūshì

16. Xiǎo Yún says that her shopping urge "has not been satisfied" (a rough translation of bù guòyǐn 不過癮 / 不过瘾). She suggests that you go shopping with her, and that the two of you can "dǎdī qù 打的去." Can you guess what this means? Check one:

☐ take a cab

☐ go in leisurely fashion

Answer:

"的" here is pronounced "dī," and is a shortened form of the Cantonese term "的士 dīksí," for "taxi." "打" is popular lingo for "to take, to ride."

17. Write a brief response to Xiǎo Yún:

Unit D

彭瓊：你好！

余修明：你好！

彭瓊：這裏是北大的學生商店。
哦，這裏是賣布料的地方。
這些是布料。這是藍顏色
的。這些是花的布料。你喜
歡哪種布料？

余修明：我喜歡藍色的布料。

彭瓊：嗯…這些是毛巾。毛巾。
嗯，這些是T恤衫。你喜歡T
恤衫嗎？

余修明：我要買兩件T恤衫。

彭瓊：好的。小姐，我們想買兩件
T恤衫。

售貨員：可以。您要甚麼樣的？

余修明：哦，我要那個灰色的T恤
衫。

售貨員：灰色的？甚麼碼的？

余修明：嗯，加大。

售貨員：加大碼啊？還要甚麼樣的？

余修明：還有我要買那個T恤衫。

售貨員：這個樣子的？

余修明：Yeah.

售貨員：這個加大碼。

余修明：多少錢？

售貨員：這是二十，這是十五，一
共三十五元。您這是四十元
啊。找您五元。您拿好。不
用謝。

彭瓊：謝謝。

售貨員：不用謝。

彭琼：你好！

余修明：你好！

彭琼：这里是北大的学生商店。
哦，这里是卖布料的地方。
这些是布料。这是蓝颜色
的。这些是花的布料。你喜
欢哪种布料？

余修明：我喜欢蓝色的布料。

彭琼：嗯…这些是毛巾。毛巾。
嗯，这些是T恤衫。你喜欢T
恤衫吗？

余修明：我要买两件T恤衫。

彭琼：好的。小姐，我们想买两件
T恤衫。

售货员：可以。您要什么样的？

余修明：哦，我要那个灰色的T恤
衫。

售货员：灰色的？什么码的？

余修明：嗯，加大。

售货员：加大码啊？还要什么样的？

余修明：还有我要买那个T恤衫。

售货员：这个样子的？

余修明：Yeah.

售货员：这个加大码。

余修明：多少钱？

售货员：这是二十，这是十五，一
共三十五元。您这是四十元
啊。找您五元。您拿好。不
用谢。

彭琼：谢谢。

售货员：不用谢。

Lesson 15

Péng Qióng: Nǐ hǎo!

Yú Xiūmíng: Nǐ hǎo!

Péng Qióng: Zhèli shì Běidà de xuéshēng shāngdiàn. O, zhèli shì mài bùliào de dìfāng. Zhè xiē shì bùliào. Zhè shì lányánsè de. Zhè xiē shì huā de bùliào. Nǐ xǐhuān něi zhǒng bùliào?

Yú Xiūmíng: Wǒ xǐhuān lánsè de bùliào.

Péng Qióng: Ng... zhè xiē shì máojīn. Máojīn. Ng, zhè xiē shì T-xù shān. Nǐ xǐhuan T-xùshān ma?

Yú Xiūmíng: Wǒ yào mǎi liǎng jiàn T-xùshān.

Péng Qióng: Hǎo de. Xiǎojiě, wǒmen xiǎng mǎi liǎng jiàn T-xùshān.

Shòuhuòyuán: Kěyǐ. Nín yào shénmeyàng de?

Yú Xiūmíng: O, wǒ yào nèige huīsè de T-xùshān.

Shòuhuòyuán: Huīsè de? Shénme mǎ de?

Yú Xiūmíng: Ng, jiādà.

Shòuhuòyuán: Jiādà mǎ a? Háiyào shénmeyàng de?

Yú Xiūmíng: Háiyou wǒ yào mǎi nèi ge T-xùshān.

Shòuhuòyuán: Zhèi ge yàngzi de?

Yú Xiūmíng: Yeah.

Shòuhuòyuán: Zhèi ge jiādà mǎ.

Yú Xiūmíng: Duōshǎoqián?

Shòuhuòyuán: Zhè shì èrshí, zhè shì shíwǔ, yīgòng sānshíwǔ yuán. Nín zhè shì sìshí yuán a. Zhǎo nín wǔ yuán. Nín ná hǎo. Bùyòng xiè.

Yú Xiūmíng: Xièxiè.

Shòuhuòyuán: Bùyòng xiè.

Peng Qiong: Hello!

Robyn: Hello!

Peng Qiong: This is the Peking University student store. Oh, this is where they sell cloth. These are materials. This is blue. This is patterned material. What kind of material do you like?

Robyn: I like the blue material.

Peng Qiong: Er, these are towels. Towels. Mmm, these are T-shirts. Do you like T-shirts?

Robyn: I want to buy a couple T-shirts.

Peng Qiong: Okay. Miss, we'd like to buy a couple T-shirts.

Salesclerk: Fine. What kind do you want?

Robyn: Oh, I want that grey T-shirt.

Salesclerk: Grey? In what size?

Robyn: Mmm, extra-large.

Salesclerk: Extra-large, huh? What other kind do you want?

Robyn: And I want to buy that T-shirt.

Salesclerk: This style?

Robyn: Yeah.

Salesclerk: This one is extra-large.

Robyn: How much is it?

Salesclerk: This is twenty, this is fifteen, thirty-five altogether. You're giving me forty. I'll give you back five. Keep it safe. You're welcome.

Robyn: Thank you.

Salesclerk: You're welcome.

Unit D

Lesson 16:

Buying Souvenirs

*Robyn shops for an item she
doesn't know the name of,
on the Beida campus.*

Previewing Activity

1. If you wanted to buy something, but you don't know what it's called, what would you do?

Number the choices below in the order you would be most likely to choose them (1 = most likely).

_____Look in the dictionary

_____Go find the item in the store

_____Point out the item to the salesclerk

_____Go shopping with someone who knows Chinese and English

_____Describe the item to a salesclerk

_____Other (describe):_____

2. Match the Chinese expressions below with the English ones above.

A. dào diàn lǐ qù zhǎo nǐ yào de dōngxi

到店裏去找你要的東西 / 到店里去找你要的东西

B. gěi diànyuán miáoshù nǐ yào de dōngxi

給店員描述你要的東西 / 给店员描述你要的东西

C. qítā fāngfǎ (jiěshì) 其他方法（解釋）/ 其他方法（解释）

D. zhǐ gěi diànyuán kàn nǐ yào de dōngxi

指給店員看你要的東西 / 指给店员看你要的东西

E. chá zìdiǎn 查字典

F. gēn huì shuō Zhōngwén Yīngwén de rén qù mǎi dōngxi

跟會說中文英文的人去買東西 / 跟会说中文英文的人去买东西

First Viewing: Global Information

3. Which techniques does Robyn use? Go back to Exercise 1 and circle any that pertain.

Second Viewing: Specific Information

4. Fill in the blanks in the statement below:

Robyn wanted to buy _____ of the pencil holders she saw, but she could only buy _____ because _____. They cost _____ each, for a total of _____. Robyn paid with a _____-yuan bill and received _____ in change. The salesclerk walked away for a moment because she went to fetch a _____.

Third Viewing: Linguistic Information

5. Link the items below.

剩	sùliàodàir	two
塑料袋兒 / 塑料袋儿	liǎng	plastic bag
倆 / 俩	shèng	remain, be left

6. The salesclerk in this exchange uses a particle three times, to indicate a *change of state*: "There are only two left, there are no more" (where there once were many, there are now just a few). What is the particle used to express such a change of state? Fill in the blanks.

現在就剩倆 _____ ... 這個沒有_____。就這倆 _____ /
现在就剩俩 _____ ... 这个没有_____。就这俩 _____。

7. The salesclerk says, "I'll go look for a plastic bag for you." How does she express this? Fill in the blanks below:

Wǒ qù _____ _____ zhǎo yī (ge) sùliàodàir.

我去给你找一（個）塑料袋兒 /
我去给你找一（个）塑料袋儿。

Note: She omits the "ge" here by carelessness or laziness; dropping the measure word in this context is not standard speech.

Unit D

Post-Viewing Activities
Speaking

8. Suppose you were in a department store speaking to a salesclerk, trying to get him or her to understand what it was you were looking for. You could try describing the item's appearance. Think of an item currently in your possession, and then use 3–4 of the expressions below (or some versions of these expressions) to describe it.

it's about this big (add a gesture) dàgài zhènme dà 大概這麼大 / 大概这么大

it's ___ inches high ____ cùn gāo _____ 寸高

it's ___ inches wide ____ cùn kuān _____ 寸寬 / 寸宽

it's ___ inches long ____ cùn cháng _____ 寸長 / 寸长

it's ___ inches thick ____ cùn hòu _____ 寸厚

it's hard shì yìng de 是硬的

it's soft shì ruǎn de 是軟的 / 是软的

it's round shì yuán de 是圓的 / 是圆的

it's square shì fāng de 是方的

it's made of _____ shì _____ de 是____的

        cloth bù 布

        plastic sùliào 塑料

        rubber xiàngpí 橡皮

        wood mùtou 木頭 / 木头

        iron, metal tiě 鐵 / 铁

        stainless steel bùxiùgāng 不鏽鋼 / 不锈钢

        porcelain cíqì 瓷器

        stone shítou 石頭 / 石头

        glass bōli 玻璃

        paper, cardboard zhǐ 紙 / 纸

9. Or you could tell what the item is used for. Use the structure below, and fill in your own meaning—state the usage of the item you are thinking of. Some examples are:

it's used to _____ shì yònglái _____ de 是用來____的 / 是用来___的

        hold CDs zhuāng CD 裝 C D / 装 C D

        hold water zhuāng shuǐ 裝水 / 装水

        draw with huàhuàr 畫畫兒 / 画画儿

        wipe the table cā zhuōzi 擦桌子

Lesson 16

Reading / Writing

10. Some forgetful Chinese friends have written descriptions of items they want to buy, but cannot name. Can you match the English names for these items with the descriptions?

a. a visor; b. a can opener; c. a keychain; d. a paperweight; e. a notepad; f. a plastic container

1。我要买一个塑料的盒子，长方形的，两寸长，三寸宽，六寸高，带盖子的，可以用来装糖或其他吃的。

2。我想买一个纪念品，水晶的，或者玻璃的。是个球，可是有一个平面。平面上刻有长城的图案，有个标志，还有一些汉字。

3。我要买一个小工具，是厨房里用的。是不锈钢的，有两个把手。是用来开罐头的。

4。我需要买一个用来遮太阳的帽子，前面有一个又大又软的橡皮或者塑料做的帽沿，后面只有一根松紧带。

5。我需要一个用来挂钥匙的东西，有很多样式，但一般都有一个串钥匙的铁环或铁链，和一个装饰用的坠子。

6。我找一个正方形的，有很多张纸粘在一起的小本子，差不多两寸宽，两寸长。

11. Now match the English with the Chinese terms .

a. a visor

b. a can opener

c. a keychain

d. a paperweight

e. a notepad

_____ i. kāiguànqì 開罐器 / 开罐器

_____ ii. yàoshiliànr 鑰匙鏈 / 钥匙链

_____ iii. sùliào hézi 塑料盒子

_____ iv. biànqiān 便籤 / 便签

_____ v. zhènzhǐ 鎮紙 / 镇纸

_____ vi. zhēyángmào 遮陽帽 / 遮阳帽

Unit D

12. Match the characters to their pinyin and English glosses.

___長方形 / 长方形   a. jìniànpǐn *souvenir*

___帶蓋子 / 带盖子   b. gēn *(measure word for a strand, a line)*

___糖   c. tiěhuán *metal ring*

___紀念品 / 纪念品   d. gōngjù *tool*

___水晶   e. qiú *globe, ball*

___球   f. tiěliàn *metal chain*

___平面   g. màozi *hat*

___刻   h. bǎshǒu *handle*

___長城的圖案 / 长城的图案   i. dài gàizi *comes with a lid*

___標志 / 标志   j. yàngshì *a style*

___工具   k. zhuāngshì yòng de *for decorative purposes*

___厨房   l. zhuìzi *a tag, a pendant*

___把手   m. sōngjǐndài *elastic*

___罐頭 / 罐头   n. zhē tàiyang *keep off the sun*

___遮太陽 / 遮太阳   o. Chángchéng de tú'àn *picture of the Great Wall*

___帽子   p. chángfāngxíng *rectangle*

___又大又軟 / 又大又软   q. píngmiàn *flat surface*

___帽沿   r. yòu dà yòu ruǎn *big and soft*

___根   s. táng *candy*

___松緊帶 / 松紧带   t. zhèngfāngxíng *square shape*

___掛 / 挂   u. xiǎo běnzi *small notepad*

___鑰匙 / 钥匙   v. biāozhì *trademark, logo*

___樣式 / 样式   w. yàoshi *a key*

___串   x. guà *to hang*

___鐵環 / 铁环   y. chúfáng *kitchen*

___鐵鏈 / 铁链   z. shuǐjīng *crystal*

___裝飾用的 / 装饰用的   aa. kè *carve, etch*

___墜子 / 坠子   ab. màoyán *hat brim*

___正方形   ac. guàntou *can, tin*

___粘   ad. chuàn *thread through*

___小本子   ae. zhān *glue, attach*

Lesson 16

13. Write three facts in English about each of the six items described, based on the reading:

container			
paperweight			
can opener			
visor			
keychain			
notepad			

14. Try to write a brief description about an item you might want to buy, but that you don't know the name of. After correction, share your description with your classmates, and see if, together, you can come up with the name of this object.

Name of the object:
(in English)   (in Chinese)

_____   _____

Unit D   258

余修明：小姐！你好！我要買
　　　三個那個東西。

售貨員：三個這個呀？現在就
　　　剩倆了。

余修明：噢。

售貨員：這個沒有了。就這倆
　　　了。

余修明：好。我要買兩個。多
　　　少錢一個？

售貨員：十一塊三一個。十一
　　　塊三，是，兩個是二十二
　　　塊六。我去給你找一
　　　（個）塑料袋兒...二十二
　　　塊六。找你七十七塊四。

余修明：好。謝謝！

余修明：小姐！你好！我要买
　　　三个那个东西。

售货员：三个这个呀？现在就
　　　剩俩了。

余修明：噢。

售货员：这个没有了。就这俩
　　　了。

余修明：好。我要买两个。多
　　　少钱一个？

售货员：十一块三一个。十一
　　　块三，是，两个是二十二
　　　块六。我去给你找一
　　　（个）塑料袋儿...二十二
　　　块六。找你七十七块四。

余修明：好。谢谢！

Lesson 16

Yú Xiūmíng: Xiǎojie! Wǒ yào mǎi sān ge nèige dōngxi.

Shòuhuòyuán: Sān ge zhèige ya? Xiànzài jiù shèng liǎngr le.

Yú Xiūmíng: Ou.

Shòuhuòyuán: Zhèige méiyǒu le. Jiù zhèi liǎngr le.

Yú Xiūmíng: Hǎo. Wǒ yào mǎi liǎng ge. Duōshǎo qián yī ge?

Shòuhuòyuán: Shíyī kuài sān yī ge. Shíyī kuài sān, shì, liǎng ge shì èrshíèr kuài liù. Wǒ qù gěi nǐ zhǎo yī (ge) sùliàodàir ... èrshíèr kuài liù. Zhǎo nǐ qīshíjiǔ kuài sì.

Yú Xiūmíng: Hǎo. Xièxie!

Robyn: Miss! I want to buy three of that thing.

Salesclerk: Three of this? We only have two left.

Robyn: Oh.

Salesclerk. We don't have any more of this. Just these two.

Robyn: Okay. I'll buy these two. How much are they, each?

Salesclerk: 11.30 yuan each. 11.30, that's 22.60 for two. I'll go find a plastic bag for you ... 22.60. Here is 77.40 in change.

Robyn: Great. Thanks!

Unit D

Unit D: Shopping

Lesson 17:
Buying Postcards

Péng Qióng takes Todd Pavel shopping in the sundry goods store on the Beida campus.

Previewing Activity

1. Check five items that you think might be sold in this campus store:

<table>
<tr><td>☐</td><td>*daily use items* rìyòngpǐn 日用品</td><td>☐</td><td>*maps* dìtú 地圖 / 地图</td></tr>
<tr><td>☐</td><td>*magazines* zázhì 雜誌 / 杂志</td><td>☐</td><td>*drinks* yǐnliào 飲料 / 饮料</td></tr>
<tr><td>☐</td><td>*stationery* wénjù 文具</td><td>☐</td><td>*souvenirs* jìniànpǐn 紀念品 / 纪念品</td></tr>
<tr><td>☐</td><td>*shoes* xiézi 鞋子</td><td>☐</td><td>*snacks* xiǎochī 小吃</td></tr>
<tr><td>☐</td><td>*backpacks* bēibāo 背包</td><td>☐</td><td>*postcards* míngxìnpiàn 明信片</td></tr>
</table>

First Viewing: Global Information

2. Confirm the predictions you made by underlining the items above that were actually mentioned/shown as available in the store.

3. How many items does Todd buy? Circle one.

one item （一樣東西 / 一样东西）	two items （兩樣東西 / 两样东西）	three items （三樣東西 / 三样东西）

Second Viewing: Specific Information

4. Number the following items in the order by which they were introduced.

_____ postcards   _____ snacks   _____ makeup   _____ slippers   _____ cups

_____ jogging shoes   _____ watches

5. Number the following postcards in the order in which Péng Qióng and Todd describe them.

_____   _____   _____   _____

6. Péng Qióng and Todd look at two cups. Number the following attributes in the order in which they are mentioned when Péng Qióng and Todd discuss the first thermal cup.

_____ It costs ¥7

_____ It can be used to hold coffee or tea

_____ It is green

_____ It sports a trademark logo

7. In looking over the second cup, Todd wonders if it can be used to hold (check one):

_____ water   _____ food

8. The clerk replies that it is generally used to hold (check one):

_____ water   _____ food

9. Péng Qióng suggests that they look at another one of the second cup, because there is a problem with the quality (a small chip) on the original. Eventually, Todd purchases (check one):

_____ the original cup   _____ the substitute cup.

Unit D

10. When Todd pays for the cup, the transaction might have sounded like this (fill in the blanks):

Clerk (cost of cup):　　　　　　　　"總共是 / 总共是＿＿＿＿圓 / 元。"

Todd (amount tendered):　　　　　　"給您 / 给您 ＿＿＿＿圓 / 元。"

Clerk (change received):　　　　　　"找您 ＿＿＿＿圓 / 元。"

Third Viewing: Linguistic Information

11. Fill in the following vocabulary chart (items follow the order in which they appear):

商店	shāngdiàn	store
各種各樣 / 各种各样		all different kinds
小吃		
食物		
拖鞋		slippers
涼鞋 / 凉鞋		sandals
旅遊鞋 / 旅游鞋		jogging shoes
明信片		
供你選擇 / 供你选择		offer you a choice
化妝品 / 化妆品		makeup
梳子		comb
錶 / 表	biǎo	
著名		famous
水塔		water tower
湖邊 / 湖边		
廟 / 庙		temple
菏花 / 菏花		lotus blossoms
校長 / 校长		

Lesson 17

蔡元培先生		*Mr. Cai Yuanpei*
雕像		*statue*
套	tào	
杯子	bēizi	
清楚		
非常對不起 / 非常对不起		
保温杯		*thermal cup*
注冊商標 / 注册商标	zhùcè shāngbiāo	
沏茶 / 沏茶		*to steep tea*
選擇 / 选择		
質量 / 质量		*quality*

12. Utilizing the vocabulary chart above, fill in the classification chart below, writing in *pinyin*, characters, or a combination of both:

四種穿或戴的東西 / 四种穿或戴的东西 (4 things to wear on the body)

_____   _____   _____   _____

兩種化妝品 / 两种化妆品 (2 toiletry items)

_____   _____

兩種茶具 / 两种茶具 (2 tea utensils)

_____   _____

四種在明信片上看到的東西 / 四种在明信片上看到的东西

(4 things seen in the postcards)

_____   _____   _____   _____

兩個動詞 / 两个动词 (two verbs)

_____   _____

Unit D   264

13. This interchange in the store features a number of descriptive adjectives. Match the adjectives with the nouns they describe, based on the video.

gèzhǒnggèyàng de
各種各樣的 / 各种各样的   shuǐtǎ
                                                          水塔

zhùmíng de
著名的

húbiān de
湖邊的 / 湖边的   diāoxiàng
                                                          雕像

Cài Yuánpéi Xiānsheng de
蔡元培先生的

liǎng kuài qián yī tào de
兩塊錢一套的 / 两块钱一套的   bǎowēnbēi
                                                          保温杯

lǜsè de
綠色的 / 绿色的

dài zhùcè shāngbiāo de
帶注冊商標的 / 带注册商标的   míngxìnpiàn
                                                          明信片

qīchá de
沏茶的 / 沏茶的

zhìliàng hǎo yīdiǎr de
質量好一點兒的 / 质量好一点儿的   dōngxi
                                                          東西 / 东西

14. Rearrange (by numbering them) the phrases below to express the following English sentence:
"The big black cup on top with the gold trademark design is best in quality, and is therefore the most expensive."

| 杯子 | 上邊的那個 / 上边的那个 | 所以價錢最貴 / 所以价钱最贵 |
| 黑色的 | 帶金色商標的 / 带金色商标的 | 大大的 | 質量最好 / 质量最好 |

Speaking

15. Pretend you are opening a sundry goods store on campus. Select ANY TWENTY items from the list below by checking the spaces provided.

___textbooks kèběn 課本 / 课本

___atlases dìtúcè 地圖冊 / 地图册

___dictionaries zìdiǎn 字典

___encyclopedias bǎikē quánshū
百科全書 / 百科全书

___thesaurus tóngyìcí cídiǎn
同義詞詞典 / 同义词词典

___flashcards shēngcí kǎpiàn
生詞卡片 / 生词卡片

___notebooks bǐjìběn 筆記本 / 笔记本

___graph paper zuòbiāozhǐ 坐標紙 / 坐标纸

___binders wénjiàn jiā 文件夾

___pens bǐ 筆 / 笔

___pencils qiānbǐ 鉛筆 / 铅笔

___highlighters yíngguāngbǐ
熒光筆 / 荧光笔

___correction fluid xiūgǎiyè 修改液

___erasers xiàngpí 橡皮

___gluesticks jiāobàng 膠棒 / 胶棒

___scissors jiǎndāo 剪刀

___staplers dìngshūjī 訂書機 / 订书机

___staples dìngshūdīng 訂書釘 / 订书钉

___memo pads biàntiáoběn 便條本 / 便条本

___computers diànnǎo 電腦 / 电脑

___printers dǎyìnjī 打印機 / 打印机

___diskettes cípán 磁盤 / 磁盘

___calculators jìsuànqì 計算器 / 计算器

___software ruǎnjiàn 軟件 / 软件

___newspapers bàozhǐ 報紙 / 报纸

___magazines zázhì 雜誌 / 杂志

___candy bars qiǎokèlì 巧克力

___lollipops bàngbàngtáng 棒棒糖

___icecream bīngjilíng 冰激凌

___drinks yǐnliào 飲料 / 饮料

___breath mints bòhetáng 薄荷糖 / 薄荷糖

___chewing gum kǒuxiāngtáng 口香糖

___cookies bǐnggān 餅乾 / 饼干

___backpacks bēibāo 背包

___sweatshirts yùndòngshān
運動衫 / 运动衫

___T-shirts T-xùshān T恤衫

___slippers tuōxié 拖鞋

___umbrellas yǔsǎn 雨傘 / 雨伞

___coffee mugs kāfēi bēi 咖啡杯

___keychains yàoshiliànr
鑰匙鏈 / 钥匙链

___razors guāhúdāo 刮胡刀

___lip balm chúngāo 唇膏

___lipsticks kǒuhóng 口紅 / 口红

___toothbrush yáshuā 牙刷

___toothpaste yágāo 牙膏

___nylon stockings liánkùwà
連褲襪 / 连裤袜

___sanitary napkins wèishēngjīn
衛生巾 / 卫生巾

___tampons wèishēng miántiáo
衛生棉條 / 卫生棉条

___aspirin āsīpǐlín 阿斯匹林

___bandages chuàngkětiē 創可貼 / 创可贴

___bus passes yuèpiào 月票

___ATM zìdòng qǔkuǎnjī
自動取款機 / 自动取款机

Unit D

266

16. Now pretend you are an on-campus shopper. Write the Chinese for any FOUR items you want to buy, and write at least one specification (color? size? price? quality? quantity?) for each. Then walk around the classroom, talking to your classmates until you find someone who is "selling" each of the items you want to buy.

Dì yī yàng dōngxi:_____

tèdìng特定 (specification):

_____

Available from: _____
(write name of classmate)

Dì èr yàng dōngxi:_____

tèdìng特定 (specification):

_____

Available from: _____
(write name of classmate)

Dì sān yàng dōngxi:_____

tèdìng特定 (specification):

_____

Available from: _____
(write name of classmate)

Dì sì yàng dōngxi:_____

tèdìng特定 (specification):

_____

Available from: _____
(write name of classmate)

Lesson 17

Reading / Writing

17. A friend named Cuī Yuè has left you the following note. Highlight what you can decipher of the text, and then summarize what you understand that she wants you to do.

听说你今天下午要开车去中国城买东西，正好我有几样东西要买，麻烦你帮我带回来。我刚到夏威夷，人生地不熟，很多东西都没买齐，这次全靠你了。一共有七样。

① 《现代汉语词典》，2000年版的。

② 荧光笔两支，最好是黄色的，越细越好，比如说0.4的。

③ 修改液一支，形状像笔的那种。

④ 背包一个，粉红色；什么牌子都行，要最结实的。

⑤ 唇膏一个，要草莓香型的。

⑥ 3.5寸软盘十张，价钱在十块钱以下。

⑦ 一箱可口可乐饮料，要无糖的。

希望不会太麻烦你。回来以后，请给我打电话。我来取东西，顺便把钱还给你。拜托了！

崔越

18. Match the Chinese with the English terms below.

_____聽說 / 听说   a. máfan nǐ *may I trouble you*

_____中國城 / 中国城   b. fěnhóngsè *pink (pastel red)*

_____正好   c. xíngzhuàng *shape*

_____麻煩你 / 麻烦你   d. páizi *brand*

_____幫 / 帮   e. jiēshi *sturdy*

_____帶回來 / 带回来   f. Zhōngguóchéng *Chinatown*

_____剛到 / 刚到   g. yuè xì yuè hǎo *the finer the better*

_____人生地不熟   h. bàituō *make a request of someone*

_____買齊 / 买齐   i. yíngguāngbǐ *fluorescent pen*

_____全靠你   j. zhènghǎo *it just happens that*

_____一共   k. bāng *help*

_____現代漢語詞典 / 现代汉语词典   l. ruǎnpán *floppy disk*

_____版   m. dàihuilai *bring back*

_____熒光筆 / 荧光笔   n. jiàqian *price*

_____支   o. mǎi qí *buy till complete*

_____越細越好 / 越细越好   p. chúngāo *lip balm*

_____比如說 / 比如说   q. yī gòng *altogether*

_____修改液   r. Xiàndài Hànyǔ Cídiǎn

_____形狀 / 形状   *Dictionary of Modern Chinese*

_____背包   s. wútáng *sugarless*

_____粉紅色 / 粉红色   t. zhī *(measure word for stick-like objects)*

_____牌子   u. bǐrúshuō *for example*

_____結實 / 结实   v. tīngshuō *I hear people say*

_____唇膏   w. xiūgǎiyè *correction fluid*

_____草莓香型   x. bēibāo *backpack*

_____寸   y. shùnbiàn *conveniently, in passing*

_____軟盤 / 软盘   z. cǎoméi xiāng xíng *strawberry-flavored type*

_____价錢 / 价钱   aa. cùn *inch*

_____以下   ab. yǐxià *below*

_____箱   ac. bǎn *edition*

_____飲料 / 饮料   ad. gāng dào *just arrived*

_____無糖 / 无糖   ae. rénshēng dì bùshú

_____取   *be a stranger in a strange place*

_____順便 / 顺便   af. xiāng *case*

_____拜托   ag. quán kào nǐ *rely entirely on you*

                                         ah. yǐnliào *soft drink*

                                         ai. qǔ *obtain, fetch*

Lesson 17   269

19. Now fill out the form below IN ENGLISH, to remind you of what Cuī Yuè is asking of you.

when you will pick up the items _____

what you should do after you have them _____

how Cuī Yuè will repay you _____

	name of item	number desired	any specifications?
1.			
2.			
3.			
4.			
5.			
6.			
7.			

20. If you were to entrust a Chinese friend or family member to pick up some items you needed from the store, and you needed to write them a note giving them the best instructions you could, what would you write? Compose a note asking for at least FIVE items, with some specifications for each item.

彭瓊：這裏是北大的學生商店，有
　　各種各樣的吃的東西。你看這
　　是北京的小吃。

彭德：啊！好吃嗎？

彭瓊：很好吃。你應該 ...

彭德：你最喜歡的是甚麼？

彭瓊：我想我最喜歡的是 ... 這個！
　　這是我 ... 一種 ...

彭德：很甜的，對不對？

彭瓊：對，很甜的一種食物。

彭德：啊。

彭瓊：很好吃。

彭德：是嗎？

彭瓊：嗯，你喜歡甜的食物嗎？

彭德：喜歡。

彭瓊：這裏賣的是各種各樣的鞋
　　子。這樣的叫拖鞋，這樣的叫
　　涼鞋，這樣的叫旅遊鞋，或者
　　叫運動鞋。你覺得怎麼樣？

彭德：很好，好多。

彭瓊：對，很多。

彭德：那我想買名信片。

彭瓊：嗯，好。

彭德：有沒有？

彭瓊：有，這裏有很多名信片，可
　　以供你選擇。看！這，這邊是
　　化妝品，這些是梳子，這些是
　　表。有各種各樣的東西。

彭瓊：这是北大的学生商店，有各
　　种各样的吃的东西。你看这
　　是北京的小吃。

彭德：啊！好吃吗？

彭瓊：很好吃。你应该 ...

彭德：你最喜欢的是什么？

彭瓊：我想我最喜欢的是 ... 这个！
　　这是我 ... 一种 ...

彭德：很甜的，对不对？

彭瓊：对，很甜的一种食物。

彭德：啊。

彭瓊：很好吃。

彭德：是吗？

彭瓊：嗯，你喜欢甜的食物吗？

彭德：喜欢。

彭瓊：这里卖的是各种各样的鞋
　　子。这样的叫拖鞋，这样的叫
　　凉鞋，这样的叫旅游鞋，或者
　　叫运动鞋。你觉得怎么样？

彭德：很好，好多。

彭瓊：对，很多。

彭德：那我想买名信片。

彭瓊：嗯，好。

彭德：有没有？

彭瓊：有，这里有很多名信片，可
　　以供你选择。看！这，这边是
　　化妆品，这些是梳子，这些是
　　表。有各种各样的东西。

Péng Qióng: Zhè shì Běidà de xuéshēng shāngdiàn, yǒu gèzhǒng-gèyàng de chī de dōngxi. Nǐ kàn zhè shì Běijīng de xiǎochī.

Péng Dé: A! Hǎochī ma?

Péng Qióng: Hěn hǎochī. Nǐ yīnggāi ...

Péng Dé: Nǐ zuì xǐhuan de shì shénme?

Péng Qióng: Wǒ xiǎng wǒ zuì xǐhuan de shì ... zhège! Zhè shì wǒ ... yī zhǒng ...

Péng Dé: Hěn tián de, duì bù duì?

Péng Qióng: Duì, hěn tián de yī zhǒng shíwù.

Péng Dé: A.

Péng Qióng: Hěn hǎochī.

Péng Dé: Shì ma?

Péng Qióng: N, nǐ xǐhuan tián de shíwù ma?

Péng Dé: Xǐhuan.

Péng Qióng: Zhèr mài de shì gèzhǒng-gèyàng de xiézi. Zhèyàng de jiào tuōxié, zhèyàng de jiào liángxié, zhèyàng de jiào lǚyóuxié, huòzhě jiào yùndòngxié. Nǐ juéde zěnmeyàng?

Péng Dé: Hěn hǎo, hǎo duō.

Péng Qióng: Duì, hěn duō.

Péng Dé: Nà wǒ xiǎng mǎi míngxìnpiàn.

Péng Qióng: Ng, hǎo.

Péng Dé: Yǒu méiyǒu?

Péng Qióng: Yǒu, zhèli yǒu hěn duō míngxìnpiàn, kěyǐ gòng nǐ xuǎnzé. Kàn! Zhè, zhèbiān shì huàzhuāngpǐn, zhèxiē shì shūzi, zhèxiē shì biǎo. Yǒu gèzhǒng-gèyàng de dōngxi.

Peng Qiong: This is Beida's student store, it has all kinds of things to eat. See, these are Beijng snacks.

Todd: Ah! Are they good?

Peng Qiong: Very good. You ought to ...

Todd: What do you most like to eat?

Peng Qiong: I think that what I like is ... this! This is what I ... it's a kind of ...

Todd: It's very sweet, right?

Peng Qiong: Right. It's a very sweet sort of foodstuff.

Todd: Oh.

Peng Qiong: It's very good.

Todd: Is it?

Peng Qiong: Uh-huh. Do you like sweets?

Todd: I do.

Peng Qiong: Here they sell all kinds of shoes. These are called slippers, these are called sandals, these are called sneakers, or exercise shoes. What do you think of them?

Todd: They're great, so many.

Peng Qiong: Right, there are so many.

Todd: Well, I'd like to buy some postcards.

Peng Qiong: Oh, okay.

Todd: Are there any?

Peng Qiong: Yes, there are lots of postcards here, plenty for you to choose from. See! This, on this side is makeup, these are combs, these are watches. There are all kinds of things.

Unit D

啊！名信片，這個就是名信
片。

彭德：對，可不可以看一下。

彭瓊：當然。小姐，小姐！你好，
我想看一看這個名信片。

售貨員：就這兩種。

彭瓊：甚麼？

售貨員：就這兩種。

彭瓊：嗯，好。就這兩種。

彭德：裏面有幾個？一、二、三、
四、五 ... 六張。那，冬天的。

彭瓊：對，晚上的。這是北大最著
名的水塔，博雅塔。

彭德：在湖邊的。

彭瓊：在湖邊，對。

彭德：旁邊。

彭瓊：對，對。

彭德：很漂亮。

彭瓊：再看看這個怎麼樣？這也是
在未名湖邊的一個小的一個
廟。

彭德：嗯，蠻，很漂亮的。

彭瓊：對，對。

彭德：哦，在校園的旁邊，對不對？

彭瓊：對，對，對。荷花。

彭德：哦，他是誰呀？

彭瓊：這就是北大的以前的校長蔡
元培先生。這是一個雕像。

彭德：雕像？

彭瓊：嗯。

啊！名信片，这个就是名信
片。

彭德：对，可不可以看一下。

彭琼：当然。小姐，小姐！你好，我
想看一看这个名信片。

售货员：就这两种。

彭琼：什么？

售货员：就这两种。

彭琼：嗯，好。就这两种。

彭德：里面有几个？一、二、三、
四、五 ... 六张。那，冬天的。

彭琼：对，晚上的。这是北大最著
名的水塔，博雅塔。

彭德：在湖边的。

彭琼：在湖边，对。

彭德：旁边。

彭琼：对，对。

彭德：很漂亮。

彭琼：再看看这个怎么样？这也是
在未名湖边的一个小的一个
庙。

彭德：嗯，蛮，很漂亮的。

彭琼：对，对。

彭德：哦，在校园的旁边，对不对？

彭琼：对，对，对。荷花。

彭德：哦，他是谁呀？

彭琼：这就是北大的以前的校长蔡
元培先生。这是一个雕像。

彭德：雕像？

彭琼：嗯。

Lesson 17

A! Míngxìnpiàn, zhège jiù shì míngxìnpiàn.

Péng Dé: Duì, kě bu kěyǐ kàn yīxià?

Péng Qióng: Dāngrán. Xiǎojiě, xiǎojiě! Nǐ hǎo, wǒ xiǎng kàn yī kàn zhège míngxìnpiàn.

Shòuhuòyuán: Jiù zhè liǎng zhǒng.

Péng Qióng: Shénme?

Shòuhuòyuán: Jiù zhè liǎng zhǒng.

Péng Qióng: Ng, hǎo. Jiù zhè liǎng zhǒng.

Péng Dé: Lǐmiàn yǒu jǐ ge? Yī, èr, sān, sì, wǔ ... liù zhāng. Nà, dōngtiān de.

Péng Qióng: Duì, wǎnshang de. Zhè shì Běidà zuì zhùmíng de shuǐtǎ—Bóyǎtǎ.

Péng Dé: Zài hú biān de.

Péng Qióng: Zài hú biān, duì.

Péng Dé: Pángbiān.

Péng Qióng: Duì, duì.

Péng Dé: Hěn piàoliang.

Péng Qióng: Zài kànkan zhège zěnmeyàng? Zhè yě shì zài Wèimínghú biān de yī ge xiǎo de yī ge miào.

Péng Dé: Ng, mán, hěn piàoliang de.

Péng Qióng: Duì, duì.

Péng Dé: O, zài xiàoyuán de pángbiān, duì bù duì?

Péng Qióng: Duì, duì, duì. Héhuā.

Péng Dé: O, tā shì shuí ya?

Péng Qióng: Zhè jiùshì Běidà de yǐqián de xiàozhǎng Cài Yuánpéi xiānsheng. Zhè shì yī ge diāoxiàng.

Péng Dé: Diāoxiàng?

Péng Qióng: Ng.

Ah! Postcards, these right here are postcards.

Todd: Right, can I take a look?

Peng Qiong: Of course. Miss, miss! Hello, I'd like to take a look at these postcards.

Clerk: There are just these two kinds.

Peng Qiong: What?

Clerk: There are just these two kinds.

Peng Qiong: Oh. There are just these two kinds.

Todd: How many are there inside? One, two, three, four, five ... six. Here, of the wintertime.

Peng Qiong: Right, in the evening. This is Beida's best known water tower—Boya Tower.

Todd: By the lake.

Peng Qiong: By the lake, right.

Todd: Next to it.

Peng Qiong: Right, right.

Todd: It's beautiful.

Peng Qiong: Let's take a look and see what this one is like. This is a small little temple also by the side of No-name Lake.

Todd: Uh-huh, it's quite, it's very pretty.

Peng Qiong: Right, right.

Todd: Oh, this is over by the edge of campus, right?

Peng Qiong: Right, right, right. Lotus blossoms.

Todd: Oh, and who is this?

Peng Qiong: This is a former president of Beida, Mr. Cai Yuanpei. This is a statue.

Todd: Statue?

Peng Qiong: Uh-huh.

Unit D

彭德：好，好。我想買這個。

彭瓊：多少錢？

售貨員：兩塊。

彭德：兩塊錢。

售貨員：兩塊錢一套。

彭德：好，想買這個。兩塊錢。
　　那你覺得漂亮嗎？

彭瓊：嗯，很漂亮。你還想買些
　　甚麼其它的東西嗎？

彭德：我也想買 ... 哦 ... 一個杯
　　子。

彭瓊：嗯。

彭德：好不好。

彭瓊：嗯，好主意。

彭德：好，謝謝。商店裏有沒有？
　　在哪兒？

彭瓊：在這邊。

彭德：一個杯子多少錢？

彭瓊：哦，這個我也不是很清楚，
　　非常對不起。

彭德：沒關係呀！

彭瓊：嗯。

彭德：看一看。

彭瓊：小姐！

彭德：那個綠色的，可以看一看？

售貨員：這是保溫杯。

彭德：注，啊，怎麼講？怎麼看？

彭瓊：注冊商標。

彭德：For coffee，咖啡，茶。

售貨員：沏茶的。

彭德：好，好。我想买这个。

彭琼：多少钱？

售货员：两块。

彭德：两块钱。

售货员：两块钱一套。

彭德：好，想买这个。两块钱。
　　那你觉得漂亮吗？

彭琼：嗯，很漂亮。你还想买些
　　什么其它的东西吗？

彭德：我也想买 ... 哦 ... 一个杯
　　子。

彭琼：嗯。

彭德：好不好。

彭琼：嗯，好主意。

彭德：好，谢谢。商店里有没有？
　　在哪儿？

彭琼：在这边。

彭德：一个杯子多少钱？

彭琼：哦，这个我也不是很清楚，
　　非常对不起。

彭德：没关系呀！

彭琼：嗯。

彭德：看一看。

彭琼：小姐！

彭德：那个绿色的，可以看一看？

售货员：这是保温杯。

彭德：注，啊，怎么讲？怎么看？

彭琼：注册商标。

彭德：For coffee，咖啡，茶。

售货员：沏茶的。

Lesson 17

Péng Dé: Hǎo, hǎo. Wǒ xiǎng mǎi zhège.

Péng Qióng: Duōshao qián?

Shòuhuòyuán: Liǎng kuài.

Péng Dé: Liǎng kuài qián.

Shòuhuòyuán: Liǎng kuài qián yī tào.

Péng Dé: Hǎo, xiǎng mǎi zhège. Liǎng kuài qián. Nà nǐ juéde piàoliang ma?

Péng Qióng: Ng, hěn piàoliang. Nǐ hái xiǎng mǎi xiē shénme qítā de dōngxi ma?

Péng Dé: Wǒ yě xiǎng mǎi ... o ... yī ge bēizi.

Péng Qióng: Ng.

Péng Dé: Hǎo bù hǎo?

Péng Qióng: N, hǎo zhǔyì.

Péng Dé: Hǎo, xièxie. Shāngdiàn li yǒu méiyǒu? Zài nǎr?

Péng Qióng: Zài zhèbiān.

Péng Dé: Yī ge bēizi duōshao qián?

Péng Qióng: O, zhège wǒ yě bù shì hěn qīngchu, fēncháng duìbuqǐ.

Péng Dé: Méi guānxi ya!

Péng Qióng: N.

Péng Dé: Kàn yī kàn.

Péng Qióng: Xiǎojiě!

Péng Dé: Nàge lùsè de, kěyǐ kàn yī kàn?

Shòuhuòyuán: Zhè shì bǎowēnbēi.

Péng Dé: Zhù, a, zěnme jiǎng? Zěnme kàn?

Péng Qióng: Zhùcè shāngbiāo.

Péng Dé: For coffee, kāfēi, chá.

Shòuhuòyuán: Qīchá de.

Todd: Good, good. I'd like to buy this.

Peng Qiong: How much is it?

Clerk: Two yuan.

Todd: Two yuan.

Clerk: Two yuan for the set.

Todd: Fine, I'd like to buy it. Two yuan. Do you think they're pretty, then?

Peng Qiong: Uh-huh, they're beautiful. Is there anything else you want to buy?

Todd: I'd like to buy ... er ... a mug.

Peng Qiong: Okay.

Todd: Is that all right?

Peng Qiong: Uh-huh, good idea.

Todd: Fine, thanks. Is there any in the store? Where is it?

Peng Qiong: Over here.

Todd: How much is it for a mug?

Peng Qiong: Oh, I'm not too sure of that, sorry.

Todd: That's all right!

Peng Qiong: Uh-huh.

Todd: Let's take a look.

Peng Qiong: Miss!

Todd: That green one, can I take a look at it?

Clerk: This is a thermal mug.

Todd: "Reg-", er, how do you say this? How do you read this?

Peng Qiong: The registered trademark.

Todd: "For coffee," coffee, tea.

Clerk: It's to steep tea.

Unit D

彭德：那多少錢？

售貨員：七塊。

彭德：那，那個上面的杯子 ...

售貨員：這個？

彭德：啊。

彭瓊：這個好象不錯。

彭德：比較大。可以，可以放吃的東西。

彭瓊：甚麼？

彭德：可不可以放吃的東西在裏面？

彭瓊：當然可以放吃的東西。

售貨員：可以放。

彭德：飯，還是別的東西？

售貨員：這 ...喝水，要放飯就太小了。

彭德：好哦，我想買這個了。

售貨員：十六塊錢。

彭德：十六？

售貨員：對。

彭德：好。

彭瓊：我們是不是可以再選擇一個 ... 好一些的？

彭德：嗯？

彭瓊：我們是不是可以再選擇一些好一些的？因爲這個質量好象有的地方不是很好。

彭德：啊，是嗎？

彭瓊：對吧？是嗎？

彭德：差不 ...哦，對對對，謝謝。

彭德：那多少钱？

售货员：七块。

彭德：那，那个上面的杯子 ...

售货员：这个？

彭德：啊。

彭琼：这个好象不错。

彭德：比较大。可以，可以放吃的东西。

彭琼：什么？

彭德：可不可以放吃的东西在里面？

彭琼：当然可以放吃的东西。

售货员：可以放。

彭德：饭，还是别的东西？

售货员：这 ...喝水，要放饭就太小了。

彭德：好哦，我想买这个了。

售货员：十六块钱。

彭德：十六？

售货员：对。

彭德：好。

彭琼：我们是不是可以再选择一个 ... 好一些的？

彭德：嗯？

彭琼：我们是不是可以再选择一些好一些的？因为这个质量好象有的地方不是很好。

彭德：啊，是吗？

彭琼：对吧？是吗？

彭德：差出 ...哦，对对对，谢谢。

Lesson 17

Péng Dé: Nà duōshao qián?

Shòuhuòyuán: Qī kuài.

Péng Dé: Na, nàge shàngmian de bēizi ...

Shòuhuòyuán: Zhège?

Péng Dé: A.

Péng Qióng: Zhège hǎoxiàng bù cuò.

Péng Dé: Bǐjiào dà. Kěyǐ, kěyǐ fàng chī de dōngxi.

Péng Qióng: Shénme?

Péng Dé: Kě bù kěyǐ fàng chī de dōngxi zài lǐmiàn?

Péng Qióng: Dāngrán kěyǐ fàng chī de dōngxi.

Shòuhuòyuán: Kěyǐ fàng.

Péng Dé: Fàn, háishi bié de dōngxi?

Shòuhuòyuán: Zhè ... hē shuǐ, yào fàng fàn jiù tài xiǎo le.

Péng Dé: Hǎo wo, wǒ xiǎng mǎi zhège le.

Shòuhuòyuán: Shíliù kuài qián.

Péng Dé: Shíliù?

Shòuhuòyuán: Duì.

Péng Dé: Hǎo.

Péng Qióng: Wǒmen shì bù shì kěyǐ zài xuǎnzé yī ge ... hǎo yīxiē de?

Péng Dé: N?

Péng Qióng: Wǒmen shì bù shì kěyǐ zài xuǎnzé yīxiē hǎo yīxiē de? Yīnwéi zhège zhìliàng hǎoxiàng yǒude dìfang bù shì hěn hǎo.

Péng Dé: A, shì ma?

Péng Qióng: Duì ba? Shì ma?

Péng Dé: Chàbù ... o, duì, duì, duì, xièxie.

Todd: How much is it, then?

Clerk: Seven yuan.

Todd: Er, that mug on top ...

Clerk: This one?

Todd: Uh-huh.

Peng Qiong: This doesn't look bad.

Todd: It's bigger. You can, you can put food in it.

Peng Qiong: What?

Todd: Can you put things to eat in it?

Peng Qiong: Of course you can use it for things to eat.

Clerk: Yes, you can.

Todd: Rice, or something else?

Clerk: This ... is for drinking water. If you want to use it for food, it's a bit small.

Todd: Oh, fine then, I'd like to buy this then.

Clerk: Sixteen yuan.

Todd: Sixteen?

Clerk: Right.

Todd: Okay.

Peng Qiong: Should we pick one that is ... somewhat better?

Todd: Huh?

Peng Qiong: Should we pick some better ones? Because the quality of this one doesn't seem too good in places.

Todd: Oh, is that right?

Peng Qiong: Right? Don't you think so?

Todd: It's not much diff...oh, right, right, right. Thanks.

Unit D

售貨員：就這兩個了。沒甚麼了。

彭瓊：哦，就這兩個了。

彭德：沒有別的？

彭瓊：這個好象更不好啊。質量上
面…

彭德：沒有關係。

彭瓊：沒有關係？

彭德：沒有關係。

彭瓊：那好象這個好。

售貨員：那還是這個…這個。

彭德：比較好。

彭瓊：這個好一些。

彭德：你要不要買？

彭瓊：嗯，不，謝謝。我有很多。

彭德：哦，是嗎！二十塊。

售貨員：四塊。

彭德：謝謝你。

售貨員：不客氣。

售货员：就这两个了。没甚么了。

彭琼：哦，就这两个了。

彭德：没有别的？

彭琼：这个好象更不好啊。质量上
面…

彭德：没有关系。

彭琼：没有关系？

彭德：没有关系。

彭琼：那好象这个好。

售货员：那还是这个…这个。

彭德：比较好。

彭琼：这个好一些。

彭德：你要不要买？

彭琼：嗯，不，谢谢。我有很多。

彭德：哦，是吗！二十块。

售货员：四块。

彭德：谢谢你。

售货员：不客气。

Lesson 17

Shòuhuòyuán: Jiù zhè liǎng ge le. Méi
    shénme le.
Péng Qióng: O, jiù zhè liǎng ge le.

Péng Dé: Méiyǒu bié de?
Péng Qióng: Zhège hǎoxiàng gèng bù hǎo a.
    Zhìliàng shàngmian ...
Péng Dé: Méiyǒu guānxi.
Péng Qióng: Méiyǒu guānxi?
Péng Dé: Méiyǒu guānxi.
Péng Qióng: Nà hǎoxiàng zhège hǎo.

Shòuhuòyuán: Nà háishi zhège ... zhège.

Péng Dé: Bǐjiào hǎo.
Péng Qióng: Zhège hǎo yīxiē.
Péng Dé: Nǐ yào bù yào mǎi?
Péng Qióng: N, bù, xièxie. Wǒ yǒu hěn duō.
Péng Dé: O, shìma! Èrshí kuài.
Shòuhuòyuán: Sì kuài.
Péng Dé: Xièxie nǐ.
Shòuhuòyuán: Bù kèqi.

Clerk: There are just the two of these. There
    are no more.
Peng Qiong: Oh, there are just the two of
    these left.
Todd: There's no other?
Peng Qiong: This one seems even worse. In
    quality ...
Todd: It doesn't matter.
Peng Qiong: It doesn't matter?
Todd: It doesn't matter.
Peng Qiong: Then it seems that this one is
    better.
Clerk: Then you'd better go with this
    one ... this one.
Todd: It's better.
Peng Qiong: This one is somewhat better.
Todd: Do you want to buy (one)?
Peng Qiong: Er, no, thanks. I have lots.
Todd: Oh, is that so! Twenty yuan.
Clerk: Four yuan.
Todd: Thank you.
Clerk: You're welcome.

Unit D

Unit D: Shopping

Lesson 18:
Buying Snacks

*James Yao shops for
something to snack on,
in a Beida shop.*

Previewing Activity

1. Match the English with the Chinese terms, and underline the items you think might appear in this segment.

_____*sandwiches*   a. 糖果 tángguǒ

_____*beef jerky*   b. 汽水 qìshuǐ

_____*cookies*   c. 果汁 guǒzhī

_____*crackers*   d. 土豆片 tǔdòupiàn

_____*potato chips*   e. 玉米片 yùmǐpiàn

_____*corn chips*   f. 炸麵圈 / 炸面圈 zhámiànquān

_____*pretzels*   g. 堅果 / 坚果 jiānguǒ

_____*nuts*   h. 酸奶 suānnǎi

_____*yogurt*   i. 三明治 sānmíngzhì

_____*fruit*   j. 牛肉乾 / 牛肉干 niúròugān

_____*ice cream*   k. 餅乾（甜）/ 饼干（甜）bǐnggān (tián)

_____*popsicles*   l. 餅乾（鹹）/ 饼干（咸）bǐnggān (xián)

_____*candy*   m. 水果 shuǐguǒ

_____*soda*   n. 冰激凌 bīngjilíng

_____*juice*   o. 冰棍兒 / 冰棍儿 bīnggùnr

First Viewing: Global Information

2. List two facts about what James bought in this store.

_____

_____

Second Viewing: Specific Information

3. List three more facts about what James bought in this store.

_____

_____

_____

Third Viewings: Linguistic Information

4. James wants to know what a particular item is. He asks,

請問這個叫甚麼/请问这个叫什么？　Qǐngwèn zhège jiào shénme?

Write two more questions he could have asked to obtain the same information.

_____

_____

5. The salesclerk tells James the snack is "haw hamburgers": a triple-layered snack that looks like a tiny hamburger, that is made of haw (the berry or fruit of the hawthorn). Fill in the blanks below:

這_____山楂漢堡/这_____山楂汉堡。

Zhè jiào shānzhā _____.

6. James wants to know what is in the haw hamburger. Write the *pinyin* for what he says.

裏面有甚麼東西/里面有什么东西？

_____

Unit D

7. Write two more questions he could have asked to obtain the same information.

_____

_____

8. The salesclerk tells James there is fruit leather, haw flakes, etc. in the confection. Match the English, *pinyin*, and Chinese characters below.

guǒdānpí

山楂片

haw flake

fruit leather

果丹皮

shānzhāpiàn

9. James wants to know whether the haw hamburgers are sweet or sour. Match the English and Chinese terms below, and circle the two that James uses.

甜 tián

salty

苦 / 苦 kǔ

bitter

sour / tart

辣 là

鹹 / 咸 xián

酸 suān

sweet

spicy hot

10. So, what do you suppose that "suān-tiān de" means? _____

11. Chinese people often say of human life that it is "suān-tián-kǔ-là." What does this mean, both literally and figuratively? Write your guess, and then turn the page upside down for an answer.

"Sour, sweet, bitter, and spicy." Life has its high points and low points. It is made up of events that will elicit sorrow, joy, disappointment, hope—all the emotions that make up the spectrum of human experience. As one delights in all the flavors that engage the palate, one should expect and accept all the emotions that constitute a rich and full life.

Lesson 18

12. James asks, "一斤要多少？ *Yī jīn yào duōshao?*" If he were to speak in a complete sentence, he would have asked:

山楂漢堡一斤多少錢/ 山楂汉堡一斤多少钱？

Shānzhā hànbǎo yī jīn duōshao qián?

How much for a jin of the haw hamburgers?

Following this pattern, figure out how to ask how much the following items cost. Fill in the blanks, using the vocabulary listed within the boxed area as clues.

Example: a bottle of juice	*Guǒzhī*	yī	*píng*	duōshao qián?
a glass of juice	_____	yī	_____	duōshao qián?
a box of juice	_____	yī	_____	duōshao qián?
a pound of chocolate	_____	yī	_____	duōshao qián?
an ounce of chocolate	_____	yī	_____	duōshao qián?
a piece of chocolate	_____	yī	_____	duōshao qián?
a dozen oranges	_____	yī	_____	duōshao qián?
a pound of oranges	_____	yī	_____	duōshao qián?
a single orange	_____	yī	_____	duōshao qián?

兩 / 两 liǎng ounce

巧克力 qiǎokèlì *chocolate*

瓶 píng *bottle*

打 dá *dozen*

盒 hé *box*

橘子 júzi *orange(s)*

磅 bàng *pound*

杯 bēi *cup, glass, mug*

果汁 guǒzhī *juice*

個 / 个 gè *piece (general measure word)*

粒 lì *piece, pellet (for small things, like grains of rice)*

Unit D

13. Finally, James asks for a half *jin*. He says the following.

可以來半斤嗎/可以来半斤吗？　Kěyǐ lái bàn jīn ma?

How else could he have said the same thing? Suggest at least two ways:

_____

_____

Post-Viewing Activities

Speaking

14. Pretend you have a snack available for sale. Take some notes in the space provided below, indicating a) what the snack is, b) what it contains, c) how it tastes, d) how much it costs, and e) how you sell it (by the piece? by the pound? etc.).

15. Work with a partner. Sell what you have to offer, and buy something from him/her. Take notes about the transaction below.

What you sold (how much you sold, to whom, and for how much money)

What you bought (from whom, what it was, how it tastes, how much you bought, for how much money)

16. Report on your transaction to the class.

Reading / Writing

17. Following are descriptions of five of the snack items listed in Exercise 1 of this lesson. Identify the items, and write their names in the boxes provided.

一。 這是一種由兩片麵包夾著火腿、雞蛋、奶酪、魚、蔬菜或者其他東西的食物 / 这是一种由两片面包夹著火腿、鸡蛋、奶酪、鱼、蔬菜或者其他东西的食物。

（一）

二。 這種食物是由土豆制成的，先將土豆切成薄片，然後放在油裏炸得脆脆的 / 这种食物是由土豆制成的，先将土豆切成薄片，然后放在油里炸得脆脆的。

（二）

三。 這種食物是牛奶發酵制成的，味道有一點酸，有時候也加糖，還有各種不同的水果口味 / 这种食物是牛奶发酵制成的，味道有一点酸，有时候也加糖，还有各种不同的水果口味。

（三）

四。 這是一種很涼的食物。是由巧克力、牛奶或者各種水果口味的冰制成的。冰的中間夾著一根小木棒，吃的時候可以拿著小木棒 / 这是一种很涼的食物。是由巧克力、牛奶或者各种水果口味的冰制成的。冰的中间夹著一根小木棒，吃的时候可以拿著小木棒。

（四）

五。 這是一種含有很多氣的水，一般裝在小鋁罐或塑料瓶裏，可以有各種不同的口味 / 这是一种含有很多气的水，一般装在小铝罐或塑料瓶里，可以有各种不同的口味。

（五）

Unit D

18. Match the Chinese and English terms below, then reread the descriptions and see if you still agree with the answers you wrote previously.

_____ 種 / 种	_____ 炸
_____ 由	_____ 脆
_____ 兩片麵包 / 两片面包	_____ 牛奶
_____ 夾著 / 夹著	_____ 發酵 / 发酵
_____ 火腿	_____ 味道
_____ 雞蛋 / 鸡蛋	_____ 各種 / 各种
_____ 奶酪	_____ 不同的
_____ 蔬菜 / 蔬菜	_____ 口味
_____ 或者	_____ 巧克力
_____ 其他	_____ 冰
_____ 食物	_____ 根
_____ 制成	_____ 小木棒
_____ 將 / 将	_____ 含有
_____ 切成	_____ 氣 / 气
_____ 薄片 / 薄片	_____ 一般
_____ 放在	_____ 裝在 / 装在
_____ 油	_____ 小鋁罐 / 小铝罐
	_____ 塑料瓶

a. qì *air*
b. yībān *normally, usually*
c. zhuāng zài *packed in*
d. xiǎo lǚguàn *little tin can*
e. sùliàopíng *plastic bottle*
f. jīdàn *(chicken) egg*
g. nǎilào *cheese*
h. shūcài *vegetable*
i. huòzhě *or*
j. qítā *other*
k. zhǒng *type*
l. yóu *from*
m. liǎng piàn miànbāo *two slices of bread*
n. jiāzhe *encasing, press from two sides*
o. huǒtuǐ *ham*
p. shíwù *foodstuff*
q. zhìchéng *made from*
r. jiāng *(a preposition that marks the object of the verb; similar in function to* bǎ 把 *)*
s. qiēchéng *slice into*
t. báo piàn *thin slices*
u. fā jiào *ferment*
v. wèidào *flavor, taste*
w. gèzhǒng *many different kinds*
x. bù tóng de *different, unalike*
y. kǒuwèi *flavor, taste*
z. fàng zài *place into*
aa. yóu *oil*
ab. zhá *deep-fry*
ac. cuì *crispy*
ad. niúnǎi *(cow's) milk*
ae. qiǎokèlì *chocolate*
af. bīng *ice*
ag. gēn *(measure word for root-like objects)*
ah. xiǎo mù bàng *little wooden stick*
ai. hányǒu *contain*

19. Now describe a snack of your own choice in the space provided below. After editing, share your description with a classmate, and see if he or she can identify what you have described.

姚守正：你好！

售貨員：你好！

姚守正：請問這個叫甚麼？

售貨員：這叫山楂漢堡。

姚守正：山楂漢堡。裏面有甚麼東西？

售貨員：就是果丹皮、山楂片甚麼的。

姚守正：哦，是甜的還是酸的？

售貨員：酸甜的。

姚守正：酸甜的是吧？一斤要多少？

售貨員：一斤六塊錢。

姚守正：一斤六塊錢。可以來半斤嗎？

售貨員：可以。三塊錢的可以嗎？

姚守正：可以，可以。

售貨員：那找你兩塊錢。

姚守正：你好！

售货员：你好！

姚守正：请问这个叫什么？

售货员：这叫山楂汉堡。

姚守正：山楂汉堡。里面有什么东西？

售货员：就是果丹皮、山楂片什么的。

姚守正：哦，是甜的还是酸的？

售货员：酸甜的。

姚守正：酸甜的是吧？一斤要多少？

售货员：一斤六块钱。

姚守正：一斤六块钱。可以来半斤吗？

售货员：可以。三块钱的可以吗？

姚守正：可以，可以。

售货员：那找你两块钱。

Yáo Shǒuzhèng: Nǐ hǎo!

Shòuhuòyuán: Nǐ hǎo!

Shǒuzhèng: Qǐngwèn zhège jiào shénme?

Shòuhuòyuán: Zhè jiào shānzhā hànbǎo.

Shǒuzhèng: Shānzhā hànbǎo. Lǐmiàn yǒu shénme dōngxi?

Shòuhuòyuán: Jiù shì guǒdànpí, shānzhāpiàn shénme de.

Shǒuzhèng: O, shì tián de háishi suān de?

Shòuhuòyuán: Suān-tián de.

Shǒuzhèng: Suān-tiān de shì ba? Yī jīn yào duōshao?

Shòuhuòyuán: Yī jīn liù kuài qián.

Shǒuzhèng: Yī jīn liù kuài qián. Kěyǐ lái bàn jīn ma?

Shòuhuòyuán: Kěyǐ. Sān kuài qián de kěyǐ ma?

Shǒuzhèng: Kěyǐ, kěyǐ, .

Shòuhuòyuán: Nà zhǎo nǐ liǎng kuài qián.

James: Hello!

Salesclerk: Hello!

James: May I ask what this is called?

Salesclerk: This is called haw hamburger.

James: Haw hamburger. What is inside?

Salesclerk: It's just fruit leather, haw flakes and the like.

James: Oh. Is it sweet or is it tart?

Salesclerk: Sweet and tart.

James: It's sweet and tart, huh? How much is it for one *jin?*

Salesclerk: It's six *yuan* for a *jin.*

James: Six *yuan* for a *jin.* Could you give me a half *jin,* then?

Salesclerk: Okay. Is enough for three *yuan* okay?

James: Fine, fine.

Salesclerk: I'll give you two *yuan* back, then.

Unit D

288

Lesson 19:
Buying Magazines

Péng Qióng and her girlfriend browse a vendor's stall for newspapers and magazines.

Previewing Activity

1. Match the U.S. periodicals with their Chinese titles.

a. *Time*   ___Guójiā Dìlǐ Zázhì 國家地理雜誌／国家地理杂志

b. *Newsweek*   ___Niǔyuē Shíbào 紐約時報／纽约时报

c. *USA Today*   ___Rénwù 人物

d. *New York Times*   ___Tǐyù Huàbào 體育畫報／体育画报

e. *People*   ___Měiguó Xīnwén Zhōukān 美國新聞週刊／美国新闻周刊

f. *National Geographic* ___Shídài 時代／时代

g. *Sports Illustrated*   ___Jīnrì Měiguó 今日美國／今日美国

First Viewing: Global Information

2. Péng Qióng and her friend look at a number of periodicals. On which of the following areas do they focus?

☐ celebrities   ☐ sports   ☐ movies   ☐ current events

☐ intellectual themes   ☐ young people's interests   ☐ women's interests   ☐ education

Second Viewing: Specific Information

3. Which of the following do Péng Qióng and her friend look at or purchase?

☐ *People's Daily*	☐ *World Affairs Pictorial Weekly*
☐ *South China Morning Post*	☐ *Beijing Youth*
☐ *Soccer News*	☐ *Global Screen*
☐ *The Evening News*	☐ *Soccer World Cup*
☐ *Southern Weekend*	☐ *The College Student*

4. What are the names of the periodicals that feature stories on the following?

Hillary Clinton _____

Titanic (the movie) _____

German soccer _____

5. In which magazine was the printing a problem (the colors did not match up)?

_____

6. For which magazine did the vendor "throw in yesterday's issue" for free?

_____

7. Fill out the following chart about the running balance of the purchases Péng Qióng and her friend have made, based on the vendor's calculations:

Item	Total to date
Periodical #1	
plus #2	*1.30*
plus #3	
plus #4	
plus #5	*10.00*
plus #6	
plus #7	

Unit D

8. Fill out the following chart, based on the exchange of currency between the vendors and Péng Qióng:

Cost of periodicals: _____

Amount tendered: _____

Change received: _____

Third Viewing: Linguistic Information

9. Write the numbers and letters for the *pinyin* and characters for each of the following.

___ ___ *People's Daily*	1. 足球世界杯	a. Dàxuéshēng
___ ___ *World Affairs Pictorial*	2. 晚報/晚报	b. Nánhuá Zǎobào
___ ___ *South China Morning Post*	3. 大學生/大学生	c. Zhīshí Huàbào
___ ___ *Beijing Youth*	4. 北京青年報/北京青年报	d. Zúqiú Shìjièbēi
___ ___ *Soccer News*	5. 南華早報/南华早报	e. Rénmín Rìbào
___ ___ *Global Screen*	6. 環球銀幕/环球银幕	f. Nánfāng Zhōumò
___ ___ *The Evening News*	7. 知識畫報/知识画报	g. Wǎnbào
___ ___ *Soccer World Cup*	8. 南方週末/南方周末	h. Huánqiú Yínmù
___ ___ *Southern Weekend*	9. 人民日報/人民日报	i. Zúqiú Bào
___ ___ *The College Student*	10. 足球報/足球报	j. Běijīng Qīngnián Bào

10. Which of the following measure words are used in this video, in conjunction with newspapers?

一 ___?___ 報紙 / 报纸

☐ běn 本   ☐ zhāng 張 / 张   ☐ ge 個 / 个   ☐ fèn 份   ☐ tiáo 條 / 条

11. How about magazines?

一 ___?___ 雜誌 / 杂志

☐ běn 本   ☐ zhāng 張 / 张   ☐ ge 個 / 个   ☐ fèn 份   ☐ tiáo 條 / 条

Lesson 19

12. How do you say, "the fifth issue of *The College Student*"? Fill in the blank.

Dàxuéshēng dì wǔ _____

《大學生》第五期 / 《大学生》第五期

13. Fill in the blanks in the *pinyin* in the following vocabulary chart:

a. US First Lady _____ _____ _____ _____ *fū* _____

b. table of contents *mù* _____ _____

c. the will of Aryan peoples *rì* _____ *ěr* _____ *màn* _____ _____ *yì* _____

d. German soccer _____ _____ _____ _____

14. Now match up these terms with the character equivalents by writing the letters below :

_____ 目錄 / 目录   _____ 德國足球 / 德国足球

_____ 日耳曼人的意志   _____ 美國第一夫人 / 美国第一夫人

15. On several occasions, Péng Qióng responds "Yes" to a question simply by grunting, much like an English speaker might say "uh-huh." What best approximates the sound she makes?

☐ o...   ☐ ng...   ☐ m...   ☐ a...

16. Match the utterances on the left with those one the right.

a. 還有其他的嗎 / 还有其他的吗？

b. 晚報來了嗎 / 晚报来了吗？

c. 請給我看看那份雜誌，好嗎 / 请给我看看那份杂志，好吗？

d. 她應該也會來吧 / 她应该也会来吧？

e. 這兒有一點壞了，沒關係吧 / 这儿有一点坏了，没关系吧？

f. 來，拿好了啊 / 来，拿好了啊。

_____ 好，謝謝，謝謝 / 好，谢谢，谢谢。

_____ 說不定是的 / 说不定是的。

_____ 沒事。

_____ 還沒呢 / 还没呢。

_____ 來 / 来。

_____ 對不起，就這些，沒有了 / 对不起，就这些，没有了。

Unit D

12. Rearrange (by numbering them) the phrases below to express the following English sentence:

"Are there some other newspapers (as well)?"

" _____ _____ _____ _____ _____ ?"

a. 甚麼 / 什么   b. 報紙 / 报纸   c. 還有 / 还有   d. 是不是   e. 其他的

Post-Viewing Activities

Speaking

13. Pretend you are opening a vendor's stall on campus selling periodical literature. Write the titles of five US or Chinese publications named in this unit (or that your class decides on as a whole) in the blanks below: One copy of each of these is what you have available for sale.

Name of publication	Price
1. _____	_____
2. _____	_____
3. _____	_____
4. _____	_____
5. _____	_____

Now list three periodicals that you DON'T have available for sale. Go around the room and try to "purchase" them from your classmates. Make sure you carry on full, polite conversations IN CHINESE with them.

Name of publication	"Purchased" from	Price
1. _____	_____	_____
2. _____	_____	_____
3. _____	_____	_____

Finally, report back to the class on what you "purchased," from whom, and for how much.

Lesson 19   293

Reading / Writing

14. Following are two notes from recent visitors to your home, asking for follow-up information about magazines they saw on your table. Highlight what you can read of them.

a. 上次我去你家的時候，看到桌上有一本雜誌、那本雜誌的內容是介紹世界各地的景緻情況及其歷史背景，其中有包括海洋生物，叢林，火山等等⋯，我很喜歡那本雜誌、所以可不可以麻煩你告訴我它的名字，謝謝。

b. 你好！上次在你家看到一本杂志，我非常喜欢。杂志的封面是美国著名影星汤姆·克鲁司和尼寇·基德曼。杂志的主要内容是报道电影明星，电视明星，以及其它各种名人的生活，家庭和工作经历及近况，并配有大量有关这些名人的精美照片和插图。你能告诉我那本杂志的名字吗？我很想自己也订一份，谢谢！

15. Write the names of these two magazines in English (clue: they are in the list given in Exercise 1 in this lesson):

a.

_____

b.

_____

16. Fill in the blanks in the texts below with selections from the list provided.

a. 上次我去你家的时候，看到桌上有一本_____，那本杂志的_____是_____世界_____的_____情况及_____历史_____。_____有_____海洋_____、丛林、火山_____ ... 我很喜欢那本杂志，所以可不可以_____你告诉我它的名字，谢谢。

其	杂志	景致	背景
包括	介绍	内容	各地
生物	麻烦	等等	其中

b. 你好！上次在你家看到一本雜誌，我_____喜歡。雜誌的_____是美國著名_____湯姆·克魯司和_____·基德曼。雜誌的_____內容是_____電影明星、電視明星、_____其它各種_____的_____、_____和工作_____及近況，並_____大量_____這些名人的_____照片和_____。你能告訴我那本雜誌的名字嗎？我很想自己也_____一份。

封面	尼寇	非常	以及
經歷	訂	報道	插圖
影星	生活	有關	家庭
精美	主要	配有	名人

17. Fill in the missing items in the list below.

雜誌／杂志 _____
magazine

內容 nèiróng _____

介紹／介绍 _____
introduce

世界 shìjiè _____

各地 _____
every region

_____ jǐngzhì scenery

情況／情况 qíngkuàng

_____

及 _____ and

_____ qí its, their

歷史／历史 lìshǐ

_____

背景 _____
background

其中 _____
in, among (their midst)

_____ bāokuò include

_____ hǎiyáng ocean

生物 _____
living thing, organism

_____ cónglín forest

火山 _____ volcano

等等 _____ et cetera

麻煩你／麻烦你 _____
may I trouble you

非常 _____
extremely, extraordinarily

_____ fēngmiàn cover

著名 _____ famous

影星 _____ movie star

湯姆／汤姆 _____ Tom

克魯司／克鲁司 Kèlǔsī

_____

尼寇 Níkòu _____

基德曼 Jīdémàn _____

主要 _____
primary, principal

_____ bàodào report on

電影明星／电影明星

_____ movie star

電視明星／电视明星 diànshìmíngxīng

_____

_____ yǐjí
as well as, along with

其它 qítā _____

各種／各种 _____
many kinds of

名人 míngrén _____

生活 _____ life

Unit D

_____ jiātíng

family, household

工作經歷／工作经历 _____

work experience

及 _____ *and*

_____ jìnkuàng

recent circumstances

並／并 _____

and, furthermore

_____ pèiyǒu

accompanied by

大量 _____

great quantity

_____ yǒuguān

pertinent to

精美 _____ *exquisite*

照片 zhàopiàn _____

_____ chātú *illustration*

自己 _____ *oneself*

訂一份／订一份 dìng yī fèn

_____

18. Check your answers against the list below.

雜誌／杂志 zázhì *magazine*

內容 nèiróng *content*

介紹／介绍 jièshào *introduce*

世界 shìjiè *world*

各地 gèdì *every region*

景緻／景致 jǐngzhì *scenery*

情況／情况 qíngkuàng *circumstances*

及 jí *and*

其 qí *its, their*

歷史／历史 lìshǐ *history*

背景 bèijǐng *background*

其中 qízhōng *in, among (their midst)*

包括 bāokuò *include*

海洋 hǎiyáng *ocean*

生物 shēngwù *living thing, organism*

叢林／丛林 cónglín *forest*

火山 huǒshān *volcano*

等等 děngděng *et cetera*

麻煩你／麻烦你 máfannǐ

may I trouble you

非常 fēicháng *extremely*

封面 fēngmiàn *cover*

著名 zhùmíng *famous*

影星 yǐngxīng *movie star*

湯姆／汤姆 Tāngmǔ *Tom*

克魯司／克鲁司 Kèlǔsī *Cruise*

尼寇 Níkòu *Nicole*

基德曼 Jīdémàn *Kidman*

主要 zhǔyào *primary, principal*

報道／报道 bàodào *report on*

電影明星／电影明星

diànyǐngmíngxīng *movie star*

電視明星／电视明星

diànshìmíngxīng *TV star*

以及 yǐjí *as well as, along with*

其它 qítā *other*

Lesson 19

各種／各种　gèzhǒng　*many kinds of*

名人　míngrén　*famous person*

生活　shēnghuó　*life*

家庭　jiātíng　*family, household*

工作經歷／工作经历

　　gōngzuò jīnglì　*work experience*

及　jí　*and*

近況／近况　jìnkuàng

　　recent circumstances

並／并　bìng　*and, furthermore*

配有　pèiyǒu　*accompanied by*

大量　dàliàng　*great quantity*

有關／有关　yǒuguān　*pertinent to*

精美　jīngměi　*exquisite*

照片　zhàopiàn　*photograph*

插圖／插图　chātú　*illustration*

自己　zìjǐ　*oneself*

訂一份／订一份　dìng yī fèn

　　order a copy

19. Now describe a magazine of your choice without naming it. After editing, share your description with a classmate, and see if he or she can identify it.

Unit D

298

彭瓊：咱們...咱們買幾份報紙吧？
朋友：好吧。買甚麼報紙？
彭瓊：嗯，不知道。
朋友：我要買《足球報》。
彭瓊：好的，咱們看看吧。
朋友：最近不是有世界杯嗎？
彭瓊：對。
賣報人：要甚麼世界杯？
朋友：足球。
賣報人：《足球世界杯》就這個，沒有了。
朋友：沒有了嗎？
賣報人：啊，就這個。
朋友：我看看這個。
賣報人：哎，好咧！
男1：《晚報》來了嗎？
賣報人：沒來呢！來，給您這個。
朋友：你買甚麼報紙？
彭瓊：我想買《南方週末》。
男2：有沒有《大學生》第五期？
賣報人：有《大學生》。
彭瓊：這個好像不錯。這個報紙很好。小姐，您可以拿一本《環球銀幕》嗎？
賣報人：《環球銀幕》啊？

彭琼：咱们...咱们买几份报纸吧？
朋友：好吧。买什么报纸？
彭琼：嗯，不知道。
朋友：我要买《足球报》。
彭琼：好的，咱们看看吧。
朋友：最近不是有世界杯吗？
彭琼：对。
卖报人：要什么世界杯？
朋友：足球。
卖报人：《足球世界杯》就这个，没有了。
朋友：没有了吗？
卖报人：啊，就这个。
朋友：我看看这个。
卖报人：哎，好咧！
男1：《晚报》来了吗？
卖报人：没来呢！来，给您这个。
朋友：你买什么报纸？
彭琼：我想买《南方周末》。
男2：有没有《大学生》第五 期
卖报人：有《大学生》。
彭琼：这个好象不错。这个报纸很好。小姐，您可以拿一本《环球银幕》吗？
卖报人：《环球银幕》啊？

Lesson 19

Péng Qióng: Zánmen … zánmen mǎi jǐ fèn bàozhǐ ba?

Péngyou: Hǎo ba. Mǎi shénme bàozhǐ?

Péng Qióng: Nng, bù zhīdào.

Péngyou: Wǒ yào mǎi *Zúqiúbào*.

Péng Qióng: Hǎo de, zánmen kànkan ba.

Péngyou: Zuìjìn bù shì yǒu *Shìjièbēi* ma?

Péng Qióng: Duì.

Màibàorén: Yào shénme Shìjièbēi?

Péngyou: Zúqiú.

Màibàorén: *Zúqiú Shìjièbēi* jiù zhège, méiyǒu le.

Péngyou: Méiyǒu le ma?

Màibàorén: A, jiù zhège.

Péngyou: Wǒ kànkan zhège.

Màibàorén: Ai, hǎo lei!

Nán 1: *Wǎnbào* lái le ma?

Màibàorén: Méi lái ne! Lái, gěi nín zhège.

Péngyou: Nǐ mǎi shénme bàozhǐ?

Péng Qióng: Wǒ xiǎng mǎi *Nánfāng Zhōumò*.

Nán 2: Yǒu méiyǒu *Dàxuéshēng* dì-wǔ qī?

Màibàorén: Yǒu *Dàxuéshēng*.

Péng Qióng: Zhège hǎoxiàng bù cuò. Zhèige bàozhǐ hěn hǎo. Xiǎojiě, nín kěyǐ ná yī běn *Huánqiú Yínmù* ma?

Màibàorén: *Huánqiú Yínmù* a?

Peng Qiong: Let's … let's buy a few newspapers, okay?

Friend: Okay. What newspapers?

Peng Qiong: Er, I don't know.

Friend: I want to buy the *Soccer News*.

Peng Qiong: Okay, let's take a look.

Friend: Isn't there a World Cup soon?

Peng Qiong: Right.

Vendor: What World Cup do you want?

Friend: Soccer.

Vendor: This is the only *Soccer World Cup* there is, there aren't any more.

Friend: Isn't there any other?

Vendor: No, just this one.

Friend: Let me take a look at this one.

Vendor: Okay, here you go.

Male 1: Is the *Evening News* here yet?

Vendor: Not yet! Here, this is for you.

Friend: What newspaper will you buy?

Peng Qiong: I want the *Southern Weekend*.

Male 2: Do you have *The College Student* issue 5?

Vendor: We have *The College Student*.

Peng Qiong: This looks pretty good. Miss, can you give me a copy of *Global Screen*?

Vendor: *Global Screen*?

Unit D

彭瓊：對。

賣報人：哎！《環球銀幕》...這兒
　　　　呢！

彭瓊：不是，不是這個，是那
　　　個，雜誌！

賣報人：雜誌啊。

彭瓊：對對對。可以嗎? 有嗎?

賣報人：可以。

彭瓊：不是，在外面掛著。有
　　　一個 ...

賣報人：《環球銀幕》沒有啦！

彭瓊：就是 ...這本，這本！

賣報人：哦，哦，哦，這本呀！

彭瓊：對。

賣報人：新的。

彭瓊：就買這本、這個報紙嗎?

朋友：嗯，我買這個報紙。

賣報人：來。

彭瓊：好，謝謝。啊，泰，泰
　　　坦尼克號。

朋友：啊真好啊。我也想買一本。

彭瓊：咱們一起先看看。

朋友：好的。

彭瓊：這好像沒有泰坦尼克號
　　　的介紹。

朋友：這個雜誌挺好的。

彭瓊：對，這本多少錢?

彭琼：对。

卖报人：哎！《环球银幕》... 这儿
　　　　呢！

彭琼：不是，不是这个，是那
　　　个，杂志！

卖报人：杂志啊。

彭琼：对对对。可以吗? 有吗?

卖报人：可以。

彭琼：不是，在外面挂著。有
　　　一个 ...

卖报人：《环球银幕》没有啦！

彭琼：就是 ...这本，这本！

卖报人：哦，哦，哦，这本呀！

彭琼：对。

卖报人：新的。

彭琼：就买这本、这个报纸吗?

朋友：嗯，我买这个报纸。

卖报人：来。

彭琼：好，谢谢。啊，泰，泰
　　　坦尼克号。

朋友：啊真好啊。我也想买一本。

彭琼：咱们一起先看看。

朋友：好的。

彭琼：这好象没有泰坦尼克号
　　　的介绍。

朋友：这个杂志挺好的。

彭琼：对，这本多少钱?

Lesson 19

Péng Qióng: Duì.

Màibàorén : Ai! *Huánqiú Yínmù* … zhèr ne!

Péng Qióng: Bù shì, bù shì zhège, shì nàge, zázhì!

Màibàorén: Zázhì a.

Péng Qióng: Duì duì duì. Kěyǐ ma? Yǒu ma?

Màibàorén: Kěyǐ.

Péng Qióng: Bù shì, zài wàimian guàzhe. Yǒu yī ge …

Màibàorén: *Huánqiú Yínmù* méiyǒu la!

Péng Qióng: Jiùshì … zhè běn, zhè běn!

Màibàorén: O, o, o, zhè běn ya!

Péng Qióng: Duì.

Màibàorén: Xīn de.

Péng Qióng: Jiù mǎi zhè běn, zhège bàozhǐ ma?

Péngyou: Ng, wǒ mǎi zhège bàozhǐ.

Màibàorén: Lái.

Péng Qióng: Hǎo, xièxie. A, Tài, Tàitǎnníkèhào.

Péngyou: A, zhēn hǎo a. Wǒ yě xiǎng mǎi yī běn.

Péng Qióng: Zánmen yìqǐ xiān kànkan.

Péngyou: Hǎo de.

Péng Qióng: Zhèr hǎoxiàng méiyǒu Tàitǎnníkèhào de jièshào.

Péngyou: Zhège zázhì tǐng hǎo de.

Péng Qióng: Duì, zhè běn duōshao qián?

Peng Qiong: Right.

Vendor: Yes. *Global Screen* … Here it is!

Peng Qiong: No, not this one, it's that one, the magazine.

Vendor: A magazine?

Peng Qiong: Right, right, right. Can you? Do you have it?

Vendor: I can.

Peng Qiong: That's not it, it's hanging outside. There's a ...

Vendor: There's no other *Global Screen!*

Peng Qiong: It's … this one, this one!

Vendor: Oh, oh, oh, this one!

Peng Qiong: Right.

Vendor: It's new.

Peng Qiong: Are we buying this, (and) this newspaper?

Friend: Uh-huh, I'm buying this newspaper.

Vendor: Here.

Peng Qiong: Okay, thanks. Oh, Ti ..., Titanic.

Friend: Oh, that's great. I want one too.

Peng Qiong: Let's share it first.

Friend: All right.

Peng Qiong: There doesn't seem to be any story about the Titanic here.

Friend: This is a pretty good magazine.

Peng Qiong: Right, how much is it?

Unit D

朋友：六塊五。

彭瓊：好，買這個雜誌，咱一起看吧。

朋友：好的，我買這份報紙。

彭瓊：還有。

朋友：兩份報紙，一個雜誌。

彭瓊：還有甚麼其它的嗎？請問這個《知識畫報》…

賣報人：這個…

彭瓊：可以看看嗎？

賣報人：可以。

彭瓊：希拉里，希拉里，哈哈！

朋友：德國足球。看看目錄在哪兒？

彭瓊：啊，泰坦尼克…目錄是不是在後邊呢！嗯？沒有目錄嗎？那你自己看。

朋友：好的。日耳曼人的意志。克林頓。

彭瓊：克林頓。

朋友：美國第一夫人。

彭瓊、朋友：希拉里·克林頓。

彭瓊：她這次也會來到中國嗎？

朋友：應該是吧。克林頓六月底來到北大，他的…

彭瓊：太好了，說不定能見他。

朋友：六块五。

彭琼：好，买这个杂志，咱一起看吧。

朋友：好的，我买这份报纸。

彭琼：还有。

朋友：两份报纸，一个杂志。

彭琼：还有什么其它的吗？请问这个《知识画报》…

卖报人：这个…

彭琼：可以看看吗？

卖报人：可以。

彭琼：希拉里，希拉里，哈哈！

朋友：德国足球。看看目录在哪儿？

彭琼：啊，泰坦尼克…目录是不是在后边呢！嗯？没有目录吗？那你自己看。

朋友：好的。日耳曼人的意志。克林顿。

彭琼：克林顿。

朋友：美国第一夫人。

彭琼、朋友：希拉里·克林顿。

彭琼：她这次也会来到中国吗？

朋友：应该是吧。克林顿六月底来到北大，他的…

彭琼：太好了，说不定能见到他。

Lesson 19

Péngyou: Liù kuài wǔ.

Péng Qióng: Hǎo, mǎi zhège zázhì, zánmen
  yīqǐ kàn ba.

Péngyou: Hǎo de, wǒ mǎi zhè fèn bàozhǐ.

Péng Qióng: Háiyǒu.

Péngyou: Liǎng fèn bàozhǐ, yī ge zázhì.

Péng Qióng: Háiyǒu shénme qítā de ma?
  … Qǐngwèn zhège *Zhīshi Huàbào* …

Màibàorén: Zhège …

Péng Qióng: Kěyǐ kànkan ma?

Màibàorén: Kěyǐ.

Péng Qióng: Xīlālǐ, Xīlālǐ, ha ha!

Péngyou: Déguó zúqiú. Kànkàn mùlu zài nǎr?

Péng Qióng: A, Tàitǎnníkè ... mùlù shì bu shì
  zài hòubiān ne! Ng? Méiyǒu mùlù ma?
  Nà nǐ zìjǐ kàn.

Péngyou: Hǎo de. Rìěrmànrén de yìzhì.
  Kèlíndùn.

Péng Qióng: Kèlíndùn.

Péngyou: Měiguó dì-yī fūrén.

Péng Qióng, Péngyou: Xīlālǐ Kèlíndùn.

Péng Qióng: Tā zhè cì yě huì láidào
  Zhōngguó ma?

Péngyou: Yīnggāi shì ba. Kèlíndùn liùyuè dǐ
  láidào Běidà, tā de …

Péng Qióng: Tài hǎo le, shuōbudìng néng
  jiàndào tā.

Friend: Six fifty.

Peng Qiong: Okay, we'll buy this magazine.
  Let's read it together.

Friend: Okay. I'm buying this newspaper.

Peng Qiong: There's more.

Friend: Two newspapers and a magazine.

Peng Qiong: Is there something else?
  May I ask about this *World Affairs
  Pictorial* …

Vendor: This one …

Peng Qiong: Can I have a look?

Vendor: Okay.

Peng Qiong: Hilary, Hilary, ha ha!

Friend: German soccer. Let's see where the
  table of contents is?

Peng Qiong: Ah, Titanic... the table of con
  tents is probably in the back. Hmm?
  Isn't there a table of contents? Then
  look through it yourself.

Friend: Okay. The will of Aryan peoples.
  Clinton.

Peng Qiong: Clinton.

Friend: The American First Lady.

Peng Qiong, Friend: Hilary Clinton.

Peng Qiong: Will she come to China too,
  this time?

Friend: Probably. Clinton will come to
  Peking University at the end of June,
  his ...

Peng Qiong: Great. Maybe we'll see him.

Unit D

朋友：他的夫人應該也來。

彭瓊：嗯。這本雜誌多少錢...四塊八。是不是還有甚麼其他的報紙。嗯，有《北京青年報》嗎？

賣報人：《北京青年報》？

彭瓊：嗯。

賣報人：還有一份。

彭瓊：就是今天的嗎？

賣報人：對，就是今天的。

彭瓊：嗯，看看《北京青年報》。

賣報人：這個彩頁有點壞了，沒事吧？

彭瓊：嗯，我想還是不要青年報了。全都是足球。全都是足球。你喜歡足球嗎？

朋友：我喜歡足球。

彭瓊：那好，那要一份這個，好嗎？

賣報人：這個彩頁壞了，對不起了啊。

彭瓊：没…没關係吧？

朋友：我看看。

彭瓊：你看呢？

朋友：好的，那要一份吧。

朋友：他的夫人应该也来。

彭琼：嗯。这本杂志多少钱...四块八。是不是还有什么其他的报纸。嗯，有《北京青年报》吗？

卖报人：《北京青年报》？

彭琼：嗯。

卖报人：还有一份。

彭琼：就是今天的吗？

卖报人：对，就是今天的。

彭琼：嗯，看看《北京青年报》。

卖报人：这个彩页有点坏了，没事吧？

彭琼：嗯，我想还是不要青年报了。全都是足球。全都是足球。你喜欢足球吗？

朋友：我喜欢足球。

彭琼：那好，那要一份这个，好吗？

卖报人：这个彩页坏了，对不起了啊。

彭琼：没…没关系吧？

朋友：我看看。

彭琼：你看呢？

朋友：好的，那要一份吧。

Lesson 19

Péngyou: Tā de fūrén yīnggāi yě lái.

Péng Qióng: Ng. Zhèben zázhì duōshao qián
... sì kuài bā. Shì bù shì háiyǒu
shénme qítā de bàozhǐ. Ng, yǒu *Běijīng
Qīngniánbào* ma?

Màibàorén: *Běijīng Qīngniánbào*?

Péng Qióng: Ng.

Màibàorén: Háiyǒu yī fèn.

Péng Qióng: Jiùshì jīntiān de ma?

Màibàorén: Duì, jiùshì jīntiān de.

Péng Qióng: Ng, kànkan *Běijīng
Qīngniánbào*.

Màibàorén: Zhège cǎiyè yǒudiǎnr huài le, méi
shìr ba?

Péng Qióng: Ng, wǒ xiǎng háishi bùyào
Qīngniánbào le. Quán dōu shì zúqiú.
Quán dōu shì zúqiú. Nǐ xǐhuan zúqiú
ma?

Péngyou: Wǒ xǐhuan zúqiú.

Péng Qióng: Nà hǎo, nà yào yī fèn zhège hǎo
ma?

Màibàorén: Zhège cǎiyè huài le, duìbuqǐ le a.

Péng Qióng: Méi ... méi guānxi ba?

Péngyou: Wǒ kànkan.

Péng Qióng: Nǐ kàn ne?

Péngyou: Hǎo de, nà yào yī fèn ba.

Friend: His wife will probably come too.

Peng Qiong: Uh-huh. How much is this
magazine ... four eighty. Do you have
some other newspapers still. Um, do you
have *Beijing Youth?*

Vendor: *Beijing Youth?*

Peng Qiong: Uh-huh.

Vendor: I have one more copy.

Peng Qiong: Is it today's?

Vendor: Right, it's today's.

Peng Qiong: Um, let me see *Beijing Youth.*

Vendor: The color page is a little off on this,
that's not a problem, right?

Peng Qiong: Mmm, I think maybe we won't
take *Beijing Youth* . It's all about
soccer. It's all about soccer. Do you
like soccer?

Friend: I like soccer.

Peng Qiong: Well then, we'll take a copy of
this, okay?

Vendor: The color pages are bad, sorry.

Peng Qiong: That's not ... not a problem?

Friend: Let me see.

Peng Qiong: What do you think?

Friend: Fine, let's take a copy.

Unit D

彭瓊：好的。嗯⋯《足球報》，
　　　還看看要甚麼呢？

賣報人：要不我送你一個別天
　　　　的，昨天的。

彭瓊：啊，好的，好的。

賣報人：好嗎？

彭瓊：好的，好，謝謝。非常
　　　感謝。

賣報人：不用。

彭瓊：就這些吧。

賣報人：啊，好唻。

彭瓊：請您看一下，一共多少錢？

賣報人：好唻！這是八毛錢，一
　　　　塊三，兩塊一，三塊一，
　　　　九塊六⋯九塊六⋯十塊
　　　　⋯十四塊，十四塊四。

彭瓊：嗯，好，給你二十。

朋友：應該找五塊六。

賣報人：對，找你五塊六。來，
　　　　拿好了啊。

彭瓊：好，謝謝，謝謝。

賣報人：不用。

彭瓊：哎呀，今天有事幹啦。

朋友：嗯，回去讀報紙吧。

彭瓊：對，走吧。

朋友：走吧。

彭瓊：再見。

彭琼：好的。嗯⋯《足球报》，
　　　还看看要什么呢？

卖报人：要不我送你一个别天
　　　　的，昨天的。

彭琼：啊，好的，好的。

卖报人：好吗？

彭琼：好的，好，谢谢。非常
　　　感谢。

卖报人：不用。

彭琼：就这些吧。

卖报人：啊，好　　。

彭琼：请您看一下，一共多少钱？

卖报人：好唻！这是八毛钱，一
　　　　块三，两块一，三块一，
　　　　九块六⋯九块六⋯十块
　　　　⋯十四块，十四块四。

彭琼：嗯，好，给你二十。

朋友：应该找五块六。

卖报人：对，找你五块六。来，
　　　　拿好了啊。

彭琼：好，谢谢，谢谢。

卖报人：不用。

彭琼：哎呀，今天有事干啦。

朋友：嗯，回去读报纸吧。

彭琼：对，走吧。

朋友：走吧。

彭琼：再见。

Lesson 19

Péng Qióng: Hǎo de. Nng … *Zúqiúbào*, hái kànkan yào shénme ne?

Xiǎofàn: Yàobù wǒ sòng nǐ yī ge bié tiān de, zuótiān de.

Péng Qióng: A, hǎo de, hǎo de.

Xiǎofàn: Hǎo ma?

Péng Qióng: Hǎo de, hǎo, xièxie. Fēicháng gǎnxiè.

Xiǎofàn: Bùyòng.

Péng Qióng: Jiù zhèxiē ba.

Xiǎofàn: A, hǎo lei.

Péng Qióng: Qǐng nín kàn yīxià, yīgòng duōshao qián?

Xiǎofàn: Hǎo lèi! Zhè shì bā máo qián, yī kuài sān, liǎng kuài yī, sān kuài yī, jiǔ kuài liù … jiǔ kuài liù … shí kuài … shísì kuài, shísì kuài sì.

Péng Qióng: Ng, hǎo, gěi nǐ èrshí.

Péngyou: Yīnggāi zhǎo wǔ kuài liù.

Xiǎofàn: Duì, zhǎo nǐ wǔ kuài liù. Lái, náhǎo le a.

Péng Qióng: Hǎo, xièxie, xièxie.

Xiǎofàn: Bùyòng.

Péng Qióng: Aiya, jīntiān yǒu shìr gàn la.

Péngyou: Ng, huíqu dú bàozhǐ ba.

Péng Qióng: Duì, zǒu ba.

Péngyou: Zǒu ba.

Péng Qióng: Zàijiàn.

Peng Qiong: Okay. Um ... *Soccer News,* let's see what else we want?

Vendor: Or else I'll give you another day's issue for free, yesterday's.

Peng Qiong: Oh, good, good.

Vendor: Okay?

Peng Qiong: Good, that's fine, thanks. Thank you very much.

Vendor: You're welcome.

Peng Qiong: That'll be it, then?

Vendor: Oh, all right then.

Peng Qiong: Could you please take a look to see how much it is, altogether?

Vendor: All right then! This is eighty cents, one thirty, two ten, three ten, nine sixty ... nine sixty ... ten yuan ... fourteen yuan, fourteen forty.

Peng Qiong: Um, fine. Here's twenty.

Friend: We should get five sixty back.

Vendor: Right, here's five sixty in change. Here, hold on to it.

Peng Qiong: Right, thank you, thank you.

Vendor: You're welcome.

Peng Qiong: Wow, we have lots to do today.

Friend: Uh-huh. Let's go back and read newspapers.

Peng Qiong: Right, let's go.

Friend: Let's go.

Peng Qiong: Good bye.

Unit D

Unit D: Shopping

Lesson 20:
Advice on How to Shop

Zhāng Shēnlán comments briefly on what foreign visitors to China might want to keep in mind when they shop on the streets (not in major department stores).

Previewing Activity

1. What do you think she might say? Select one.

☐ *1. Don't shop on the street.*

☐ *2. Watch for pickpockets.*

☐ *3. Walk away if the price is too high.*

☐ *4. Make sure you bargain.*

2. Match the Chinese below with the English above.

_____ 價錢太高你就走 / 价钱太高你就走。Jiàqián tài gāo nǐ jiù zǒu.

_____ 一定要討價還價 / 一定要讨价还价。Yídìng yào tǎojià huánjià.

_____ 小心扒手。Xiǎoxīn páshǒu.

_____ 別在街上買東西 / 别在街上买东西。Bié zài jiēshang mǎi dōngxi.

First Viewing: Global Information

3. Which of the predictions given above matches Zhāng Shēnlán's comments? #

_____

4. She predicts that local vendors **will / will not** (circle one) try to take advantage of a "foreigner."

5. She states that it would be _____ (fill in the blank) if you could speak Chinese.

Second Viewing: Specific Information

6. Number the following statements in the order in which Zhāng Shēnlán makes them.

_____ "Then you can walk away."

_____ "Things in China are cheaper than in America."

_____ "People will suspect you are a foreigner, and easy to 'rip off.'"

_____ "They'll state a more realistic price."

_____ "The price will drop immediately."

_____ "Since you speak Chinese, ask them to tell you the true price."

Third Viewing: Linguistic Information

7. Fill in the following vocabulary chart (items follow the order in which they appear):

被人敲竹杠		*to be taken advantage of, fleeced*
宰人		*to rip someone off*
實價 / 实价		
	gěi tā shuō qīngchu	
不合適 / 不合适		
真實 / 真实		*true, real*
降下來 / 降下来		

Unit D

8. Fill in the blanks in the Chinese based on the English:

•*When you go shopping on the streets, because, as soon as people see you, they'll think you are a foreigner, you'll easily be, what is called "taken advantage of," our "ripped off."*

Nǐ _____ mǎi dōngxi de shíhou, yīnwéi, nǐ _____, rénjiā

juéde nǐ shi yī ge wàiguórén, hěn róngyì bèi rén, _____ "qiāo zhúgàng," wǒmen

de _____.

•*It's best if you can speak Chinese.*

Nǐ huì shuō Zhōngguóhuà _____.

Rearrange the sentence above to produce another way to say the same thing:

_____

[How would you say in Chinese, "You speak Chinese the best of all" (better than you speak any other language, or better than anyone else speaks it)?

_____]

•*If he wants you to buy his stuff, he will call you, "Come back, come back, come back."*

Tā _____ nǐ mǎi tāde dōngxi, tā _____ hǎn nǐ, "_____,

_____, _____."

Post-Viewing Activities

Speaking

9. Do you feel Zhāng Shēnlán's advice is well-taken? Do you intend to follow it when you go to China? Jot a few notes below, expressing your position. Then speak to your classmates. Find someone who agrees with you, and someone who disagrees with you, and jot down their reasons. Report your findings to the class.

Your thoughts:_____

_____

Someone who agrees:_____

Someone who disagrees:_____

Lesson 20   311

Reading / Writing

10. The following is an excerpt from a long letter. Highlight what you can decipher of it.

对于一个外国人，在中国买东西，你应该知道几条基本的规律。

第一，完全一样的东西，从小商店或超市买要比从大商场买便宜得多。道理很简单：大商场的装修、维修、水电、房租、员工的工资、上缴的营业税等都要比小商店高很多，而这些额外费用自然都平摊到了商品的价格中。所以，买一般的日常用品去小商店或超市比较合算。另外，因为中国不对顾客直接征收消费税，商品的标价就是实价，不用再交税。

第二，除非商品的质量存在问题，中国的商店一般不允许顾客退货。当然，有些商店也有变通的规定。比如，你可以换成别的价钱相近的商品，但一旦顾客把钱交给了商店，想再拿回来可就难了。另外，中国有很多假冒伪劣商品，所以购物时一定要小心。与小商店比，大商场的商品质量更保险，所以如果要买电器或家具等比较昂贵的商品，最好去大商场。

第三，一般的商店不能讲价，但如果去自由市场或个体摊位买东西，就一定要学会"讨价还价"。所谓"讨价"就是要卖主接受你给出的价格，"还价"就是压低卖主给出的价格。"讨价还价"又叫"砍价"或"杀价"，意思是狠狠地压低价格。不要觉得这样做不道德或不好意思，因为其实卖主给出的价格要远远高出商品的实价。换句话说，卖主已经给顾客留出了"砍价"的余地，如果你不砍，可就傻了！中国人讲，"砍价"的基本规律是"见一面，砍一半。"比如，卖主说他的东西要卖１００元，那么你还的价应该不超过５０元。

当然，一切规律都不是绝对的，所以最明智的选择是请一位当地的中国朋友作你的购物顾问，这样就不容易上当或被"宰"了。

同学们，你们能告诉我这个外国人，在美国买东西和在中国买东西有什么不一样的规律吗？

Unit D

11. Here is the same excerpt in traditional characters. Can you read as much (if not more) of this version? Highlight what you can read.

對于一個外國人，在中國買東西，你應該知道幾條基本的規律。

第一，完全一樣的東西，從小商店或超市買要比從大商場買便宜得多。道理很簡單：大商場的裝修、維修、水電、房租、員工的工資、上繳的營業稅等都要比小商店高很多，而這些額外費用自然都平攤到了商品的價格中。所以，買一般的日常用品去小商店或超市比較合算。另外，因爲中國不對顧客直接征收消費稅，商品的標價就是實價，不用再交稅。

第二，除非商品的質量存在問題，中國的商店一般不允許顧客退貨。當然，有些商店也有變通的規定。比如，你可以換成別的價錢相近的商品，但一旦顧客把錢交給了商店，想再拿回來可就難了。另外，中國有很多假冒偽劣商品，所以購物時一定要小心。與小商店比，大商場的商品質量更保險，所以如果要買電器或家俱等比較昂貴的商品，最好去大商場。

第三，一般的商店不能講價，但如果去自由市場或個體攤位買東西，就一定要學會"討價還價"。所謂"討價"就是要賣主接受你給出的價格，"還價"就是壓低賣主給出的價格。"討價還價"又叫"砍價"或"殺價"，意思是狠狠地壓低價格。不要覺得這樣做不道德或不好意思，因爲其實賣主給出的價格要遠遠高出商品的實價。換句話説，賣主已經給顧客留出了"砍價"的餘地，如果你不砍，可就傻了！中國人講，"砍價"的基本規律是"見一面，砍一半"。比如，賣主説他的東西要賣１００元，那麼你還的價應該不超過５０元。

當然，一切規律都不是絕對的，所以最明智的選擇是請一位當地的中國朋友作你的購物顧問，這樣就不容易上當或被"宰"了。

同學們，你們能告訴我這個外國人，在美國買東西和在中國買東西有甚麼不一樣的規律嗎？

Lesson 20

12. What <u>main points</u> does the author think the shopper should keep in mind? Check all that apply below.

_____ Use a Chinese friend as your "shopping consultant."

_____ The same items are going to much cheaper at small stores and markets than the big department stores.

_____ Watch for newspaper or television ads for sales or special buying opportunities.

_____ Chinese stores generally do not give refunds.

_____ Most stores do not allow bargaining, but at free markets and peddlers' stands, bargaining is a must.

13. The following questions pertain to some details mentioned in the essay. Please respond to them as best you can, based on the contents of the essay.

What is the sales tax in China?

_____

If refunds are difficult to get, are exchanges possible?

_____

Is counterfeiting a problem? Where, generally?

_____

What percentage of the asking price is a good "opening bid" in effective bargaining?

_____

What does the author ask about, at the conclusion of the essay?

_____

14. Can you try to guess the meanings of the following terms, based on context?

Paragraph 2, line 2: 水電 / 水电 _____

Paragraph 2, line 4: 合算 _____

Paragraph 3, line 2: 價錢相近 / 价钱相近 _____

Paragraph 4, line 2: 賣主 / 卖主 _____

Paragraph 4, line 5: 換句話說 / 换句话说 _____

Unit D

15. Fill in the missing items in the list below.

對于 / 对于 _____ for, pertaining to

條 / 条 _____ (measure word for guīlù)

基本 jīběn basic, fundamental

規律 / 规律 guīlù rule

完全 _____ completely, entirely

超市 chāoshì _____

_____ dà shāngchǎng big shopping center

_____ dàoli reason

簡單 / 简单 jiǎndān _____

_____ zhuāngxiū renovate; renovations

_____ wéixiū repair, maintain; maintenance

水電 / 水电 shuǐdiàn _____

房租 _____ rent

_____ yuángōng de gōngzī employee wages

上繳的營業稅 / 上缴的营业税 shàng jiǎo de yíngyèshuì _____

等 _____ etc.

_____ ér furthermore

_____ éwài fèiyòng additional expenses

自然 _____ naturally

_____ píngtān distribute, spread out

商品的價格 / 商品的价格 shāngpǐn de jiàgé _____

一般 yībān _____

日常用品 rìcháng yòngpǐn _____

比較 / 比较 bǐjiào _____

Lesson 20   315

合算 _____ *worthwhile*

另外 lìngwài _____

_____ gùkè *customer*

直接 / 直接 _____ *directly*

_____ zhēngshōu *levy, collect*

消費税 / 消费税 xiāofèishuì *consumption tax*

_____ biāojià jiùshi shíjià *the price indicated is the real price*

再交税 zài jiāo shuì _____

_____ chúfēi *unless*

_____ zhìliàng *quality*

存在問題 / 存在问题 cúnzài wèntí _____

_____ bù yúnxǔ *not be permitted*

退貨 / 退货 tuìhuò _____

變通 / 变通 _____ *be flexible*

規定 / 规定 _____ *regulation*

換成 / 换成 huànchéng _____

別的 _____ _____

價錢相近 / 价钱相近 jiàqián xiāngjìn _____

商品 _____ *merchandise*

_____ yīdàn *as soon as*

假冒 jiǎmào *counterfeit*

偽劣 / 伪劣 wěiliè *inferior*

_____ gòuwù shí *while shopping*

一定要 _____ *must*

小心 xiǎoxīn _____

Unit D

_____ yǔ xiǎo shāngdiàn bǐ   *compared to small stores*

更保險 / 更保险 gèng bǎoxiǎn   *safer*

如果 rúguǒ _____

電器 / 电器 _____ *electric appliance*

家俱 / 家具 jiājù _____

昂貴 / 昂贵 ángguì _____

講價 / 讲价 jiǎngjià _____

自由市場 / 自由市场 _____ *free market*

_____ gètǐ tānwèi   *individual stall, peddler*

學會 / 学会 _____ *learn how to*

_____ tǎojià huánjià   *to haggle, bargain*

_____ màizhǔ   *seller*

接受 _____ *accept*

給出的 / 给出的 _____ *proposed*

_____ jiàgé   *price*

壓低 / 压低 yādī   *bring down, lower*

又叫 _____ *be also called*

砍價 / 砍价 kǎn jià   *"hack" at the price*

殺價 / 杀价 shā jià   *"kill" the price*

意思 yìsi _____

_____ hěnhěn de   *forcefully*

這樣做 / 这样做 _____ *act in this way*

不道德 _____ *immoral*

不好意思 _____ *embarrassed*

_____ qíshí   *actually, in reality*

Lesson 20

遠遠高出 / 远远高出 _____ *exceed by far*

_____ shíjià *real price, actual price*

換句話說 / 换句话说 _____ *in other words*

留出了X的餘地 / 留出了X的余地 liúchū X de yúdì *leave room for X*

可就傻了 kě jiù shǎ le *that would be stupid*

見一面，砍一半 / 见一面，砍一半 _____

　　　　right at the outset, cut (the price) by half

不超過 / 不超过 bù chāoguò _____

當然 / 当然 _____ *of course*

一切 _____ *every, all*

絕對 / 绝对 _____ *absolute*

_____ míngzhì *wise*

選擇 / 选择 xuǎnzé *choice*

當地 / 当地 _____ *local*

購物顧問 / 购物顾问 gòuwù gùwèn _____

_____ shàngdàng *cheated, fooled*

被宰 bèi zǎi *be ripped off, be fleeced*

16. Check your answers against the list below.

對于 / 对于 duìyú *for, pertaining to*
條 / 条 tiáo *(measure word for* guīlù*)*
基本 jīběn *basic, fundamental*
規律 / 规律 guīlù *rule*
完全 wánquán *completely, entirely*
超市 chāoshì *market, supermarket*
大商場 / 大商场 dà shāngchǎng
　　big shopping center
道理 dàoli *reason*
簡單 / 简单 jiǎndān *simple*

裝修 / 装修 zhuāngxiū *renovate; renovations*
維修 / 维修 wéixiū
　　repair, maintain; maintenance
水電 / 水电 shuǐdiàn
　　utilities (water & electricity)
房租 fángzū *rent*
員工的工資 / 员工的工资
　　yuángōng de gōngzī *employee wages*
上繳的營業稅 / 上缴的营业税
　　shàng jiǎo de yíngyèshuì *business taxes paid*

Unit D

等　děng　*etc.*

而　ér　*furthermore*

額外費用／额外费用　éwài fèiyòng
　　additional expenses

自然　zìrán　*naturally*

平攤／平摊　píngtān　*distribute, spread out*

商品的價格／商品的价格　shāngpǐn de
　　jiàgé　*prices of the commercial goods*

一般　yìbān　*normally, usually*

日常用品　rìcháng yòngpǐn　*daily use items*

比較／比较　bǐjiào　*comparatively*

合算　hésuàn　*worthwhile*

另外　lìngwài　*in addition*

顧客／顾客　gùkè　*customer*

直接／直接　zhíjiē　*directly*

征收　zhēngshōu　*levy, collect*

消費稅／消费税　xiāofèishuì
　　consumption tax

標價就是實價／标价就是实价
　　biāojià jiùshi shíjià
　　the price indicated is the real price

再交稅　zài jiāo shuì　*pay taxes in addition*

除非　chúfēi　*unless*

質量／质量　zhìliàng　*quality*

存在問題／存在问题　cúnzài wèntí
　　a problem exists

不允許／不允许　bù yúnxǔ
　　not be permitted

退貨／退货　tuìhuò　*return merchandise*

變通／变通　biàn tōng　*be flexible*

規定／规定　guīdìng　*regulation*

換成／换成　huànchéng　*exchange for*

別的　biéde　*other*

價錢相近／价钱相近
　　jiàqián xiāngjìn　*close in price*

商品　shāngpǐn　*merchandise*

一旦　yìdàn　*as soon as*

假冒　jiǎmào　*counterfeit*

偽劣／伪劣　wěiliè　*inferior*

購物時／购物时　gòuwù shí
　　while shopping

一定要　yīdìng yào　*must*

小心　xiǎoxīn　*be careful*

與小商店比／与小商店比　yǔ xiǎo
　　shāngdiàn bǐ　*compared to small stores*

更保險／更保险　gèng bǎoxiǎn　*safer*

如果　rúguǒ　*if*

電器／电器　diànqì　*electric appliance*

家俱／家具　jiājù　*furniture*

昂貴／昂贵　ángguì　*expensive, costly*

講價／讲价　jiǎngjià　*to bargain*

自由市場／自由市场　zìyóu shìchǎng
　　free market

個體攤位／个体摊位　gètǐ tānwèi
　　individual stall, peddler

學會／学会　xuéhuì　*learn how to*

討價還價／讨价还价　táojià huánjià
　　to haggle, bargain

賣主／卖主　màizhǔ　*seller*

接受　jiēshòu　*accept*

給出的／给出的　gěi chū de　*proposed*

價格／价格　jiàgé　*price*

壓低／压低　yādī　*bring down, lower*

又叫　yòu jiào　*be also called*

砍價／砍价　kǎn jià　*"hack" at the price*

殺價／杀价　shā jià　*"kill" the price*

意思　yìsi　*meaning*

狠狠地　hěnhěn de　*forcefully*

這樣做／这样做　zhè yàng zuò
　　act in this way

不道德　bù dàodé　*immoral*

不好意思　bùhǎoyìsi　*embarrassed*

其實／其实　qíshí　*actually, in reality*

遠遠高出／远远高出　yuǎnyuǎn gāo chū
　　exceed by far

實價／实价　shíjià　*real price, actual price*

換句話說／换句话说　huànjùhuàshuō
　　in other words

Lesson 20　　　　　　　　　　　　　　　　　319

留出了X的餘地 / 留出了X的余地

    liúchū le X de yúdì *leave room for X*

可就傻了 kě jiù shǎ le *that would be stupid*

見一面，砍一半 / 见一面，砍一半

    jiàn yīmiàn, kǎn yībàn

    right at the outset, cut (the price) by half

不超過 / 不超过 bù chāoguò

    to not exceed

當然 / 当然 dāngrán *of course*

一切 yīqiè *every, all*

絕對 / 绝对 juéduì *absolute*

明智 míngzhì *wise*

選擇 / 选择 xuǎnzé *choice*

當地 / 当地 dāngdì *local*

購物顧問 / 购物顾问 gòuwù gùwèn

    shopping consultant

上當 / 上当 shàngdàng *cheated, fooled*

被宰 bèi zǎi *be ripped off, be fleeced*

17. Write a response to the person who wrote you. What advice can you give about shopping in the U.S.?

Unit D

Transcript of video segment

張申藍：

你上街買東西的時候，因為，你一看，人家覺得你是一個外國人，很容易被人 ...叫做"敲竹杠"，我們的"宰人"。那，你會說中國話最好。你就告訴他："請你說實價。請你 ..."給他說清楚："我知道你要得太多了，不合適，我不買你的。"你就走。你走，他想你買他的東西，他會喊你，"回來，回來，回來。"然後就給你一個真實的價錢，就可以了。你，你應該知道中國的東西比美國便宜。你不要，哦，"我要一百塊。"你馬上給他。不行！你說："我要走。我，我不買你的。"他（會說）："哎，回來，回來。"價錢就下來了。

張申蓝：

你上街买东西的时候，因为，你一看，人家觉得你是一个外国人，很容易被人 ...叫做"敲竹杠"，我们的"宰人"。那，你会说中国话最好。你就告诉他："请你说实价。请你 ..."给他说清楚："我知道你要得太多了，不合适，我不买你的。"你就走。你走，他想你买他的东西，他会喊你，"回来，回来，回来。"然后就给你一个真实的价钱，就可以了。你，你应该知道中国的东西比美国便宜。你不要，哦，"我要一百块。"你马上给他。不行！你说："我要走。我，我不买你的。"他（会说）："哎，回来，回来。"价钱就下来了。

Lesson 20

Zhāng Shēnlán:

Nǐ shàngjiē mǎi dōngxi de shíhou, yīnwéi, nǐ yī kàn, rénjia juéde nǐ shì yī ge wàiguórén, hěn róngyì bèi rén ... jiàozuò "qiāo zhúgàng", wǒmen de "zǎi rén." Nà, nǐ huì shuō Zhōngguóhuà zuì hǎo. Nǐ jiù gàosu tā, "Qǐng nǐ shuō shíjià. Qǐng nǐ..." Gěi tā shuō qīngchu: "Wǒ zhīdao nǐ yào de tài duō le, bù héshì, wǒ bù mǎi nǐ de." Nǐ jiù zǒu. Nǐ zǒu, tā xiǎng nǐ mǎi tā de dōngxi, tā huì hǎn nǐ, "Huílai, huílai, huílai." Ránhòu jiù gěi nǐ yī ge zhēnshí de jiàqian, jiù kěyǐ le. Nǐ, nǐ yīnggāi zhīdao Zhōngguó de dōngxi bǐ Měiguó piányi. Nǐ bù yào, o, "Wǒ yào yī bǎi kuài." Nǐ mǎshàng gěi tā. Bù xíng! Nǐ shuō, "Wǒ yào zǒu. Wǒ bù mǎi nǐ de." Tā (huì shuō): "Ai, huílai, huílai." Jiàqian jiù xiàlai le.

Zhang Shenlan:

When you go shopping on the streets, because, when they look at you, people will think you're a foreigner, you'll easily be, what is called "ripped off," our "soaked." In that case, it'd be best if you could speak Chinese. Just tell them, "Please give me the real price. Please..." Tell them clearly: "I know you are asking too much, it's not appropriate, I won't buy from you." Then you walk away. When you walk away, if they want you to buy their stuff, they'll call to you, "Come back, come back, come back." Thereafter they'll give you a realistic price, and that'll be all right. You, you ought to know that Chinese goods are cheaper than American. Don't, er, "I want a hundred dollars." And you give it to them immediately. That won't do! Say, "I'm leaving. I won't buy from you." They (will say): "Hey, come back, come back." And the price will come down.

Unit D